Cotton was King

Indian Farms
to

Lawrence County Plantations

Alabama Plantation Series

Rickey Butch Walker

Bluewater Publications
BWPublications.com

Published in the United States by Bluewater Publications.
Printed in the United States of America.

This work is based on the authors' personal interpretation of research.

Library of Congress Control Number: 2019938221

Bluewater Publications
books by
Rickey Butch Walker

Cotton Was King – Franklin – Colbert County – Alabama Plantation Series, ISBN 978-1-949711-08-0, $19.95

Cotton Was King - Lauderdale County – Alabama Plantation Series, ISBN 978-1-934610-99-2, $19.95

Appalachian Indians of the Warrior Mountains: History and Culture, ISBN 978-1-934610-72-5, $19.95

Appalachian Indian Trails of the Chickamauga: Lower Cherokee Settlements, ISBN 978-1-934610-91-6, $19.95

Celtic Indian Boy of Appalachia: A Scots Irish Cherokee Childhood, ISBN 978-1-934610-75-6, $19.95

Chickasaw Chief George Colbert: His Family and His Country, ISBN 978-1-934610-71-8, $19.95

Doublehead: Last Chickamauga Cherokee Chief, ISBN 978-1-934610-67-1, $19.95

Hiking Sipsey: A Family's Fight for Eastern Wilderness, ISBN 978-1-934610-93-0, $19.95

Soldier's Wife: Cotton Fields to Berlin and Tripoli, ISBN-978-1-934610-12-1, $19.95

Warrior Mountains Folklore: American Indian and Celtic History in the Southeast, ISBN 978-1-934610-65-7, $24.95

Warrior Mountains Indian Heritage-Teacher's Edition, ISBN 978-1-934610-27-5, $39.95

Warrior Mountains Indian Heritage-Student Edition, ISBN 978-1-934610-66-4, $24.95

Cotton Was King
Volume III

Acknowledgements

Yoland Morgan Smith, a local historian, was very helpful in the completion of this book. She provided family information on many of the cotton planters of Lawrence County (Colbert), Alabama. Her work was very valuable in the development of "Cotton was King," Volume III. I greatly appreciate her writing the excellent book review.

My sister, June Reed, was very helpful in editing the book, "Cotton was King," Volume III. She spent many hours making corrections, and I greatly appreciate her help and dedication in getting this book finished.

Wendy Hazle of the Lawrence County Archives provided many pictures and information that contributed to the quality of "Cotton was King," Volume III. I very much appreciate Wendy for her time and help.

I would also like to thank Ms. Bruce Lipscombe, Director of Pond Spring, and Alabama Historical Commission for their help in completing this book.

I also must thank my wife, Mary Anne Walker, and my family for putting up with all the hours I spent in writing this book. Mary Anne and my children were very understanding and provided much encouragement to which I am extremely grateful.

Contents

Cotton Was King
Volume III
Lawrence/Colbert

Introduction

The first documentation of cotton grown with the use of black slaves in Lawrence County, Alabama, along the Elk River Shoals and Big Muscle Shoals of the Tennessee River was by Chickamauga Cherokee Chief Doublehead and his white brother-in-law Irishman John Melton. Before 1800, Doublehead and Melton were not the only black slave holders on Indian lands of North Alabama. By 1782, Scotsman James Logan Colbert living in the Chickasaw Nation near the northwest corner of Alabama at the mouth of Bear Creek owned 150 black slaves. The Chickasaws were given the area of Lawrence County by the Hopewell Treaty of January 10, 1786; at that time, the Chickamauga Cherokees were occupying North Alabama but were still at war with the United States and white settlers encroaching on their homelands.

Even though the Chickamauga Cherokee Indians did not own the land by treaty with the United States government, they were occupying the area of the Muscle Shoals from 1770 until their removal under the terms of the Turkey Town Treaty of September 16 and 18, 1816. The treaty lands ceded in 1816 included southwest Madison, Morgan, Limestone, Lawrence (Colbert), Franklin (Colbert), and Lauderdale Counties of western North Alabama. Today, mixed blood remnants of those Chickamaugan Cherokees still live in Lawrence County, Alabama, and other counties ceded by the treaty.

In January 1818, northwestern Alabama opened for white settlers to make land claims; however, most of the prime fertile river and creek bottoms were claimed by wealthy land barons who owned large numbers of black slaves to work their cotton plantations. The newly acquire Indian lands by the United States Government caused a land rush of cotton planters to the Tennessee Valley of northwest Alabama which was referred to as "Alabama Fever." The majority of these planters were from Virginia and the Carolinas, and they had been told that cotton in the Tennessee River bottoms grew taller than an average man.

Background

The Muscle Shoals of the Tennessee River were very important to the Chickamauga faction of the Lower Cherokee Indians, and later the wealthy cotton planters from the east who occupied the area that became Lawrence County, Alabama. The Native American Indian people inhabiting North Alabama referred to the Muscle Shoals as "Chake Thlocko" which means Great Crossing Place or Big Ford. In approximately 37 miles, the Tennessee River dropped about 134 feet vertically. The shoals stretched along the Tennessee River from the vicinity of the mouth of Fox's Creek on the present-day county line of Lawrence and Morgan Counties of North Alabama westward to the Mississippi State line. Beginning upstream, the six Tennessee River shoals of northwest Alabama included Elk River Shoals, Big Muscle Shoals, Little Muscle Shoals, Colbert Shoals, Bee Tree Shoals, and Waterloo Shoals.

The shoals were created by a geologic feature consisting of layers of very hard rock known as chert (flint). These rocky outcroppings were very resistant to erosion and formed stretches of rushing waters cascading over sharp rocky defiles which created very hazardous conditions for water travel. In addition, the shoals also had numerous sand bars and islands that only experienced Indian guides were able to safely navigate during rainy seasons of the year which created high water levels in the river.

The Cherokee Indian people had claimed the area of the Muscle Shoals for hundreds of years. Professor Henry Sale Halbert (1/14/1837-5/9/1916) stated that, "The Cherokee's belong to the Iroquois family, as is evidence by their language. Under the name Taligewi, they are first mentioned in the Delaware Migration Legend and lived in the upper Ohio Valley. After a long war, they were expelled from their country and driven southward. After moving southward, the maximum boundaries of the Cherokees once included southwest Virginia, the western part of North and South Carolina, North Georgia, East Tennessee, and the Tennessee Valley of North Alabama. Tradition and archaeology agree the Cherokee were occupants of the Tennessee Valley in North Alabama in prehistoric times. How long they have lived in this area is not known, but some time before 1650, (after Desoto's visit in 1540) they abandoned this region, and retired beyond the Cumberland and Sand Mountain, but reserving their abandoned country as a hunting ground."

Nina Leftwich states in <u>Two Hundred Years at the Shoals</u>, (1935), "Both the French and the English contended for the Indian trade along the western waters; the French planted a post at Muscle Shoals before 1715. Because of the increasing importance of trade with the whites, the Cherokees planted villages near the Muscle Shoals area in the last quarter of the eighteenth century. There was Doublehead's village on the Tennessee and a large settlement (Shoal Town) at the mouth of Town Creek, extending a mile along the river and far up the creek."

Doublehead-the Warrior

Prior to the story of cotton and slaves among the Chickamauga faction of Lower Cherokee Indians and white cotton planters inhabiting Lawrence County, Alabama, the text will focus on life of Doublehead, first as a warrior and then as a black slave owning planter. He was responsible for the first cotton gin that was placed in Lawrence County of North Alabama as part of the January 7, 1806, Cotton Gin Treaty. The following is the story of Doublehead as a Chickamauga Cherokee warrior prior becoming a wealthy trading post merchant and cotton planter of North Alabama.

The Cherokees had claimed the Muscle Shoals as their hunting grounds as early as the 1600's. However, Cherokees and Chickasaws initially cooperated in expelling the invading Shawnee from the shoals during the early 1700's. The Cherokee presence in the Muscle Shoals portion of the Tennessee River came about as a result of their alliance with an old enemy, the Chickasaws. Their purpose was to check Shawnee attempts to occupy the territory along the Cumberland and Tennessee Rivers.

Doublehead-Chickamauga Warrior

In 1715, and again in 1745, both the Chickasaw and Cherokee nations joined forces to expel the Shawnees from the Big Bend of the Tennessee River Valley.

After forcing the Shawnee from the hunting grounds of the Cherokee, the Chickasaws established a number of their own settlements in and around the Muscle Shoals section of the Great Bend of the Tennessee River and as far east as Chickasaw Island south of present-day Huntsville, Alabama. The intrusion with villages by their Chickasaw ally into some prime hunting grounds along the shoals angered the Cherokees who attacked the Chickasaws in 1769. The Cherokees were consequently defeated in what has been called the "Battle of the Chickasaw Old Fields." Shortly after the battle, the Chickasaws began a westward migration. The void was filled by the Chickamauga faction of the Lower Cherokees under the leadership of Doublehead. By early 1770, Doublehead and his Lower Cherokee followers had migrated into the Muscle Shoals area of the Tennessee River and established several towns of their own.

Under the leadership of Doublehead during the 1770's, Mouse Town at the mouth of Fox's Creek, Doublehead's Town at the Browns Ferry Crossing, Melton's Bluff on the south bank of Elk River Shoals, Shoal Town on Big Muscle Shoals at the mouths of Big Nance's Creek, Shoal Town Creek, and Bluewater Creek, and other Indian villages were established along the Muscle Shoals in present-day Lawrence County, Alabama. The shoals became the stronghold of Doublehead, his Lower Cherokee followers, and their Chickamauga allies. These Muscle Shoals towns were used by Chickamauga Confederacy to keep out early white land speculators and to fight the Cumberland settlers for the buffalo hunting grounds in middle Tennessee.

During the Chickamauga War beginning with the signing of the Treaty of Sycamore Shoals in 1775, Doublehead and his warriors fought the encroachment of white settlers on Cherokee hunting grounds along the Cumberland River in central Tennessee. Doublehead became the most influential Chickamauga leader at the Muscle Shoals of North Alabama with the tribes making up the Indian alliance.

By the middle of the1770's, the fierce and feared Chickamauga Cherokee Chief Doublehead, along with many warriors of the various tribes making up the Chickamauga Confederacy and their families, lived at Doublehead's Town between present day Mallard Creek and Fox's Creek. Doublehead's Town at the head of the Elk River Shoals was located on the south bank of the Tennessee River at Brown's Ferry. Doublehead's Town was across from the present-day Brown's Ferry Nuclear Plant. The nuclear facility is located in present-day Limestone County, Alabama, and Doublehead's Town was on the south side of the river in Lawrence County.

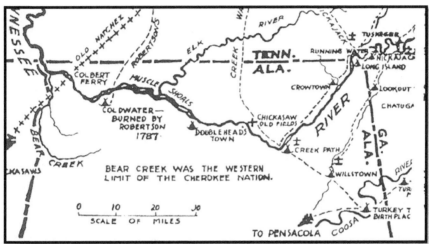
Doublehead's Town at head of Elk River Shoals

At times during the war, Doublehead's Town was occupied by warriors and their families of the Lower Cherokee, Upper Creek, Chickasaw, Shawnee, and other followers of the Chickamauga Confederacy. Some members of all these tribes making up the confederacy lived in Doublehead's Town at Elk River Shoals which was at the upstream end of the great Muscle Shoals of northwest Alabama. They were determined to stop white settlers from intruding into their hunting lands. From this strong hold at the southeast end of Elk River Shoals, these Chickamaugans under Doublehead's leadership waged war against the Cumberland Settlements in middle Tennessee.

Doublehead's personal war against encroaching white settlers lasted for some twenty years, from 1775 through June 1795. From Doublehead's Town in the southwestern most portions of the Cherokee land claims along the Muscle Shoals, Doublehead made his own declarations of war against the white settlers moving into his hunting grounds. He decided when and where to attack whether it was only two, two hundred, or two thousand in his party. If they were with him, he was in charge. Occasionally, Doublehead and his warriors would join

Chickamauga forces from the five lower towns of Dragging Canoe and the Coosa River towns of John Watts Jr. to conduct large scale raids into east Tennessee, but on most of these raids, Doublehead caused more controversy because he wanted to do things his way.

During his years on the war path, Doublehead focused primarily on the Cumberland River in order to protect his favorite buffalo hunting grounds, to prevent further white encroachment, and to steal horses and black slaves. The Cumberland was originally called the Warioto River by the Indians and the Shauvanon River by the French traders. But the early white settlers named it in honor of the Duke of Cumberland, the Prime Minister of England. For several years, these first white people who settled in the area of the French Lick (Nashville) or Big Lick on the Cumberland River in 1780's suffered under the raids of Doublehead's Chickamauga warriors with their own blood, scalps, horses, black slaves, and other valuables. Doublehead was fighting to save his ancestral hunting grounds and nothing was off-limits in his blood thirsty revenge.

Doublehead's Chickamauga Confederacy

After the Treaty of Sycamore Shoals or Henderson Treaty in 1775, Doublehead, Dragging Canoe, and John Watts, Jr. established the Indian alliance known as the Chickamauga Confederacy. John Watt's allied tribes controlled the Chickamauga towns along Big Wills Creek and other Coosa River drainage towns. Dragging Canoe's faction of Chickamauga warriors controlled the five lower towns of Lookout Mountain, Running Water, Nickajack, Crow Town, and Long Island Town. Doublehead's confederacy was an alliance established along the Muscle Shoals of the Tennessee River of North Alabama to stop white encroachment on Indian territory.

With the assistance of the Chickamauga Confederacy, Doublehead enforced his supreme control of the Muscle Shoals area of the Great Bend with his followers known as Chickamauga warriors. Even though there were previous conflicts among the Indian tribes that occupied the area of the Muscle Shoals, Doublehead worked with the local tribes to form alliances in order to organize the strongest historic Indian confederacy to ever occupy the Tennessee River shoals. Doublehead and his Chickamauga alliance was the last Indian people to occupy and control this valuable piece of Tennessee River real estate at the Muscle Shoals.

Sometimes warriors of several tribes making up the confederacy would unite with the three primary leaders of the Chickamauga faction of Lower Cherokee to attack white settlements they consider illegal occupants on their homelands. The confederacy was a motley mix of warriors from the Lower Cherokee, Upper Creek, Chickasaw, Shawnee, Delaware, and other tribes.

Upper Creek Indians

The Upper Creek Indians claimed their territory extended to the south banks of the Tennessee River including the Muscle Shoals of North Alabama. The boundary line between the Creeks and Cherokees remained in question for many years with the Creeks denying that a boundary existed in the Muscle Shoals area of the Tennessee River; however, as reported by Phil Hawkins, Jr., "In the year 1793, the Cherokees had a settlement at the Muscle Shoals (Shoal Town on Big Muscle Shoals), Doublehead and Katagiskee were the chiefs, and the Creeks had a small settlement….The Cherokee settlement extended southwardly from the shoal probably a mile and a half" (Powell, John Wesley, et al, 1887). The Creeks claimed their lands included the south bank of the Tennessee River where Doublehead and Katagiskee lived at Shoal Town.

The Upper Creeks befriended Chickamauga Cherokee Chief Doublehead and became one of his strongest allies. As they had wanted for many years, the Creeks united in a confederacy with Doublehead to carry their war to the white settlers who were invading their frontiers, killing their people, and taking their lands. The Creeks assisted Doublehead in establishing villages along the Great Bend of the Tennessee River and followed him as their leader on many raiding parties into the Cumberland settlements. At times, as many as 700 Creek warriors would follow Doublehead on the warpath; Doublehead's brother Old Tassel was best friends with Creek Chief Alexander McGillivary.

In his days as a Chickamauga warrior, not one Cherokee, Creek, or any other warrior would challenge Doublehead's authority. At times, Doublehead would lead over 1,000 of his warriors on raids into Tennessee. According to Annals of Tennessee (1853), "…Doublehead, crossed the Tennessee River, below the mouth of Holston, and marched all night in the direction of Knoxville. Of this large force, seven hundred were Creeks-the rest were Cherokees."

A cloud of impending doom for Doublehead's Creek alliance began to spread over the Tennessee Valley after Doublehead agreed to peaceful relations with President George Washington of the United States government on June 26, 1794, meeting in Philadelphia. The break in friendly relations with the Creeks was due in part to the response Doublehead received from Governor William Blount telling him to control the Creeks living in his territory if he wanted to maintain peace. The issue with the Creeks played a major role in Doublehead's acceptance by the government officials; at the time, Doublehead was a lesser of two evils. The bribes offered to Doublehead by the government were of assistance in maintaining peace, controlling the Creeks, and encouraging him to give up Cherokee lands. As the Creek alliance that Doublehead had nurtured weakened, so did his power and authority. Doublehead was drawn into conflicts with the Creeks by government officials who ultimately were responsible for the downfall of both Doublehead and his supporters in the Creek Nation. On August 9, 1807, Doublehead was assassinated by fellow Cherokees because of his personal benefits in deals with the government.

Some seven years after the death of Doublehead on March 27, 1814, the Cherokees would join forces with General Andrew Jackson to defeat the Red Stick Creeks at Horseshoe Bend on the Tallapoosa River. The Creeks fought to the bitter end but were eventually defeated by General Andrew Jackson forces. Over 800 Creek Indian people died at Horseshoe Bend making this single battle the largest loss of American Indian lives in the history of the United States.

The death of Doublehead and the defeat of his Creek alliance at Horseshoe Bend was the beginning of the end for all Southeastern Indian people east of the Mississippi River. Total Indian removal to the west of the Mississippi River was not many years in the future following the defeat of the Red Stick Creeks at Horseshoe Bend. President Andrew Jackson finally got the Indian Removal Act passed on May 28, 1830, which not only removed the Creeks from east of the Mississippi but also the other southeastern tribes including the Cherokee.

Chickasaw

After the conflict with the Shawnees ended in the mid 1700's, the Chickasaws moved east through North Alabama and controlled the Muscle Shoals. They claimed the territory east to the mouth of Flint River and north along that river into Tennessee. The Chickasaws established a town at the Chickasaw Old Fields on Chickasaw Island (Hobbs Island) in the Tennessee River south of present-day Huntsville, Alabama.

According to Professor Henry Sale Halbert (1837-1916), "Around the mid 1700's, the Chickasaw's formed the settlement in the Chickasaw Old Fields, which angered the Cherokees very much against their former allies. A great battle was fought in the Chickasaw village in 1769, in which the Chickasaw were victors, but their victory was gained at such a great loss that they retreated from the country, but the Chickasaw's continued their claims to lands on both sides of the Tennessee River." The Chickasaw boundary was established on January 10, 1786, in the Treaty of Hopewell even though the Lower Cherokees were occupying the area; at the time of the treaty, the Chickamauga Cherokees were still at war with the United States. The Chickasaws were the first historic tribe to be recognized by the United States government as having legal claim of the Muscle Shoals all the way to the Flint River east of Huntsville.

Shortly after the fight with the Cherokee in 1769, the Chickasaws moved west from the Chickasaw Old Fields beyond Caney Creek in the western portion of present-day Colbert County, Alabama. As the Chickasaws moved down the Tennessee River toward Mississippi, Doublehead and his followers moved into and occupied the Muscle Shoals. Eventually, the Chickasaws came on friendly terms because Chickasaw Chief George Colbert married two of Doublehead's oldest daughters. When questioned by government authorities about Doublehead living on Chickasaw land, George Colbert claimed that Doublehead and his Cherokee followers were living at the Muscle Shoals by his permission.

At the beginning of the Chickamauga War, the Chickasaw were a major faction of Chickamauga Confederacy, but after the death of James Logan Colbert on January 7, 1784, the alliance weakened. The Chickasaw were the first tribe of the Great Bend to abandon the confederacy. In January 1781, the great Chickasaw Chief Piomingo and General James Robertson of the Cumberland settlements agreed to terms of peace. On January 10, 1786, just two years after the death of James Logan Colbert, Piomingo negotitated the Hopewell Treaty which recognized Chickasaw claims east to the Flint River in present-day Madison County, Alabama. However, a few Chickasaws remained loyal to the Chickamauga confederacy and lived at Doublehead's Town near Brown's Ferry at the east end of Elk River Shoals. These loyal Chickasaws continued to make raids with Doublehead and the Chickamauga.

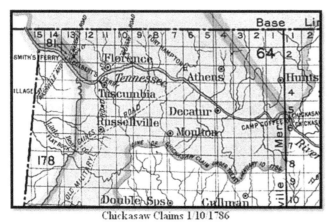

Chickasaw Claims 1/10/1786

The ancestral stronghold of the Chickasaw Indians was the upper Tombigbee River towns in northeastern Mississippi where they had defeated French invasions into their territory on three separate occasions by the mid 1700's. The Chickasaws maintained their presence in the upper Tombigbee River Valley from the time before Desoto in 1540 all the way to Indian removal in the 1830's.

Shawnee

Some years after the Cherokee and Yuchi moved from the Great Bend, bands of Shawnee migrated south and took possession of the land along the Muscle Shoals of the Tennessee River in present-day North Alabama. The Cherokee became very angry at the Shawnee intrusion upon the lands of the Tennessee Valley to which they still claimed as their primary hunting grounds. The Cherokee formed an alliance with the Chickasaw, and by 1750, the two tribes drove the Shawnee from the Muscle Shoals of the Tennessee Valley.

Eventually under the leadership of Dragging Canoe, John Watts Jr. and Doublehead, the Shawnee joined forces with the Chickamauga to fight a common enemy of white settlers who were moving into their hunting grounds, farming their lands, and building houses and towns in their country. Many Shawnee warriors fought with Lower Cherokee during the Chickamauga War with some living at Doublehead's Town at the head of Elk River Shoals. As many as 300 Shawnee warriors joined Doublehead's alliance and accompanied him on raids against the land-hungry white settlers.

The great Shawnee Tecumseh (3/1768-10/5/1813) fought in the Chickamauga War with the Lower Cherokee. Tecumseh was considered by many historians to be mixed Shawnee and Creek. Shawnee people were noted as living in North Alabama along the Muscle Shoals and some historians say that Doublehead had some Shawnee blood.

According to John Sugden in Tecumseh: A Life (1998), "In early 1789, Tecumseh traveled south with Cheeseekau to live among, and fight alongside, the Chickamauga faction of the Cherokee. Accompanied by twelve Shawnee warriors, they stayed at Running Water in Marion County, Tennessee, where Cheeseekau's wife and daughter lived. There Tecumseh met Dragging Canoe, a famous leader who was leading a resistance movement against U.S. expansion. Cheeseekau was killed while leading a raid, and Tecumseh assumed leadership of the small Shawnee band, and subsequent Chickamauga raiding parties. Tecumseh returned to Ohio in late 1790, having fathered a Cherokee daughter before leaving (according to Cherokee oral tradition). Afterward, Tecumseh took part in several battles, including that of the 1794 Fallen Timbers."

Tecumseh

After the Battle of Fallen Timbers, Tecumseh continued his struggle against white encroachment and tried to unite all the southern tribes as he had witnessed with the Chickamauga Confederacy. In 1810, the great Shawnee Tecumseh came through North Alabama with a delegation advocating to reunite an Indian confederacy. He tried to get George Colbert and the Chickasaws to join his cause. The Colbert brothers refused; however at Tukabatchee in 1811, Tecumseh encouraged the Red Stick Creeks to war against the Americans.

Delaware

Doublehead, as did Dragging Canoe, built alliances with surrounding tribes including the Delaware who were living in Kentucky along the Ohio River. Through intermarriage with a Delaware woman from the northern part of Kentucky, the tribe became members of Doublehead's extended family. His marriage to the Delaware woman was an appropriate way to establish a friendly relationship with her people who controlled a great portion of the Ohio River Basin. The Delaware alliance with the Chickamauga was helpful to Doublehead in controlling the northern portion of Tennessee and Kentucky. The Delaware were considered by some historians to be one of the oldest tribes in the northeastern United States, and the parent tribe of the Cherokee people who migrated from the north and settled in the mountainous Appalachian region of the Southeast.

According to Edward Albright in Early History of Middle Tennessee (1909), "In 1780 a group of Delaware hunting south of the Cumberland River were met by a party of men from Fort Nashborough who noted that the group of Delaware was moving south into North Alabama. The whites returned at once to the Bluff (Fort Nashborough), and a delegation was sent…to seek an interview…it was found that they were of the Delaware tribe…they quietly took their leave going south into Alabama." The Delaware were heading to the Muscle Shoals of the Tennessee River controlled by Doublehead.

Doublehead and his war parties made raids into Delaware territory against white settlers on the Rolling Fork section of the Salt River Basin in northern Kentucky and even assisted the Delaware in their fight against white encroachment into the Ohio River Valley. The Delaware were documented taking part in raids on the Cumberland settlements within the territory claimed by the Chickamauga Cherokee. Some of the Delaware warriors would take the heads of victims as war trophies; these were some of the same brutal tactics used by Doublehead and his warriors.

Dragging Canoe, in his speech to the delegation after the Treaty of Sycamore Shoals in 1775, mentions the Delaware as a vanishing people being destroyed by the encroaching white settlers. Dragging Canoe said, "The Delaware tribe is only a remnant of its once great nation." Eventually the

Delaware were defeated in 1794 by General Anthony Wayne at the Battle of Fallen Timbers, where over 100 Cherokee warriors fought with the Delaware but lost to the superior American forces.

On June 26, 1794, of the same year of the defeat at Fallen Timbers, Doublehead signed a peace agreement known as the Treaty of Philadelphia with President George Washington. Doublehead probably saw the handwriting on the wall and knew that his days on the warpath were numbered if he did not make the change from war to peace. He was the last Chickamauga Cherokee War Chief to sign a treaty of peace. The lands of Doublehead's Chickamauga stronghold along the shoals were taken by the Turkey Town Treaty of 1816. The Muscle Shoals area counties taken included Franklin, Lauderdale, Lawrence, Limestone, Morgan, and southwest Madison. By 1818, wealthy white planters along with their black slaves began occupying Doublehead's territory.

Doublehead's Allies

While living at Doublehead's Town at the head of Elk River Shoals in present-day Lawrence County, Alabama, Doublehead became very independent from other Chickamauga leaders. He would make his own decisions in the isolation of the Muscle Shoals, and he had complete control of his war against the Cumberland settlements. He made his raids without asking for permission or guidance from other Chickamauga leaders. Doublehead was the last Chickamauga Cherokee War Chief to cease hostilities in 1795.

During the Chickamauga War while living at Doublehead's Town at the head of Elk River Shoals, Doublehead was allied with other leaders of the Chickamauga faction of Lower Cherokee. These Indian leaders included Pumpkin Boy, Standing Turkey, Sequechee, WarHatchie, Black Fox, The Glass, Bowl (Duwali), Kattygisky, Cuttyatoy, Path Killer, Tahlonteeskee, The Gourd, The Bench, and Scotsman James Logan Colbert of the Chickasaw Nation. Family members allied with Doublehead providing him tremendous support included: Doublehead's nephew John Watts Jr.; his sister Ocuma, wife of Irishman John Melton, and her half blood sons—James, Charles, David, Thomas, Lewis, and Elick; his sister Big Nance; and his brothers Old Tassel, Standing Turkey, Pumpkin Boy, Sequechee, and Warhatchee.

Pumpkin Boy

Pumpkin Boy (Eyahchutlee) was born about 1746, and he was the younger brother of Doublehead. During the Chickamauga War in 1793, he was shot and killed by John Sevier's men during a scouting encounter at Ish's Station. Pumpkin Boy was a scout for Doublehead in preparation for a raid against Knoxville; however, Doublehead attacked Cavett's Station where he took out his revenge for his brother's death by killing all occupants.

Prior to his death, Pumpkin Boy and his wife Chaueukah had one daughter Catherine Spencer. For 12 years, Catherine lived with her uncle Doublehead at Doublehead's Town and at Shoal Town. She was 19 years old when Doublehead was assassinated, and she gave her personal testimony on June 8, 1838.

Standing Turkey

Standing Turkey

Standing Turkey (Gvnagadoga) was an older brother of Doublehead, and he was born about 1738. He was the great nephew of Old Hop, also known as Standing Turkey, and succeeded his uncle as chief of the Cherokee Nation for a brief period in 1761. He went to London with Henry Timberlake in 1762-1763, and he signed the Royal Proclamation of 1763, which was an agreement with the Crown of England to allow no more white people or settlements west of the Appalachians.

In 1782, he was one of a party of the Chickamaugans on a diplomatic mission to the Spanish at Fort St. Louis in Missouri to get arms for the Chickamauga War. Standing Turkey died during the Chickamauga War about 1785. The circumstances of Standing Turkey's death are not known, but for sure he was fighting with his brother Doublehead against the Cumberland settlers.

Sequechee

Sequechee (Sequechu, Sequichee) was born 1748 and died about 1816. In a letter dated August 9, 1807, Captain Addison B. Armstead of Hiwassee Garrison specifically mentioned Sequechee as Doublehead's brother. Sequechee also signed the Cotton Gin Treaty of January 7, 1806, along with his brother Doublehead and his nephew Red Bird II, who was the son of Red Bird I (brother of Sequechee and Doublehead). Sequechee also signed a letter with his brother Doublehead and his nephew Red Bird on August 9, 1805.

WarHatchie

WarHatchie (Wah-hatch, Wah-hatih, Wah-hatihi, WawHatchy, WahHatchie, Warhatchee) was mentioned by Doublehead's niece Catherine Spencer, daughter of Pumpkin Boy. Catherine stated that he was the brother of Doublehead in an affidavit given June 8, 1838. He was also mentioned by his nephew Bird Tail Doublehead, son of Doublehead, as a brother of his father in an affidavit given June 21, 1838. His date of death and birth is not known. WarHatchie signed a treaty with the Cherokee on December 26, 1817, while living in Arkansas Cherokee Territory. There is a community in Lauderdale County, Alabama, called War-hatchie. The community is the namesake of Doublehead's younger brother and lies within the old Doublehead's Reserve.

Enoli-Black Fox

After the Chickamauga War and the death of Little Turkey, Black Fox (Inali, Enoli, or Eunolee) was elected the Principal Chief of the Cherokee Nation from 1801 to his death in 1811. At one time, he lived in a Cherokee village known as Mouse Town or Monee Town near the mouth of Fox's Creek on the Tennessee River some five miles upstream from Doublehead's Town. Fox's Creek, named in honor of Black Fox, enters the Tennessee River east of the upstream end of Elk River Shoals on the county lines of Morgan and Lawrence and still bears his name.

Black Fox eventually moved a few miles west to the road junction of Brown's Ferry Road and Black Warriors' Path that became Fox's Stand which was located some three miles west of Doublehead's Town. During 1816, General John Coffee purchased supplies at Fox's Stand. The store was run by Black Fox, the son of old Chief Black Fox who died in 1811. On July 26, 1816, General John Coffee wrote in his diary, "Went to the river-crossed at Brown's Ferry-paid ferriage…This night went to Black Foxe's and lay all night…bought salt from Fox…paid bill at Fox's $6.75." On August 2, 1816, Coffee wrote again, "Come to the Black Foxe's-bought 2 ½ bushels of corn-paid the bill $1.75-Same day came on-crossed the Tennessee River at Brown's Ferry…"

Chief Black Fox and Doublehead honored each other in several treaties with the United States Government. John Watts, Doublehead, Black Fox and others signed the Treaty with the Cherokee on July 2, 1791. On October 20, 1803, Black Fox places his (X) between his name and Principal Chief; however, this treaty refers to "our beloved Chief Doublehead." Both Black Fox and Doublehead signed Cherokee treaties of October 25, 1805, and October 27, 1805.

Doublehead signed the Cotton Gin Treaty of January 7, 1806, that gave the Cherokees a machine for cleaning cotton; the gin was placed at Melton's Bluff. The treaty also gave the old Cherokee Chief Black Fox $100.00 annually for the rest of his life. The final payment made to Chief Black Fox was in October 1810 and the money was received by his representative. It is probable that Black Fox was in bad health because he had some of his people pick up the money. The old chief Black Fox died the next year in 1811.

Tauquatehee-Thomas Glass

The Glass (Tauquatehee), also known as Thomas Glass, was a true mixed blood Chickamauga warrior of the Lower Cherokee. He moved south after the Treaty of Sycamore Shoals in 1775 and Cherokee Treaty of 1776 to fight white encroachment with Dragging Canoe, Doublehead, and others. In January 1791, Glass and his warriors captured James Hubbard and 15 men who were building a blockhouse at the Muscle Shoals on one of the islands near Tuscumbia Landing. Glass released them with a warning not to return.

In April 1791, Zachariah Cox and 31 settlers arrived at the Muscle Shoals on the Tennessee River to build a fort and develop a trading post on Cox's Island south of present-day Center Star in Lauderdale County, Alabama. Cox and his associates were busy erecting a fort when Glass and his some sixty warriors suddenly appeared. Glass put an end to the plans of Cox's group settling on the Muscle Shoals. Glass warned Cox and his men that they would be put to death if they came back to the area. The white adventurers led by Cox abandoned their fort and dreams; thus, Glass' actions preserved the Muscle Shoals as Indian Territory for another quarter of a century.

On February 17, 1792, Glass waylaid the John Collingsworth family near Nashville and killed him, his wife, and daughter, and captured an eight-year-old girl. After Doublehead signed the Treaty of Philadelphia on June 26, 1794, the Lower Chickamauga Cherokees were compelled to make peace with the United States government. Glass signed the treaty at Tellico Blockhouse. After the Treaty of Tellico Blockhouse in 1794, Glass remained prominent among the Lower Cherokee and became the assistant to Chief Black Fox.

At Philadelphia on June 3, 1801, The Glass was the Lower Cherokee speaker who made a fiery speech pressing for removal of settlers from Cherokee territory, and he astounded Secretary of War Henry Dearborn and President Jefferson by the vehemence of his refusal to consider a land cessation. His verbal barrage so astonished Thomas Jefferson that the President gave assurance to Glass that the land proposal being negotiated would not be pressed. Six years later, however, like other former Lower Chickamauga Cherokee leaders, he succumbed to the government gratuity. Several times in the ensuing decade, he accepted bribes to give up Cherokee lands.

Following the assassination of Doublehead on August 9, 1807, Glass succeeded him as head of the Lower Cherokee council. Glass was considered the Chickamauga Cherokee faction principal chief until 1809, when separate councils for the Lower and Upper Cherokees were abolished. The domination of national affairs by the Lower Cherokee chiefs ended with a revolt of a group of the younger chiefs of the Upper Cherokee Towns. At Broom Town, the reunited Cherokee National Council abolished the Blood Law; however, the Old Settlers or Cherokees West got blood revenge after eastern Cherokees arrived in Indian Territory in March 1839.

Glass' activities led him to advocate for removal to Indian Territory west of the Mississippi River. He signed the Turkey Town Treaty of September 1816 which gave up the lands of the Muscle Shoals which he protected during the Chickamauga War. The lands ceded in the 1816 treaty include portions of present-day Franklin, Colbert, Lauderdale, Lawrence, Limestone, Morgan, and southwestern Madison Counties, Alabama. In 1818, Glass led 167 Cherokees to their lands west of the Mississippi. While in route west, Glass' wife and son died, and he died the following year in 1819.

Duwali-The Bowl

Chief Bowl (Duwali), born circa 1756, was a fierce half-blood of a Scots father and Cherokee mother. While fighting with Doublehead during the Chickamauga War, Duwali was leader of a band of the Chickamauga faction of Lower Cherokees who murdered 13 white people, including three women and

Duwali by William A. Berry

four children. He led a war party of Lower Cherokees on an attack of William and Alexander Scott's party from Williamsburg, South Carolina. Members of the Scott group were trying to reach the Natchez District by way of the Tennessee River.

The attack took place on the Tennessee River in North Alabama near Melton's Bluff in Lawrence County, Alabama, in 1794. Duwali's warriors killed all whites in the party except for some women and children who were set adrift on the shoals. During the assault on the flotilla at the Muscle Shoals, Chief Bowl and his warriors captured 21 black slaves. Since there is no mention of the slaves when Duwali moved west, Doublehead and John Melton probably took the black slaves for their cotton plantation and farming operations. All the goods of the Scott party were probably sold or distributed to local Lower Cherokee families. This act of piracy at the Muscle Shoals received so much publicity that the Upper Cherokees denied their nation was responsible, and Bowl was forced to flee to the Arkansas country. Not long afterwards, Chief Bowl settled with his band in Texas.

Some historians report that Duwali left the Muscle Shoals shortly after 1794; however, according to United States Agent to the Cherokees Return J. Meigs' letter of January 22, 1810, to United States Secretary of War, Chief Bowl's passport for 63 Cherokees moving west of the Mississippi was issued to him on January 10, 1810. Duwali's move west was probably because of fear that he might receive the same punishment as Doublehead. Duwali eventually settled with his band between the Neches River and the Sabine River in Texas.

According to The Texas Cherokees by Dianna Everett (1990), Bowl (Duwali) and mixed blood Richard Fields tried to get a Texas land grant from the Mexican government. Fields eventually turned against the Mexicans and Bowl maintained his allegiance to Mexico. The Texas Cherokee council approved the assassination of Fields which was carried out in February 1827. Texas revolutionists and Texas President Mirabeau Buonaparte Lamar refused to recognize Cherokee claims to Texas lands partly because Bowl sided with the Mexicans. As a consequence, the 83-year-old Chief Bowl was killed on the battle field against the Army of the Republic of Texas on July 16, 1839.

Kattygisky

Around the 1770's, Kattygisky settled in Shoal Town in the northwest corner of Lawrence County (present-day Colbert County), Alabama. Captain Edmund Pendleton Gaines identified Shoal Town in his field notes on December 28, 1807, as follows, "8th mile…at 119 chs. cross the path which leads from Shoal Town, easterly to Gourds Settlement, about 3 miles distance" (Stone, 1971). Shoal Town was one of the largest Lower Cherokee villages along the Muscle Shoals. Shoal Town was located some six miles west of the eastern end of the Big Muscle Shoals in the area around the mouths of Bluewater Creek, Town Creek, and Big Nance's Creek.

Kattygisky (Katagiskee) was a powerful Chickamauga Cherokee chief who Doublehead referred to and sought approval on white settlers leasing farming rights in the area. Kattygisky lived about one mile from the mouth of Town Creek on a hill overlooking his huge spring. Kattygisky's (present-day Kittiakaska) Creek runs northeast into Town Creek about one half mile from his home and spring. The Indian chief and the creek he lived on had several different spellings of the name on various maps including Kattygisky, Katagiskee, Katty

Gisky, Kategishee, Kittagesta, Kittikaski, Kittikaskia, Kitticaski, Kitticaska, Kittycasidda, and Kitticaski; it was no different with the Cherokee Chief Kattygisky whose name was spelled a dozen different ways. The mouth of Kattygisky's Creek is about a half mile south from the Tennessee River, and Kattygisky's home is about one half mile to the southwest of Town Creek up the small creek.

Kattygisky was involved with several treaty negotiations, and he signed several treaties with Doublehead. In a May 20, 1792 letter to General James Robertson, Governor William Blount wrote of the reception of the Chickamauga Cherokee Chief Kattygisky, The Glass, and other chiefs that came from the lower towns in North Alabama to Coyate, "At the house built there for my reception is erected the standard of the United States (a very elegant stand) on a high pole. To this they (the lower chiefs) were conducted by the Bloody Fellow and John Watts, Kittagesta and other chiefs and Captain Chisholm and Leonard Shaw walking side by side with the Bloody Fellow and Watts to the great joy of both parties, where volleys were fired by those from the lower towns in honor of it and returned by the upper…Chisholm declares he never saw more joy expressed by any people."

"In the year 1793, the Chickamauga Cherokees had a settlement at the Muscle Shoals, Doublehead and Katagiskee were the chiefs," wrote Phil Hawkins, Jr. (Powell, John Wesley, et.al., 1887). Also, Hawkins identifies Shoal Town were Doublehead and Katagiskee had a large settlement that extended a mile and half southward from the river along Town Creek. The Cherokee settlement along Town Creek is also written about in Nina Leftwich's book, Two Hundred Years at Muscle Shoals, (1935).

On January 12, 1807, Alford and Drew wrote to Doublehead and Kattygisky telling that they would help the Cherokees at the Muscle Shoals raise cotton.

"Sirs:
We wish to live at the Shoals. We will conform to laws of the Cherokee. We are willing to settle at the Shoals and help Doublehead's people with farming, raising cotton, and other produce, together with house building.

Sincerely,
Hutson Alford and Newit Drew"

On January 14, 1807, Doublehead wrote Return J. Meigs the Cherokee Indian agent the following, "I (Doublehead) am not able to ride or I should have come-I send you letters from two good men (Hutson Alford and Newit Drew) whom Kattygesky and I want to live here. I have consulted with Katty Gisky. Please give them permits.

Your Friend and Brother,
Doublehead"

Prior to the white cotton planters arriving in the Tennessee Valley, Doublehead and Kattygisky wanted the government to upgrade roads coming into the area. On February 1, 1805, Doublehead and Kattygisky requested that the Georgia Road be extended to the Muscle Shoals. "I have received a line from Doublehead, Kategishee and some others who live at the Shoals that they wish a road from Cumberland may pass-by the Shoals in such a deviation as to fall into the road to Georgia in a proper place. Return J. Meigs"

John Johnson Plantation House

Kattygisky lived on a rise just a few hundred yards above a big spring downhill from his home which was one half mile west of Town Creek on the south side of the Tennessee River. The spring was originally known as Kattygisky's Spring; the spring branch runs a short distance before entering a small creek. Today, the creek is known as Kittikaski Creek in present-day Colbert County, Alabama. From the spring, the creek runs a short distance before entering into Town Creek across from present-day Doublehead's Resort in Lawrence County, Alabama.

In the summer of 1807, John Johnson and his second wife Nance had leased a large tract of land from Doublehead just a few days prior to his assassination on August 9, 1807. In 1816, John Johnson's son-in-law Major Lewis Dillahaunty was sent to the area by President James Monroe for the peaceful removal of the Cherokees and Chickasaws. Later, Kattygisky's home eventually became the site of the Green Onion Plantation Mansion that belonged to planter John Johnson. Johnson established his home on the area that once was the home of Chief Kattygisky. Johnson was a black slave holder of a large amount of cotton land around the mouth of Town Creek.

Cuttyatoy

Cuttyatoy was a fierce and aggressive Lower Cherokee warrior who fought with Dragging Canoe and Doublehead during the Chickamauga War. He was fighting the encroachment of whites to prevent settlement of the Big Bend of the Tennessee River and to protect Cherokee lands. In 1788, Cuttyatoy led an attack on a keelboat belonging to the Brown Family near the Lower Towns of Dragging Canoe. During the raid which led to the death of the father of the Brown Family along with two of his boys, Cuttyatoy took the black slaves of the Brown family. In addition, Creeks and Lower Cherokees took Jane Brown, two daughters and two sons captive. One of the captive white boys was Joseph Brown, who was fifteen years old at that time. Later, Cuttyatoy tried to kill Joseph Brown, but he was protected by his Indian owner.

After the raid, Cuttyatoy moved west along the Tennessee River with the black slaves of the Brown Family, and he settled near the lower end of the Elk River Shoals of the Tennessee River in present-day Lawrence County, Alabama. His village was on Gilchrist Island across the river from the mouth of Elk River. The island is located near the mouth of Spring Creek on the south side of the Tennessee River in present-day Lawrence County, Alabama.

In time, Joseph Brown escaped and joined the army of Tennessee volunteers commanded by General Andrew Jackson. Joseph became a colonel during the Creek Indian War. During the Battle of Talladega on November 9, 1813, Colonel Joseph Brown learned from mixed blood Charles Butler where his father's slaves were being held by Cuttyatoy. According to the <u>American Whig Review</u>, Volume 15, Issue 87, March 1852, page 247, "Colonel (Joseph) Brown…a participant in the battle of Talledega (November 9, 1813)…met Charles Butler… and learned from him that…Chief Cuttyatoy, was still alive…he was then living on an island in the Tennessee River, near the mouth of Elle (Elk) River, and that he had with him several Negroes … taken by him at Nickajack on the 9th of May, 1788… with ten picked men, Brown proceeded to the island, went to the head man's (Cuttyatoy) lodge and exhibited to him General (Andrew) Jackson's order, and demanded that Cuttyatoy's Negroes be immediately sent over to Fort Hampton…In crossing the river, Colonel Brown and his men took up the Negroes, and Cuttyatoy's wife behind them, to carry them over the water while the Indian men crossed on a raft (Brown's Ferry) higher up (stream). Colonel Joseph Brown and his men reached Fort Hampton that morning while Cuttyatoy and his men arrived in the afternoon."

By the time Cuttyatoy reached Fort Hampton, the black slaves had already been sent to Huntsville. Colonel Joseph Brown, who was also a preacher, spared the life of old Cuttyatoy, and said, "I will let God take care of him." Joseph Brown became a landowner in the Pulaski, Tennessee area. It is ironic that the black slaves retaken by Joseph Brown wound up killing him. Some say they put poison or ground glass in his food.

Path Killer

Prior to the Turkey Town Treaty of 1816, Path Killer lived in Lawrence County, Alabama; the creek that flows through the center of the county and drains the area around the county seat of Moulton was initially named Path Killer's

Creek. According to Captain Edmund Pendleton Gaines on December 27, 1807, "We proceeded, same course…6th mile…At 116 [chains] (west of Melton's Bluff) Path Killer's Creek, 3 chains wide from tops of banks" (Stone, 1971).

The name of the creek was changed from Path Killer to Big Nance's Creek after Doublehead's sister Nance moved to the mouth of the creek just one quarter mile west of present-day Wheeler Dam. Big Nance was mentioned in a letter from John D. Chisholm from Darnelle Rock on the Arkansas River on June 28, 1812. In microcopy 208, roll 5, and number 2846, the following statement identifies that Nancy was the sister of Doublehead, "Lost nearly all my property. Two Negroes ran away in possession of Big Nance, Doublehead's sister. I have been constantly with Talluhuskee and his party."

Path Killer took over as Principal Chief of the Cherokee Nation after the death of Black Fox in 1811. He signed the Turkey Town Treaty of September 1816 that gave up Cherokee land claims to the area of the Muscle Shoals of North Alabama. On September 11, 1808, Path Killer signed an act passed by the Cherokee National Council at Broom's Town forbidding the blood law.

On October 22, 1813, during the Creek War, Path Killer informed General Andrew Jackson by a letter written from Turkey Town that the warring Creek army would take the Muscle Shoals Path. The Muscle Shoals Path was also known as the Coosa Path, and the Indian trail led through Oakville, Moulton, and then to Tuscumbia Landing to the west. Path Killer served as chief until he died on January 8, 1827. At the time of his death, Path Killer was living near Turkey Town, and he is buried at Centre, Alabama.

Tahlonteeskee

Tahlonteeskee was the great nephew of Doublehead and the son of Doublehead's niece Wurteh Watts and trader John Benge. Tahlonteeskee (Tolontuskee, Taluntuskee, Tashliske, Talohuskee, Talluhuskee) Benge was born about 1770 and died in the Spring of 1819. He lived at Shoal Town located at the Big Muscle Shoals in the Big Bend of the Tennessee River. In the summer of 1808, he sought permission from President Thomas Jefferson to take some 1,131 Chickamauga Cherokees to Arkansas.

Tahlonteeskee's group became known as the "Old Settlers or Cherokees West," and their passports were approved in January and February 1810. The Old Settlers were primarily the relatives, friends, or loyal supporters of Doublehead. Tahlonteeskee also stated that he feared assassination like his uncle Doublehead had received because he had signed some of the same treaties and received benefits just as Doublehead had. After moving west of the Mississippi River, Tahlonteeskee became Chief of the western Cherokees or Old Settlers. After his death in 1819, his half-brother John Jolly became the chief of the Arkansas Cherokee.

The Gourd

The Gourd lived at Gourd's Settlement, a Cherokee village near the present-day town of Courtland in Lawrence County, Alabama. The Indian town was named after a Cherokee Indian called The Gourd which was first written about by Captain Edmund Pendelton Gaines. On December 28, 1807, Captain Gaines made this note on his survey of the area from Melton's Bluff to Cotton Gin Port, "8ᵗʰ mile…. At 119 chs. Cross the path which leads from the Shoal Town, eastwardly, to the Gourd's Settlement, about 3 miles distance" (Stone, James H., 1971). Based on Gaines measurements of some 8.7 miles westerly from Melton's Bluff, then easterly for three miles, Gourd's settlement was near the present-day town of Courtland, Alabama.

The Gourd fought against the Red Stick Creeks with the army of General Andrew Jackson during the Creek Indian War. According to Letters from Alabama 1817-1822 written by Anne Royall on January 12, 1818, "Guide says Gourd was very kind; he knew him for fifteen years. He helped subdue the Creeks, and made an excellent soldier."

Gourd's Island in the Tennessee River south of the mouth of Elk River was named in honor of Gourd. Also, Gourd's Landing was on the south bank of the river north of present-day Courtland; an Indian road connected the landing to Courtland. The landing was thought to be near the mouth of Spring Creek and south of Gourd's Island.

In a letter dated August 15, 1816, The Gourd asked for Negro Fox to be returned to the Cherokees after members of the Burleson family attacked and killed two of their Cherokee people. These Cherokee men were killed at Mouse Town which was located on the border of present-day Lawrence County and Morgan County, Alabama, at the mouth of Fox's Creek and the Tennessee River. At one time, the Burleson family operated a ferry which crossed the Tennessee River from Mouse Town to Cow Ford Landing in present-day Limestone County, Alabama.

The Bench-Robert (Bob) Benge

Bob Benge fought with his Uncle Doublehead during the Chickamauga War. Although the name of his great nephew Robert (Bob) Benge sent fear into the hearts of settlers on the frontier, Doublehead was still considered the most ruthless and brutal Chickamauga warrior who ever lived. Even though legends say that Benge personally took forty-five scalps, historians agree that Doublehead far surpassed that mark. However, Bob Benge was known as the most notorious kidnapper of black slaves and sought out settlers who were slaveholders. Benge would sell the stolen slaves. Many of the slaves probably wound up in the possession of Doublehead and his brother-in-law John Melton.

While on his last raid in Virginia, Benge captured Susanna and Elizabeth Livingston and three black slaves. Benge asked Elizabeth about the slaveholder General Evan Shelby who lived on the North Holston River. Bob Benge then told his white female captives that, "He would pay him (General Shelby) a visit next summer and take away all of his Negroes" (Perdue, 1979). As Benge was attempting to transport his captives back to Doublehead's stronghold in northwest Alabama, he was ambushed and killed by Lieutenant Vincent Hobbs on April 9, 1794, at Stone Gap, Virginia.

James Logan Colbert

Scotsman James Logan Colbert and his half-blood Chickasaw sons were allied with Lower Cherokee Chief Doublehead and Creek Chief Alexander McGillivary during the Chickamauga War. During the war, Colbert was made a captain by the British and led the siege on Fort Jefferson in 1781.

While returning home after visiting with McGillivary, his friend and brother-in-law to his son William, James Logan Colbert was killed on January 7,

1784, by his slave Cesar or from being thrown from his horse. After the death of James Logan Colbert, Chickasaw Chief Piomingo negotiated the January 10, 1786 Treaty of Philadelphia with President George Washington. As a result of the treaty, the Chickasaw boundary included the lands occupied and controlled by Chickamauga Cherokee Chief Doublehead at the Muscle Shoals of northwest Alabama including Lawrence County. In 1786, Doublehead was still at war with the United States.

Doublehead-the Planter

At the end of the Chickamauga War, Doublehead signed the Treaty of Philadelphia in June 26, 1794, with President George Washington. Some 20 years of Doublehead's life at the Muscle Shoals of the Tennessee River was spent on the warpath—killing, scalping, stealing, burning, and destroying. However, one day in June 1795, Doublehead ceased all hostilities against the white settlers, and he was never recorded on another raid. After his time on the warpath ended, Doublehead became a very shrewd and successful planter, slave owner, and businessman.

After the 1794 treaty ended the Chickamauga War, the black slaves of Doublehead and slaves of his brother-in-law John Melton engaged in farming cotton along the fertile bottom lands adjacent to Elk River Shoals and Big Muscle Shoals of the Tennessee River. Until 1802, Doublehead lived upstream about eight miles east of Melton's Bluff at Doublehead's Town at the Brown's Ferry in Lawrence County, Alabama. Earlier, Doublehead had established a Cherokee town in Franklin County (present-day Colbert) on the south side of the Tennessee River a few miles east of his son-in-law George Colbert's Ferry known as Doublehead's Village. Near Doublehead's Village was a spring known as Doublehead's Spring, and its location is recorded on old maps.

Doublehead and his black slaves raised cotton along with his brother-in-law John Melton in present-day Lawrence County, Alabama. They were the first Cherokee cotton plantation owners with black slaves at the Elk River Shoals in the area of Lawrence County, Alabama. According to historic records, Doublehead owned some 40 black slaves who were identified in affidavits by his son Bird Doublehead, his niece Catherine Spencer, and Caleb Starr in 1838.

Doublehead's brother-in-law John Melton owned some 60 black slaves prior to 1807. Anne Royall stated in <u>Letters from Alabama 1817-1822</u>, "I saw and conversed with many of Melton's slaves…Here is a very large plantation of cotton and maize, worked by about sixty slaves, and owned by General Jackson who bought the interest of old Melton." Notice that Anne Royall refers to the black slaves of General Andrew Jackson as Melton's slaves.

Doublehead and John Melton's farming operations were primarily the flat, fertile lands along Elk River Shoals and Big Muscle Shoals of the Tennessee River. Doublehead became a very successful cotton planter and farmer with the assistance of John Melton. They became farmers of cotton, corn, and livestock. On May 7, 1799, David Henley, United States war department Indian agent, wrote a letter to Doublehead praising improvements in growing cotton and corn. Doublehead also supplied the United States Army in the Tennessee Valley with beef cattle, and he owned some of the finest horses in area.

In 1802, Doublehead requested from the government a boat to transport his cotton to New Orleans. In the 1805 Treaty of Tellico, Chief Doublehead gained the right to a ferry, and he was also promised a new boat for his own use. An 1838 affidavit by his son Bird Doublehead confirms that his father used his keel boat for transporting and selling his farm products.

In 1809, Indian agent Meigs described Doublehead's Road which was an Indian trail used as a Mobile to Nashville Trace that was upgraded by Doublehead and his warriors to a wagon road. In a letter from Return J. Meigs, Esq. to the Secretary of War, Meigs states, "Hiwassee Garrison. 1st December, 1809. These roads intersect the first-mentioned great road at different points, except one road of 100 miles in length, opened by Doublehead, commencing at Franklin County, Tennessee, and runs to the Muscle Shoals, and it is contemplated to be continued to the navigable waters of Mobile." Franklin County initially was to be part of the State of Franklin from Nashville area to the Tennessee River then east toward North Carolina. Starting in 1816, much of Doublehead's Road between Columbia and Florence was actually upgraded as Jackson's Old Military Road.

John Melton-Melton's Bluff

By the late 1700's, Melton's Bluff took its name from Irishman John Melton. John Melton's cotton plantation was an outpost of the Lower Chickamauga Cherokee near the middle of the Elk River Shoals on the south bank of the Tennessee River. From 1780 through 1815, John Melton was the first white settler and cotton planter that used black slaves in Lawrence County, Alabama.

The Chickamauga faction of Lower Cherokees village at Melton's Bluff was located on the Lower South River Road between Mallard Creek and Spring Creek on the Tennessee River. Black Warriors' Path and Gaines Trace intersected with the Lower South River Road at Melton's Bluff. This strategic site was on elevated flat lands adjacent to a high bluff overlooking the river between Tennessee River miles 287 and 288.

John was the white Irish brother-in-law of Chickamauga Cherokee Chief Doublehead. Besides John Melton, Doublehead had other white relatives who had married into his family. Most of Doublehead's white kinfolks were Celtic men who were Indian traders for English merchants in the colonies. Some historians think that John Melton was a trader to the Cherokee; and, by following the early Indian trails and trade routes, he found his way to the remote outpost of Melton's Bluff not long after it was established and controlled by Doublehead's warriors.

It is known that John Melton's Cherokee wife Ocuma was the sister of Doublehead who controlled the Muscle Shoals as a strong fearless leader of the Lower Cherokee faction of the Chickamauga. Since John Melton was married to one of Doublehead's sisters, he was considered a member of Doublehead's extended family; therefore, he had protection and refuge among the Chickamauga Cherokee at the Muscle Shoals.

According to Melton's wife Ocuma in a letter to Colonel Return J. Meigs dated June 30, 1815, John Melton "became a resident of Cherokee Nation 35 years ago and married me not long afterward according to established custom of my nation" (microcopy 208, roll 7, and number 3229). Based on a written statement by his wife, John Melton was in the area by 1780. It is not known exactly when John Melton first arrived at Melton's Bluff, but his Cherokee wife Ocuma stated that they had been married thirty-five years which would have placed Melton with the Chickamauga faction about 1780; therefore, John Melton helped establish the Chickamauga Indian town of Melton's Bluff soon afterwards.

Chickamauga War-Melton's Bluff

In the spring of 1776, General Griffin Rutherford and Andrew Williamson's colonial armies escalated the Chickamauga War. They destroyed the eastern valley, middle, and lower towns of the Cherokee Nation, killing men, women, and children; taking no prisoners. The area of Melton's Bluff became a refuge for many of the survivors of the vicious raids into Cherokee lands by the armies of Rutherford and Williamson.

The colonial armies committed genocide and destroyed many Cherokee farms and settlements in their eastern towns; therefore, Chickamauga Cherokee warriors at or near Melton's Bluff would seek to retaliate by destroying boats coming down the Tennessee River. These vulnerable flatboats floating down the Tennessee River were attacked, and those on board were captured or killed by groups of Cherokees attacking from the high cliffs at Melton's Bluff. During a declared war, conflicts with the Chickamauga warriors and white settlers encroaching on Indian lands was ongoing.

Keel boats, flat boats, and other river crafts often ran into trouble with the Indians, as well as the rapids upon reaching the Muscle Shoals. As vessels approached the turbulent rapids at the upper end of the Elk River Shoals especially during low water periods, the river journey became extremely dangerous. The fall line of the Tennessee River started at the upstream rapids of the Muscle Shoals and continued for nearly 40 miles. Luckless flatboats and keelboats often stranded as they tried to float down the river through these treacherous shoals. When these river crafts ran into trouble as they approached the turbulent waters at the beginning of the shoals, they were attacked, and the passengers and crew on board were often killed or captured by the Chickamauga faction of Cherokee Indians who lived in villages along the Muscle Shoals. The warriors would rob and take all the valuables and black slaves that were on board.

On March 12, 1780, John Donelson's flotilla was fired on by Chickamauga Cherokees at Elk River Shoals; however, the flotilla had reached the shoals when the water was high, making the passage less dangerous from the river. In addition, Donelson's group was also fired on at the lower end of the Muscle Shoals. The time of John Donelson's passage through the Muscle Shoals was at the height of the Chickamauga War; Doublehead and his warriors were trying to protect their lands from white encroachment.

From 1775 through 1795, the Melton's Bluff area of North Alabama was the stronghold of Doublehead and his warriors during the Chickamauga War. Anne Royall indicates that John Melton was a much feared pirate at the Muscle Shoals from the 1780's until the end of the war in the middle of the 1790's. Doublehead and John Melton took numerous black slaves and made a sizeable fortune preying upon invading white settlers who came down the Tennessee River in their flatboats or keelboats. These white people were encroaching on the territory owned, controlled, and protected by the Chickamauga warriors of the Lower Cherokee.

Anne Newport Royall arrives at Melton's Bluff

The most colorful accounts of Melton's Bluff can be found in <u>Letters from Alabama 1817-1822</u> written by the first professional woman journalist and correspondent in the United States, Anne Newport Royall. She was born on June 11, 1769, and she died on October 1, 1854. She is buried in the Congressional Cemetery in Washington, D. C. Anne Royall left an amazing record of the early life at Melton's Bluff in Lawrence County, Alabama.

Royall was an independent lady who traveled to the new frontier in North Alabama after her military husband died. One of her stops was at Melton' Bluff in present-day Lawrence County, Alabama. The Town of Marathon at Melton's Bluff was one of the few fortunate communities in the wilderness of Alabama to be visited and described by Anne Royall. She was an adventurous reporter who made two visits to Melton's Bluff in 1818. Her first letter was in early January when the land first opened for white settlement, and some of her other letters were in late December of 1818. In 1818, Royall spent some of her time in Lawrence County at the Town of Moulton, Alabama.

In one of Royall's letters, she describes the route to Melton's Bluff from Florence as follows, "Melton's Bluff, January 8th, 1818… I was three days on the road to this place. Melton's Bluff is at the head of Mussel Shoals...I went direct to the foot of the Shoals, 70 miles from Huntsville, crossed the river, and come upon the south side of Tennessee River…three miles in width! The largest body of water that I ever saw. It was at this time very high and muddy; and the noise produced by the water washing over the rocks was tremendous…we saw a boat hung on a rock, about the middle of the stream…I took a guide, one of the pilots, and crossed the river next morning, in a ferry boat…upon leaving the ferry…I was to pass by several Indian farms… About ten o'clock we came in sight of the first Indian farm… you cross Town Creek in a canoe and swim your horses; this will cost you one dollar…I, with my horses, were safely on the other side… Rhea (my guide's name) said I had two more creeks to pass…however, these were easily forded…this land is so clear of undergrowth that you may drive a wagon any where through the woods…we passed many Indian houses in the day, and some beautiful springs. Melton's Bluff is a town, and takes its name from…John Melton…Irishman by birth…attached himself to the Cherokee Indians…Melton's Bluff… a very large plantation of cotton and maize, worked by about sixty slaves and owned by General Jackson, who bought the interest of old Melton." A very interesting note is that she passed many Cherokee Indian homes which were still standing.

In 1818, Anne Newport Royall, a guest at Melton's Bluff, said that she was there only two years following the death of the aged John Melton. In Anne Royall's first letter from Melton's Bluff January 8, 1818, she was obviously fascinated by what she had heard about the Irishman John Melton, and wrote in some detail about his life. Her inquiries about the Bluff's first white settler were timely in that she actually talked to the black slaves of John Melton during her visits to the area.

Anne Royall wrote that Irishman John Melton was responsible for some acts of piracy at the Muscle Shoals. She also pointed out that Melton was the perpetrator of boat raids; however, these attacks on white settler boats occurred during the Chickamauga War which lasted from 1775 through 1795. There were several Chickamauga warriors who were involved in acts of piracy at or near Melton's Bluff and the Muscle Shoals.

During the war, John Melton benefited from Chickamauga attacks on early white settlers whose flatboats became stranded on the rocks, sand bars, and islands of Elk River Shoals. During this time, Melton secured some 60 black slaves and other property taken by the Chickamauga Cherokee warriors from these white intruders in Indian territory. In her letter dated January 14, 1818, Royall made the following accusation against John Melton, "He was an Irishman by birth…attached himself to Cherokee Indians and married a squaw…with the assistance of the Indians, he used to rob the boats which passed down the river, and murder the crews. By these means, he became immensely rich; owned a great number of slaves; most of who he robbed from these boats."

Melton's Plantation House

In <u>Letters from Alabama 1817 to 1822</u>, Anne Royall described Melton's house as a large cotton plantation mansion built probably between the years of 1788 and 1793. The house was built on the south bank of the Tennessee River, almost directly southeast across the river from the mouth of the Elk River in present-day Lawrence County, Alabama. Royall described the house as a large two-storied log house. Irishman John Melton, his Cherokee wife Ocuma, and his half-blood Cherokee children lived in the home on the high flat land above the river bluff. John Melton's black slaves added to and improved his home and cotton plantation over a period of years.

The Melton home was described by Anne Royall as a "mansion with an impressive courtyard that fronted the house, and a road that ran to the river. The house was a large two-storied home that was the central building with many outlying slave quarters, a cotton gin, stables, visitors' cabins that lined the bluff, and an inn for travelers. From the front of the house, one could see upriver to Brown's Ferry, about eight miles away, and about the same distance down river from the house." John Melton's home was downstream from the town of his brother-in-law Doublehead at Brown's Ferry.

The road that led to the river was the Black Warriors' Path that crossed the river at Melton's Bluff to Fort Hampton. Later, the road became a post route that connected Fort Mitchell in Russell County, Alabama, to Fort Hampton in Limestone County, Alabama, and became known as Mitchell's Trace.

In one of Royall's (1817-1822) letters, she described the John Melton house with horrible stories that she had heard and unable to erase from her mind, "The mansion was large, built with logs, shingled roof….I recoiled at the sight of a place once the habitation of such a monster." In yet another letter, the she referred to the house as, "Melton's castle… it only serves to remind us of the rapine and bloodshed of its former owner." She accuses Melton, but these were acts of war caused by the illegal invasion of white settlers. Melton's family, Doublehead, and the Chickamauga warriors were trying to save and protect their ancestral homelands and hunting grounds.

A total of sixteen letters were written by Anne Royall from Melton's Bluff in Lawrence County, Alabama. Her writings were biased against the Indian people as evidenced by her statement that the best way to deal with the Indians was with rifles. By the time Anne Royall described Melton's Bluff in January 1818, the Indian territory had just been open to white settlement; however, the village contained two large houses of entertainment, several doctors, one hatters shop, one warehouse, and several mechanics.

Cotton Plantation and Gin at Melton's Bluff

Before the end of the late 1700's, cotton became a very important Cherokee product, and the use of black slaves in the early 1800's was common among the Cherokee. Melton's Bluff was a Cherokee Indian plantation with rich cotton ground along the south bank of the Tennessee River. Doublehead and John Melton owned some 100 black slaves who planted and harvested the first cotton in present-day Lawrence County, Alabama.

According to Cherokees of the Old South, "In order to encourage the Cherokee Indians at Melton's Bluff to become cotton farmers, the newly appointed Cherokee Agent Return Jonathan Meigs at Hiwassee Garrison near the present-day town of Calhoun, Tennessee, sent them a blacksmith named Samuel Hall. In 1802, Samuel Hall, a white man, arrived at Melton's Bluff in Lawrence

County, Alabama, to teach the Cherokees. Hall was a blacksmith that was hired to train the Cherokees the art of his trade. However, while at Melton's Bluff, Samuel Hall complained about not receiving his one shilling of silver a day for training Cherokees the blacksmithing skills. Later, Indian Agent Meigs transferred Samuel Hall east to Wills Town located on Big Wills Creek in present-day Dekalb County, Alabama" (Malone, 1956).

A cotton gin was placed on the Melton's Bluff Plantation according to the Cotton Gin Treaty of January 7, 1806, when the Lower Cherokees ceded some their land claims north of the Tennessee River in northwest Alabama. Doublehead thought enough of his white Irish brother-in-law John Melton that in the Cotton Gin Treaty of 1806, he negotiated for a cotton cleaning machine to be placed at Melton's Bluff by the United States Government. The Cotton Gin Treaty had the following provision, "…that the Cherokee shall be furnished with a machine for cleaning cotton."

The following was stipulated in the Cotton Gin Treaty of January 7, 1806: "The United States agree to pay in consideration for the foregoing cession, $2,000.00 in money upon ratification; $8,000.00 in four equal annual installments; to erect a grist-mill within one year in the Cherokee country; to furnish a machine for cleaning cotton; and to pay the Cherokee Chief, Black Fox, $100.00 annually for the rest of his life." The cotton gin was placed at Melton's Bluff in Lawrence County, Alabama, and indications are that John Melton was the recipient of this equipment.

In Letters from Alabama 1817-1822, Anne Royall described the cotton gin at Melton's Bluff, "From the field we sauntered along to the cotton gin. Everyone who raises cotton, must have a gin…We found a number of boys and horses at the cotton gin…a considerable tree pulled round and round by a horse; this turned a screw which pressed the bales of cotton-the world and all the boys seemed to be made of cotton here…The pressing part of it is something like pressing cyder; but as to the ginning part of it, with its thousand wheels and saws. On our return home, we passed two lines of negro cabins…warm and comfortable."

In the same letter, Royall continued to describe the plantation. "I took a walk with some ladies to-day over the plantation, as we wished to have a nearer view of those snowy fields...together with orchards, gin houses, gardens, Melton's mansion, and a considerable negro town…We entered the court yard, fronting the house, by a stile; and the first thing we met was a large scaffold overspread with cotton: as it was in the seed, there must have been many thousands of pounds. Being damp from dew, and often rain, it must be dried in this manner. The mansion was large, built with logs and shingled roof…Jackson's overseer, who joined us here, said he lived in the lower story, the upper being filled with cotton."

In another letter, Royall continued to describe the cotton plantation and fields at Melton's Bluff, "From this we crossed another fence, and found ourselves in a cotton field of about one hundred acres, white with cotton and alive with negroes….It appears an endless business when we cast our eye over so vast plain of white with a production….But these negroes have great patience, and seem to be cut out for the business. Here are from 40 to 50….Some are erect, and others stooping, and all their hands move very fast…they work out the whole winter….These go regularly over the field, and by that time, a number of pods which were not open on the first picking, are now ready, and they return to where they first began, and go over the same ground, and so on the whole winter. Large quantities are burnt for want of hands to get it out of the way of the plow, for plowing must commence at the usual time; and they set fire to it to rid it out of the way."

Melton's Bluff Inn

Following the end of the war by the Treaty of Philadelphia on June 26, 1794, John Melton's notorious days of receiving goods from Chickamauga raids on white settlers came to an end. After the Treaty of Philadelphia was signed by his brother-in-law Doublehead, John Melton opened an inn on his property at Melton's Bluff.

Here for many years, John Melton became not only a prosperous cotton planter, but he also operated an inn for travelers at his Melton's Bluff Plantation. Early documents show that Melton had excellent service at his inn where the traveler could find plenty of meat, coffee, tea, and the best of liquors.

In her letters Royall reported, "An excellent house of entertainment…his table was furnished with the best of liquors, meat, coffee, and tea, and prepared in the best manner. I met with a gentleman who spent a week at Melton's house, in company with six others. He said he never fared better in any part of the United States; but their bill was excessively high."

A number of people interviewed by Anne Royall (1817-1822) were former slaves of John Melton. One of them had been the cook at Melton's Bluff. Melton had purchased her in Baltimore at a very high price because of her training in the culinary arts. John Melton's former chef at his inn gave an account to Anne Royall of Melton's relationship with his Cherokee wife. Royall related this colorful account of John Melton and his Cherokee wife as told to her by their former Negro cook, "…Mrs. Melton would sometimes take it into her head to go into the kitchen (particularly when she took a dram,) and kick up a dust with her about the dinner. Mrs. Melton wanted to model cooking to her own mind, that is, Indian fashion. She, the cook, being responsible to her master for the forthcoming of the dinner, would go to her master; upon which the old man would sally forth, with whip in hand, and if fair words failed, the horsewhip always restored order."

Melton Family

Ocuma, the sister of Doublehead, was born about 1750, and she married John Melton, an Irishman, about 1780. John and Ocuma Melton had a number of half Irish and half Cherokee children. The names of some of their children are believed to have been Charles, David, Elick, James, Lewis, Merida, Rhea's Wife, and Thomas. Moses Melton was the son of Lewis and a grandson to John Melton. It is said that most of the Melton children married white people.

Charles Melton

After his father and mother, John and Ocuma, moved to the north side of the Tennessee River in Limestone County, Alabama, their son Charles lived and traded from the Melton's Bluff home. During the Indian boundary surveys in April 1816, General John Coffee would stop at Melton's Bluff and trade with Charles Melton. After the Turkey Town Treaty of September 1816, Charles Melton moved eastward along the Tennessee River to about three miles above Guntersville, Alabama. About 1817, Charles established an Indian town known as Melton's Village or Meltonsville at the mouth of Watts Town Creek or later Town Creek in Marshall County, Alabama.

Oliver D. Street in <u>Indians of Marshall County</u> refers to Charles Melton as an Indian from Melton's Bluff who settled Meltonsville in Marshall County, Alabama. This village was named for Charles Melton, who was born at Melton's Bluff; Charles Melton was the half-blood Cherokee son of Irishman John Melton and his Cherokee wife Ocuma.

David Melton

On November 22, 1816, half-blood Cherokee David Melton, son of John and Ocuma Melton, sold his family's land and black slaves to General Andrew Jackson; therefore, when Andrew Jackson purchased Melton's Bluff, he also purchased Melton's slaves. David Melton signed the deed on November 22, 1816, that gave General Andrew Jackson all the Cherokee land at Melton's Bluff. The lands claimed by David Melton's family were given to Jackson in the first legal deed to white people in present-day Lawrence County, Alabama; Jackson kept the land until 1827.

In 1816 after the sale of Melton's Bluff to Andrew Jackson, David Melton moved west to be with his Old Settlers people many of whom were his relatives. The Old Settlers left the Muscle Shoals area in 1810; the passports were issued in January and February 1810.

After moving west, David Melton, formerly of Melton's Bluff, signed the 1834 treaty between the Cherokees West, Comanche, Wichita, Osage, and other tribes (the Kiowa did not attend). Also, both David Melton and Lewis Melton, sons of John and Ocuma Melton, signed the Cherokee Articles of Union on behalf of the Old Settlers; the articles unified the Old Settlers and the Cherokees who arrived in the west in March 1839 with Trail of Tears.

Elick Melton

While living at Melton's Bluff in Lawrence County, Alabama, Elick Melton signed a letter with The Gourd asking for Negro Fox to be returned to the Cherokees after members of the Burleson family attacked and killed three of their Cherokee people. These Cherokee men were killed at Mouse Town which was located on the border of present-day Lawrence County and Morgan County, Alabama, at the mouth of Fox's Creek and the Tennessee River.

James Melton

James Melton made quite a reputation for himself as a boat pilot or guide. This involved meeting the boats at the upper end of the Muscle Shoals and piloting them through the dangerous and often deadly passage over that part of the river. There were a number of these pilots who operated from Melton's Bluff. They would meet the boats at the upper end of the Elk River Shoals and guide them through the treacherous shoals of the river. These men would disembark below the Shoals at Colbert's Ferry at the Natchez Trace crossing and walk back to Melton's Bluff.

John Melton's son James was mentioned by General John Coffee. James had a reputation as an excellent pilot or guide. James became identified with the bluff that was named for his father. A number of early historians refer to James Melton as the half-blood Cherokee Indian from Melton's Bluff who guided keelboats through the Muscle Shoals.

James Melton worked mainly as a pilot for Malcolm Gilchrist who settled near Melton's Bluff before Alabama became a state. Gilchrist, whose ancestors came from Scotland, became the "Commodore Vanderbilt" of the lower Tennessee River. Malcolm, a land speculator, owned a fleet of flatboats that navigated the river from Muscle Shoals to New Orleans and made for him quite a fortune.

James Melton would hire out to the boats going down the river. After successfully guiding the boats over the hazardous Muscle Shoals, James would walk back to Melton's Bluff to wait for another river craft that needed his service. Some of James' descendants stayed in Lawrence County, Alabama; he had a great, great, great granddaughter Barbara Melton that was a resident of Moulton, Alabama.

Lewis Melton

Lewis Melton lived at Melton's Bluff when the Lower Cherokees relinquished their claims to most of their lands north of the Tennessee River in Lauderdale and Limestone Counties except Doublehead's Reserve. The treaty was signed at Washington, D.C., on January 7, 1806. After the 1806 treaty, Lewis' son Moses Melton, the grandson of John Melton, was made a beneficiary of one of the tracts of land reserved by the provisions of the Cotton Gin Treaty. The land Moses received was just west of Melton's Bluff near Spring Creek. He was given the reserve as follows: "…and the other reserved tract, of said Moses Melton, and of Charles Hicks in equal shares."

After the Turkey Town Treaty of 1816, Lewis Melton moved west with the Old Settlers along with his brother David Melton. After the Trail of Tears Cherokees arrived west in 1839, Lewis and signed for the reunification of the Cherokee Nation with his brother David.

Merida (Merrida) Melton

Merida was the son of John and Acumo Melton. Merida Melton was listed in the 1820 census of Lawrence County, Alabama, as a white male over 21 years of age. The census reported a total of eight individuals in the household of Merida Melton as follows: White males over 21, 2; White males under 21, 2; White females over 21, 1; White females under 21, 3. The census indicates that Merida Melton was born before 1799; he could very well be the half-blood Cherokee son of John Melton who died on June 7, 1815.

On September 18, 1818, Merida Melton of Lawrence County, Alabama, entered 80.13 acres of land in the South ½ of the Southeast ¼ of Section 15 in Township 7 South and Range 9 West (Cowart, 1991). The land he entered was on the northwest edge of present-day William B. Bankhead National Forest south of Mt. Hope, Alabama. Merida Melton forfeited his claim to the land in 1829 and left Lawrence County, Alabama.

According to the descendants of Merida Melton, he moved west and married a woman by the name of Mary Edington. One of their daughters, Leah Ann Melton who married William Reynolds, died on October 20, 1906, at Marion in Linn County, Iowa. Another daughter Elizabeth Melton moved to Tennessee with her husband and his family. Other descendants of John and Acumo Melton migrated from Alabama to Arkansas, Oklahoma, Texas, and California."

(Rhea's Wife) Melton

Rhea's wife was the daughter of John and Ocuma Melton. Rhea was a white man and river boat pilot who guided boats through the Muscle Shoals. He was the guide to Anne Royall when she visited the Muscle Shoals, "I learned he was from Rockbridge County, Virginia; had piloted boats through the Muscle Shoals, fifteen years; sometimes four at a time, at ten dollars each. He sails down one day, and walks back the next. He never met, in all that time, with an accident! There are several of these pilots" (Royall, 1969).

Rhea's wife was not named, but on January 12, 1818, Anne N. Royall's Letters from Alabama 1817-1822 talks about John Melton's son-in-law Rhea. Rhea had guided boats through the Shoals for some 15 years. On January 14, 1818, Royall also tells about John Melton's half-blood daughter (Rhea's Wife) leaving Melton's Bluff for lands in the west. Royall says that Rhea's wife left Melton's Bluff last fall for Indian Territory in Arkansas which would have been the Fall of 1817.

Thomas Melton

Thomas Melton is found in the 1820 United States Census of Lawrence County, Alabama. He is also mentioned as a son of John Melton in William Lindsey McDonald's, Lore of the River (2007).

Melton's Bluff Roads and Trails

During Doublehead's reign terror on the Appalachian frontier, he and his motley mix of warriors from different tribes used many ancient Indian roads and trails that crisscrossed the Big Bend of the Hogoheegee (Tennessee) River or River of the Cherokees. The major north-south Indian trails through the area of the Muscle Shoals were used to conduct raids on the Cumberland Settlements in the area of present-day Nashville, Tennessee.

Later, the Indian trails and roads were used by the cotton planters moving into the Tennessee Valley to claim the rich bottom lands for their plantations. Some of the major routes north and south included Natchez Trace, Doublehead's Trace (present-day Highway 101 and County Line Road crossing at Bainbridge),

Sipsie Trail (Lamb's Ferry Road or Cheatham Road), Black Warriors' Path, Jasper Road (present-day Highway 41), and the Great South Trail (Old Huntsville Road from Nashville).

Prior to 1776, the east to west trails were trade routes that connected the Indian tribes in North Alabama to Atlantic ports controlled by the British such as Old Charles Town (Charleston), South Carolina. Initially, the British were allied with the Cherokee and Chickasaw by way of the primitive wilderness roads. Four major trading routes to the Muscle Shoals coming from the east into the southern portion of the Tennessee Valley included:

1. The High Town Path from Olde Charles Town, South Carolina, ran along the Tennessee Divide through North Alabama south of the Muscle Shoals to Chickasaw Bluffs on the Mississippi River.
2. Coosa or Muscle Shoals Path traversed from Ten Islands on the Coosa River to Ditto's Landing south of Huntsville, Alabama, through the Moulton Valley to Tuscumbia Landing.
3. Chickasaw Trail came from the Chickasaw Old Fields south of Huntsville to Moulton, to Russellville, then to Cotton Gin Port on the Tombigbee.
4. The South River Road, traveled by Reverend Patrick Wilson in 1803, followed the south side of the Tennessee River. In most of northwest Alabama, there were the Upper and Lower River Roads; the lower road ran adjacent to the south bank passing adjacent to Doublehead's Town. The Upper South River Road ran a direct line through the Tennessee Valley connecting present-day towns of Decatur, Courtland, Leighton, Tuscumbia, and Cherokee. Through Lawrence County, the upper river road passed by Courtland and became known as the Tuscumbia Road; a historic marker in Courtland identifies the Tuscumbia Road.

As early as 1770, Doublehead's Lower Chickamauga Cherokees had established towns at Indian trail crossings along the Muscle Shoals which included

Gunter's, Brown's Village, Mouse Town, Doublehead's Town, Melton's Bluff, Shoal Town, and other villages. These Indian towns served as outposts against the encroachment of the white settlers upon their hunting lands in the Tennessee Valley. The Lower Cherokees soon began using their Muscle Shoals towns as fortresses to keep out land speculators and to block passage of white emigrants who were attempting to settle or pass through their territory by navigating the Tennessee River as a route to the Natchez District of Florida.

Melton's Bluff was a site near the junction of three early Indian trails and roads. Ganies Trace ran southwest from Melton's Bluff to Cotton Gin Port, Mississippi. Black Warriors's Path or Mitchell Trace was a north-south route from Fort Mitchell that passed by the bluff to Fort Hampton. The Lower South River Road was an east-west road that ran parallel to the south side of the Tennessee River. The Upper South River Road passed south of Melton's Bluff through the Courtland valley.

Many of these Indian trails and roads provided a steady flow of travelers for Melton's Inn. Goods and travelers would descend the Tennessee to Melton's Bluff to be transferred to pack horses, and later wagon trains, for the long journeys through the wilderness over these roads.

Gaines Trace

One of the first of these roads was Gaines Trace which was established as an effort to save the endangered American Settlements on the Tombigbee River in Mississippi and South Alabama. The road connected Melton's Bluff to Courtland in Lawrence County and passed along present-day Tennessee Street before continuing south toward the Tombigbee River Valley.

By the early 1800's, the much-travelled wilderness road known as the Gaines Trace had been established. The route commenced at Melton's Bluff, a popular river crossing, and terminated at Cotton Gin Port on the Tombigbee River in Mississippi.

The Gaines Trace was a trade route from the Muscle Shoals at Melton's Bluff in Lawrence County, Alabama, to Cotton Gin Port, Mississippi, on the Tombigbee River. The road was laid out by Captain Edmund Pendleton Gaines in

December 1807, just four months after the death of Doublehead on August 9, 1807. Captain Gaines was married to Barbara Blount, the daughter of Governor William Blount of the Southwest Territory. Governor Blount and his Indian agent Return J. Meigs were primarily responsible for making peace with Doublehead.

In October 1810, the Secretary of War appointed William S. Gaines to negotiate a treaty with the Chickasaws for the right to build this road so as to connect the Tennessee and Tombigbee Rivers. The Chickasaws resisted, but finally agreed to the horse path. The language of Gaines' original survey specified that the road was to begin "…at the house of Mr. Melton, on a bluff, left (or south) bank of the Tennessee River, near the head of the Muscle Shoals" (Stone, 1971).

Black Warriors Path-Mitchell's Trace

The Black Warriors' Path passed through Melton's Bluff. Later, the path became Mitchell's Trace which was established as a wagon road in 1811. The trace was established along the Indian trail that connected the Tennessee River to the Warrior and Chattahoochee River basins. The Black Warriors' Path was actually a Nashville to St. Augustine Trace that passed by Fort Hampton on the north side of the Tennessee River.

Early documents show a number of military crossings at Melton's Bluff during the Creek War. General John Coffee, in his report dated October 22, 1813, described one event as follows: "…I proceeded to cross the river at the upper end of the Shoals, all my efforts failed to procure a pilot. I took with me one of John Melton's sons, who said he knew not the road, he showed me a path that had been reputed the Black Warriors' Path.…"

44

When Coffee arrived at Black Warrior Town at the junction of the Sipsey and Mulberry Forks of the Black Warrior River, he found it had been deserted by the Creek Indian people. He then proceeded to burn the town to prevent it from being used again by the Creeks. It has been passed down through many generations that William Walker and Tandy Walker II warned the Creek Indians of the impending attack by General John Coffee's forces. In 1812, the Walkers had earlier secured the release of Martha Crawley from the Creeks. They were mixed blood Indian traders and scouts and are buried by each other not far from the Warrior River at Old Nectar in Blount County, Alabama.

During the troop movements crossing the Tennessee River at Melton's Bluff, famous frontiersman David Crockett was a member of General John Coffee's cavalry; his payroll and muster records reveal that he was a third sergeant in Captain John Cowan's company at the time. Crockett remembered two occasions when they crossed Melton's Bluff. The first instance was in November 1813. They actually crossed the Tennessee River twice on this first occasion in order to maneuver around the local Indians. After crossing at Huntsville, they moved westward to cross the river again at Melton's Bluff. James Richard Gillespie of Indian Tomb Hollow was with Captain Cowan and David Crockett.

At Melton's Bluff, Crockett described the river at this point as being about two miles wide. The rocky bottom of the river was rough and dangerous. While fording the river, several of the horses became stuck in the rocky crevices and had to be left there while the military command moved on to their destination. The second crossing remembered by Crockett was in October 1814.

Northwest Alabama 1823

On the 1823 map of Northwest Alabama, notice the locations of Doublehead's Spring at Shoal Town, Courtland, Ft. Hampton, Melton's Bluff, and Mooresville on the Tennessee River. The two roads marked on the map from Melton's Bluff are Gaines Trace which goes southwest to Cotton Gin Port, Mississippi, on the Tombigbee River, and Black Warriors' Path which goes south to southeast to St. Augustine, Florida, on the Atlantic coast.

South River Road

The South River Road, also known as the Tennessee River Road, ran along the south bank of the Tennessee River. This is the route traveled by Reverend Patrick Wilson in 1803 and connected the Lower Cherokee towns along the south side of the Muscle Shoals. The South River Road passed by the river ports at Chattanooga, Ditto's Landing, and Tuscumbia Landing, and ran overland to the river crossing at Savannah, Tennessee.

Today, the road is called the River Road in a few of the North Alabama counties it passes through. In Morgan and Lawrence Counties, this east-west Indian trail is divided into the upper and lower river roads. The Lower South River Road runs adjacent to the south bank of the Tennessee River, and the Upper South River Road runs parallel to the river but goes through the valley a few miles south of the river bank. Where the Upper River Road passed through Courtland, it was called the Tuscumbia Road. The Decatur-Tuscumbia Railroad ran parallel to the Upper South River Road or Tuscumbia Road from Tuscumbia Landing to Decatur.

Death of John Melton

John Melton moved to the north side of the Tennessee River in present-day Limestone County, Alabama, a few years before he died for fear of Creek raids from the south. In 1813 and 1814, the Cherokees had joined with General Jackson to defeat the Red Stick Creeks during the Creek Indian War. It is said that Melton had heard threats from the Creeks and feared attacks from the hostile Creek Indians causing him to leave the south side of the Tennessee River.

After Captain Smithe established Fort Hampton near the mouth of Elk River in 1810, John Melton and his Cherokee wife Ocuma sought refuge between Fort Hampton and the north bank of the river in present-day Limestone County, Alabama. John probably knew that the fort located nearby would deter an attack on his residence from hostile Creeks during the Creek Indian War.

Even though the Cherokee had relinquished their claim north of the Tennessee River, the Chickasaw still owned the land by treaty and demanded the whites removed from their lands; therefore, Smithe was sent to the Muscle Shoals to expel the early white settlers in the Sims Settlement and those who had leased land on Doublehead's Reserve. The site selected for the fort was probably not without coincidence since it was near to the junctions of the North River Road and the Mitchell Trace. Fort Hampton was located east of Elk River and north of the Tennessee River. The strategic site provided excellent military control over the roads, rivers, and the vulnerable upper entrance to the Elk River Shoals.

Some speculate that the assassination of his brother-in-law Doublehead was the reason John Melton moved. Chief Doublehead's assassination on August 9, 1807, may have caused John Melton to fear for his own life and that of his family. Melton and his family had personally benefitted from the Cotton Gin Treaty of January 7, 1806, negotiated by Doublehead.

Some of the Cherokee were so upset over the 1806 treaty that they assassinated Doublehead who was one of its signers; the assassins were supposedly Major Ridge, Alex Saunders, and a white man named John Rogers. Doublehead's death, plus the provisions of the treaty that possibly benefited John Melton's family, may have caused the old man to fear for his own life; however, he continued to live at the Bluff until a few years prior to his death.

By all accounts, old man John Melton was dead and in his grave before Anne Royall arrived at Melton's Bluff. According to Anne Royall (1817-1822), "…toward the latter part of his life, he became alarmed from the threats… and removed over the river (on the north side of the Tennessee River), where he also had a large farm, and built a fine house (which I have seen,) and died rich in a good old age." In a letter dated January 14, 1818, Anne Newport Royall made an important statement concerning John Melton's death. Royall said, "Melton's Bluff is a town, and takes its name from a person by the name of John Melton, a white man, deceased two years since." Royall's statement indicates the death of John Melton was about 1816. The date Anne Royall states John Melton died is within eight months of the death date identified by John Melton's wife in her letter to Indian agent Return J. Meigs.

According to his wife Ocuma Melton, John died on June 7, 1815, in present-day Limestone County, and he was reportedly buried in the place now known as McNutt Cemetery. Shortly after his death, John Melton's wife wrote a letter to Colonel Return J. Meigs voicing her concerns about her husband's brother getting all the property they had accumulated as found in microcopy 208, roll 7, and number 3229, and dated June 30, 1815. Mrs. Ocuma Melton's letter to Colonel Meigs is as follows:

"June 30, 1815-My husband John Melton died at his residence below Ft. Hampton 7 instant. He became a resident of Cherokee Nation 35 years ago and married me not long afterward according to established custom of my nation. He died of considerable property which I am told me and my children will be deprived of by his brother, a citizen of the United States who resides on Duck River in Tennessee. Please advise me what to do."

After he died on June 7, 1815, on the north side of the river, it has been passed down for years that John Melton was buried in the McNutt Cemetery in Limestone County, Alabama. The local legend that Doublehead's brother-in-law John Melton was one of the original burials in the graveyard has been passed through many generations of local folks in the area.

Cherokee Removal from Melton's Bluff

In 1810, some 1,131 Cherokees were the first to leave Melton's Bluff area for Indian Territory west of the Mississippi River; they were known as the Old Settlers. Some historical writers suggest that Colonel Return J. Meigs forced the Cherokees out of the Muscle Shoals of North Alabama shortly after the death of Doublehead on August 9, 1807. However, most of the Cherokees leaving the shoals area were eager to go west after the assassination of Doublehead by their own people.

Melton's Bluff had been used as a collecting point for Cherokee Indians going to the West because of its location at the head of the Muscle Shoals, but not all the Cherokees left shortly after Doublehead's death. Ocuma Melton's letter, letters of Anne Royall, and John Coffee's journal records confirm that the Meltons and other Cherokees were still living at the Muscle Shoals of the Tennessee River until sometime around 1816. After the death of her husband John Melton on June 7, 1815, Ocuma Melton was still residing at her residence south of Fort Hampton on the north side of the river in what is now present-day Limestone County. In January 1818, Anne Royall stated that John Melton died at his residence on the north side of the river two years hence.

During his boundary surveys of 1816, John Coffee also tells of trading with Black Fox who operated a trading post near Browns Ferry. In addition, John Coffee traded with Charles Melton at Melton's Bluff during his tribal boundary surveys of 1816; therefore, Charles, son of John, continued to live at the Melton's Bluff Plantation until the passage of the Turkey Town Treaty of September 16 and 18, 1816, took the Indian lands of Lauderdale, Franklin (Colbert), Lawrence, Limestone, Morgan, and southwest Madison Counties.

Melton's Bluff as an Indian village ended with the 1816 Turkey Town Treaty; Turkey Town was a few miles northeast of the present-day City of Gadsden, Alabama. This treaty, headed up by none other than General Andrew Jackson, took from the Cherokees all their lands south of the Tennessee River including Melton's Bluff. After the treaty, the remaining Cherokees at the Muscle Shoals joined the Indian

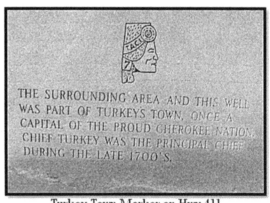

Turkey Town Marker on Hwy 411

removal to be relocated in the West or territory they still owned in the northeastern part of Alabama.

Anne Royall's guide Rhea gives a firsthand account of Cherokees leaving Melton's Bluff in 1816 after the Turkey Town Treaty. Anne Royall wrote, "The order for their removal was sudden and unexpected. Some of the Cherokees were taken up the river to wait for boats; others were picked up at Melton's Bluff and sent down the river to Arkansas. One of those transported directly to the West from the Muscle Shoals was a daughter of John Melton who was married to the river guide, Rhea, a white settler from Rockbridge County, Virginia." When the order came, according to Royall, "…Rhea, at that time was absent from home, but returned on the same day, and learned what had happened, was almost frantic– jumped into a canoe, and soon overtook the boats. He flew to his wife, and clasped her in his arms. Neither spoke a word, but both wept bitterly. In a few moments, he resumed his canoe and returned to the Bluff, and she went on."

While Anne Royall was a visitor at Melton's Bluff, boats loaded with Cherokee Indians moving west because of white man's greed often waited near Melton's Bluff for high water before they passed through the Muscle Shoals. In 1818, Anne Royall wrote about visiting some removal encampments, "Hearing (that) eleven boats had arrived about two miles hence, and had halted up the river, we set off… to see the Indians… on their way to their destination beyond the Mississippi….There were several encampments at a distance of three hundred yards from each other, containing three hundred Indians. The camps were nothing but some forks of wood driven into the ground, and a stick laid across them, on which hung a pot of boiling meat." Royall stated, "Many were of mixed-blood (offspring of white and Indian), but they were as unsociable as the others."

Conclusion of Melton's Bluff

Even though Doublehead had the first cotton gin in North Alabama placed on the Melton's Bluff Plantation of his brother-in-law John Melton, time has removed most remnants of the Cherokee people who lived in the area. To the east side of Melton's Bluff and on the west side of Jackson's (Jack's) Slough, an ancient woodland ceremonial mound indicating aboriginal occupation stands between the Lower South River Road and the Tennessee River. The mound, at the east edge of a cotton field, is the only visible reminder that the area was once occupied by aboriginal American Indian people from long ago to the time of the Cherokees under the leadership of Doublehead.

Today, the only sign of Melton's Bluff is a historic marker that stands along a lonely stretch of a narrow black topped road that at one time was the

Lower South River Road used by the Chickamauga Cherokees under Doublehead's leadership. The largest portion of land that once made up Melton's Bluff became part of the General Joseph (Fighting Joe) Wheeler Plantation and today remains a part of his estate. A narrow fringe of Melton's Bluff that runs along the backwaters of Wheeler Lake is owned by the Tennessee Valley Authority and still contains the old stone hearths of the cabin chimneys that once lined the river bluff.

Andrew Jackson-Muscle Shoals Plantation

On November 22, 1816, General Andrew Jackson became the first white cotton plantation owner with black slaves in Lawrence County, Alabama, after the Indian land cessions to the United States in September 1816. However, Andrew Jackson's wife Rachel Donelson saw the area of the Muscle Shoals before her husband purchased Melton's Bluff in Lawrence County. After the Treaty of Sycamore Shoals in 1775, where the older Cherokees leaders gave up their claims to the Cumberland River Valley, James E. Saunders (1899) wrote the following in his book Early Settlers of Alabama. "…General James Robertson, with eight others, settled at Nashville. In the fall they returned to East Tennessee for their families. It was arranged that General Robertson should proceed, first, with a number of young men to raise the necessary buildings, and that Colonel John Donelson should follow with another party of emigrants, including the women and children. To avoid the toil and peril of the route through the wilderness, Colonel Donelson conceived the idea of reaching the new settlement by water, down the Tennessee and up the Cumberland Rivers. No man, white or red, had ever attempted the voyage, which was really more dangerous than, the overland route, while there were equally as many Indians to be encountered. At the suck one of the boats hung upon a rock, and a hot skirmish with the Cherokees on the mountain side took place before they could extricate her. Among those who shared the dangers of this voyage was Rachel Donelson, the daughter of the leader, a black-eyed, black-haired brunette, as gay, as bold, and as handsome a lass as ever danced on the deck of a flatboat, or took the helm while her father took a shot at the Indians. This lass became the wife of General Andrew Jackson.…This party of Colonel Donelson boldly shot the Muscle Shoals without a pilot. They were the first whites who ever set their eyes on the soil of Lawrence County of whom we have any account. After a voyage of four months they reached their new home, and there was a happy meeting of husbands and wives, parents, and children."

During the travel down the Tennessee River, John Donelson describes his first reactions upon reaching the Elk River Shoals which borders Lawrence County on the south side of the river. According to his journal of March 12, 1780, "After running until about ten o'clock, we came in sight of the Muscle Shoals…When we approached them, they had a dreadful appearance…The water being high made a terrible roaring…the current running in every possible direction. Here we did not know how soon we should be dashed to pieces and all our troubles ended at once…I know not the length of the shoal; it had been represented to me to be twenty five or thirty miles…" It would be some 36 years later that General Andrew Jackson, the son-in-law of Colonel John Donelson, would own his Muscle Shoals Plantation at Melton's Bluff.

In a letter dated June 30, 1815, Ocuma Melton wrote Indian agent Return Jonathan Meigs stating that her and her children will be deprived of her husband's estate by his brother who was a citizen of the United States living on the Duck River in Tennessee. It appears that the mixed blood Cherokee family was forced to give up the possessions, slaves, and plantation of their father Irishman John Melton. This was one of many times that Indian people had to relinquish their property to white settlers.

On November 22, 1816, General Andrew Jackson in partnership with Rachel's nephew and his nephew-in-law, Colonel John Hutchings, purchased the Melton's Bluff Plantation from Cherokee David Melton, a half blood son of

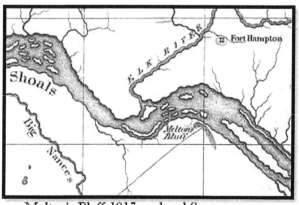

Irishman John Melton and his Cherokee wife Ocuma, sister of Doublehead. Therefore, Andrew Jackson became the first legal white plantation owner of Melton's Bluff in Lawrence County, Alabama.

In about two months and a few days after General Andrew Jackson signed the

Melton's Bluff-1817 peel and Sannoner map

52

Turkey Town Treaty in September 18, 1816, on behalf of the United States, he was handed the deed that made him part owner of Melton's Bluff. After the 1816 treaty, Anne Royall states that some of John Melton's children left Melton's Bluff for destinations to the Cherokee Nation in east Alabama or west of the Mississippi River.

Half-blood Cherokee David Melton made the transfer of the title and deed to Melton's Bluff on November 22, 1816. The following is the description of the property and its transfer to Jackson and Hutchings, "I, David Melton of the Cherokee Nation, do by these presents bargain and sell... unto General Andrew Jackson and Captain John Hutchings all my right title and interest to the tract of land where I now live, and agree to give them possession of all the improvements laying north and east of the spring, including said spring, on said tract where I live and adjoining where I live, and the houses and...land southeast of the spring. Possession to be given of as many Negro houses as will house the Negroes of the said Andrew and the said John... and possession of the other houses on or before the first day of February... For which I acknowledge to have received the consideration of sixty dollars in cash and in full of the above sale."

There was probably more involved than a mere sixty dollars in the transaction for Melton's Bluff; however, from 1816 until 1827, General Andrew Jackson wound up with one of the best known Alabama cotton plantations in Lawrence County, Alabama. Jackson referred to the town that he established at Melton's Bluff as Marathon and his cotton farm as the Muscle Shoals Plantation. With the labor of the former black slaves of John Melton's family, Jackson and Hutchings used the plantation for growing cotton and corn.

When Anne Royall arrived in January 1818, the Muscle Shoals Plantation at Melton's Bluff and Marathon was in operation as the cotton plantation and frontier town of General Jackson and his wife's nephew, John Hutchings. Immediately after her arrival, Anne Royall began writing her series of letters that reveal an interesting part of its early history. In her third letter Royall stated, "here is a very large plantation of cotton and maize, worked by about sixty slaves, and owned by General Jackson, who bought the interest of old Melton."

General Andrew Jackson made a brief visit to his Alabama plantation at Melton's Bluff while Anne Royall was there. In her letter dated January 18,

1818, Royall described his arrival, "I was devouring Phillip's Speeches when a loud cry, 'General Jackson, General Jackson comes!' and running to my window I saw him walking slowly up the hill, between two gentlemen, his aides."

Biographer Marquis James listed a number of trips that General Andrew Jackson made to Alabama. In March of 1822, the Cumberland and Tennessee Rivers were at flood stage which allowed General Jackson's cotton boats to make the water journeys to New Orleans. During this time, Jackson emptied his cotton warehouses at the Hermitage Plantation and his Muscle Shoals Plantation. Three months later, General Jackson rode his horse from Nashville to Alabama to inspect his plantation. In relating the events of the 1824 national presidential election, Marquis James wrote, "During the last weeks before the balloting began, General Jackson visited Melton's Bluff to make arrangements for the marketing of his Alabama cotton; an important detail, as the winter in Washington had been costly and the absentee planter was pressed for funds."

Marathon

In 1818, Andrew Jackson and John Hutchings had a town surveyed and marked lots to sell at Melton's Buff. The town plat showed the boundaries running south from the Tennessee River at the high bluff which formed the river's south bank. The plat showed the Lower South River Road basically running an east to west direction through the middle of the town.

The plans for Marathon was first mentioned in a letter dated May 27, 1818, from Josiah Meigs to John Coffee, a friend and kinsman of General Andrew Jackson. Jackson named the Town of Marathon for an ancient Greek city which was associated with foot races. It is said that Jackson favored the name of Marathon because of his love for horse racing and the racetrack. He employed General John Coffee to plan and survey his new town. "Marathon was spread out a little more than a mile long and a little less than a mile wide, south of the Tennessee River. It was surveyed by John Coffee and laid out in 658 lots with public grounds centrally located. John Coffee was surveyor general of Alabama from 1817 to his death in 1833" (Gentry, 1962).

According to Life and Legends of Lawrence County by Dorothy Gentry (1962), "Marathon, a settlement just west of Melton's Bluff on the Tennessee

River, was a town laid out in lots, but no field notes showing the metes and bounds of the boundary lines can be located. The lots in the Town of Marathon were offered for sale in 1818 under the Federal Credit System and Lots Numbers 1 to 564, inclusive, were sold to various parties, most of whom, after paying a part of the purchase money, made default of the remainder, thereby forfeiting their rights to the lots purchased. The sales were made pursuant to authority of Proclamation Number 24 of May 26, 1818."

A memorandum from Jon Read to Josiah Meigs on October 22, 1818, gave results of the first land sales. "The sale of Marathon closed on Saturday the 17th Ins. All the lots sold, the highest price (lot No. 8) $800; several sold for two, three, four, and five hundred dollars, some for ten, fifteen, and twenty, and many only for three dollars. No further entries were made until the year 1834 when cash entries were made for the forfeited lots, 1 to 564, except lots 68 and 196. An act was passed on June 25, 1936, by the 74th Congress, releasing interest in fractional section 25 to the owners of the equitable titles thereto" (Gentry, 1962).

In Old Land Records of Lawrence County, Alabama, by Maragret M. Cowart (1991), John W. Lane of Limestone County owned 48.91 acres on the northwest part of Section 25 of Township 3 South and Range 7 West, south of Tennessee River; the land near the area of Marathon was first entered on December 7, 1820, and received the patent dated November 28, 1822. Cowart does not show General Andrew Jackson or Colonel John Hutchings entering land in Lawrence County, Alabama. The southeast portion containing 149 acres of Section 25 in Township 3 South and Range 7 West and south of the Tennessee River is the Town of Marathon; this area was sold in town lots. Jackson's purchase of Melton's Bluff on November 22, 1816, was probably before official land records were recorded; therefore, that is probably the reason he is not listed in old land records of Lawrence County.

According to Early Settlers of Alabama by James E. Saunders (1899), "The most prominent citizen in the place then, and for many years after, was Isaac Brownlow, who died at Lamb's Ferry, in 1828, a brother of Hon. W. G. Brownlow, late United States Senator from Tennessee." James E. Saunders (1899) stated that, "Isaac died in 1828 on the north bank on the Tennessee at Lamb's Ferry a few miles south of Rogersville in Lauderdale County, Alabama."

Of course the date given by Saunders is wrong according to census and land records, or there was an Isaac Brownlow Jr.

On October 31, 1829, Isaac Brownlow entered 160 acres in Section 4 of Township 4 South and Range 7 West which was just southwest of Melton's Bluff (Cowart, 1991). On July 24, 1827, Isaac entered 79.86 acres in Section 36 of Township 2 South and Range 8 West in Lauderdale County, Alabama (Cowart, 1996). Isaac Brownlow is also listed in the 1830 federal census of Lauderdale County, Alabama.

For a number of years, Marathon served as the seat of justice for Lawrence County while Alabama was a territory. In 1818, white settlers and wealthy planters rapidly moved to the area from Virginia and North Carolina to claim the fertile bottomlands for growing cotton. The Mitchell Trace (Black Warriors' Path), Gaines Trace and South River Road were the main residential roads of the town which stretched for more than a mile along the bluff. After the county seat was moved to Moulton in 1820, Marathon was abandoned and eventually became a ghost town. Today, the rock pile remains of old chimneys and gigantic red oaks still line the bluff some 60 feet above the waters of Wheeler Reservoir of the Tennessee River.

Commerce at Marathon

Around the area of Melton's Bluff, most of the commercial shipping was by water which increased significantly on the Tennessee River after the 1816 Turkey Town Treaty ceded Indian land claims, and the Indians were removed from northwest Alabama. Steamboats, flatboats, keel or pole boats, and cotton boxes carried most of the goods transported by water in the area of Muscle Shoals; however, steamboats were limited between Florence and Decatur because of the treacherous waters. These early boats were usually loaded with building materials, farming equipment, agricultural produce, household items, and most important to planters was cotton.

Cotton was one of the main products shipped by water. Around 1820, Richard Rapier of Florence became known as the "Merchant Prince of Cotton" because of his fleet of wagons and boats. Also, Malcolm Gilchrist was very successful and became extremely rich by shipping cotton from North Alabama to New Orleans by water.

At or above the three dreaded upper Muscle Shoals, Ditto's Landing south of Huntsville in Madison County, Rhodes Ferry at Decatur in Morgan County, Lamb's Ferry near the mouth of the Elk River in Lauderdale County, and Melton's Bluff in Lawrence County became prominent as unloading points for boats to avoid the risk of losing their merchandise. Some boats would unload at a point south of Rogersville connected by an early Indian road known as the Sipsie Trail and later Lamb's Ferry Road, named for Cherokee John Lamb. The route ran from the ferry south of Rogersville in Lauderdale County, Alabama, northward to Pulaski and Nashville, Tennessee. The Black Warriors Path and Gaines Trace routes at Marathon led to points south on both the Atlantic and Gulf Coasts.

Even though the shipping merchants were careful to avoid the dangerous Muscle Shoals, accidents still happened. One entry in the early boating records shows the unloading of 114 barrels of salt at Melton's Bluff; however, across from Melton's Bluff, a salt barge was stranded on a sand bar up Elk River and unload at a place that is still known as the Salt House. As expected, a number of wrecks and other losses are mentioned in these early boating records. A shipper by the name of George Hale complained, "One boat was stove in the Muscle Shoals and the loading lost." In another incident, the John Hogan and Company had to pay a fellow named B. Start for helping to rescue their stranded boat at the Shoals, "and the Huffman boys for getting iron out of the river." At certain times of the year, Elk River Shoals near Marathon was practically impassable.

David Hutchings Smith

John Melton's mansion at Melton's Bluff was the plantation house that was used by Andrew Jackson and John Hutchings for the living quarters of their slave overseer David Hutchings Smith. Smith was one of Jackson's slaves who was appointed as manager of the Muscle Shoals Plantation at Melton's Bluff. He had been General Jackson's personal camp man during the Indian campaigns and British conflict at the Battle of New Orleans.

David Hutchings Smith, known as Old Pap, was loyal and devoted to his master, and General Jackson was loyal and devoted to his beloved slave. The General placed extreme loyalty in his overseer servant Old Pap; however, David Hutchings Smith was not the overseer and manager that Jackson needed to control his Alabama cotton plantation.

There is no record of the number of trips Andrew Jackson made to Melton's Bluff; however, his inspections of the Melton's Bluff plantation were not enough to make sure that it was properly managed. The noted historian, Donald Davidson in The Tennessee (1946) concluded that Old Hickory "…had trouble with overseers and fugitive slaves and was a rather anxious absentee landlord."

While Smith was overseer at the Melton's Bluff plantation, there was continuing trouble with his management, an almost total lack of supervision, and a number of runaway slaves. The problems at Jackson's Muscle Shoals Plantation was in large part due to his faith in the abilities of his beloved slave David Hutchings Smith, but Smith could not effectively run the Muscle Shoals Plantation.

Prior to selling the Muscle Shoals Plantation, Jackson placed Old Pap in the care of Andrew Jackson Hutchings. David Hutchings Smith's last days were lived at Ardoyne Plantation near Florence where he is buried. A number of tales were handed down through the Coffee family about Old Pap's remembrances of the time he was overseer of 'Marsa' Jackson's plantation at Melton's Bluff.

Sale of Marathon

Because of his lack of the personal management, oversight, and extended absences, General Jackson's cotton plantation in Lawrence County, Alabama, became a burden while he was campaigning for the office of President of the United States. A biographer noted, "The General's cotton seemed to have suffered from inattention, however, the 1827 crop being no better than average in quality. A plague decimated the stables leaving Jackson without a team to take him to Alabama to straighten out an overseer tangle." In addition to problems at Melton's Bluff plantation, the campaigning and political efforts of Jackson was probably another major cause for his financial trouble.

Finally, General Jackson and his partner Colonel John Hutchings sold their Muscle Shoals cotton plantation at Melton's Bluff in 1827 when he made his bid for President of the United States. Jackson was convinced that one cotton plantation was enough for a busy politician to handle. General Andrew Jackson was elected President of the United States in 1828.

Conclusion of Andrew Jackson's Plantation

General Jackson became the first legal landowner in Lawrence County, Alabama, when he initially purchased Melton's Bluff prior to the Turkey Town Treaty being approved by congress in July 1817. Jackson's victory over the Creeks at Horseshoe Bend in March 1814 eventually led to the removal of Indian people east of the Mississippi River. After Jackson was elected President of the United States, a speech he made on December 8, 1829, revealed his racism and bias against Indian people. He stated, "A portion, however, of the southern tribes, having mingled much with whites and made some progress in the arts of civilized life, have lately attempted to erect an independent government within the limits of Georgia and Alabama. These states claiming to be the only sovereigns within their territories, extended their laws over the Indians, which induced the latter to call upon the United States for protection. But it seems to me visionary to suppose that in this stated of things claims be allowed on tracts of country on which they have neither dwelt nor made improvements, merely because they have seen them from the mountains or passed them in chase" (Prucha, 1975). President Jackson got the Indian Removal Act passed on May 28, 1830.

The Marathon town site of Andrew Jackson was included in the large tract of land purchased by planter and slave holder Colonel Richard Jones in 1829; he built his home not far from the site of the Chickamauga village at Melton's Bluff and Town of Marathon. Jones became the owner of one of the largest antebellum cotton operations in the Tennessee Valley called the Caldonia Plantation. By 1850, Richard Jones owned 82 black slaves; and by 1860, he owned107 black slaves. His daughter Daniella Ellen Jones was born at Caldonia, and she first married Benjamin Sherrod who died in 1861. He was the son of Felix and grandson of Colonel Benjamin Sherrod. In 1866, Daniella became the wife of the famed Confederate Calvary General Joseph Wheeler.

Caldonia-Plantation Home of Colonel Richard Jones

On October 9, 1863, General Wheeler forded the Tennessee River from the east side of the mouth of Elk River. Wheeler and his troops crossed on Elk River Shoals and entered the Caldonia Plantation in Lawrence County. His famous move into the Tennessee Valley of northwest Alabama followed his raid down the Sequatchie Valley after the Battle of Chickamauga. Shortly after crossing the river, General Joe Wheeler met the widow Daniella Ellen Jones Sherrod at her Caldonia Plantation home. Daniella would later become the wife of General Wheeler.

A large limestone monument just west of Melton's Bluff at a site referred to as "Lock A" identifies the the place where General Joe Wheeler crossed the Tennessee River on October 9, 1863. During the 1880's, Lock A was one of the first locks of the Muscle Shoals Canal and was the site of the engineering camp of Major General George Washington Goethals, United States Army Engineer, and Major General William Crawford Gorgas, United States Surgeon General. Later, the two became very famous people for completing the Panama Canal. Even though it was never successful, Lock A was later made into a Lawrence County Park which has fell into disrepair.

Nearby the Wheeler crossing, an old abandoned well and watering hole still bears the name Dora Belle's Well. Not far away to the east along the Gaines Trace was a decaying dog trot log house which stood on the north side of the old road, but today, it has been totally destroyed. It is believed that the old log cabin was where the beloved ex-slave, Sweet Peter, and his wife once lived. I well remember the old log home near the edge of a remnant of the old trace, and it is sad that the structure was torn down.

In all its colorful history, most of the Melton's Bluff area identified by a lonely historic marker on the side of the Lower South River Road is farmland . Presently, there are no dwelling houses near the site. The area is rather isolated and sparsely settled; the old town site lies near the middle of the northern border of Lawrence County, Alabama.

The 1780 Melton's Bluff site was established as a Chickamauga faction of Lower Cherokee settlement and a black slave cotton plantation of the white Irishman John Melton and his mixed blood Indian family. This tract of historic land was at one time owned by John and Ocuma Melton of the Cherokee Nation, General Andrew Jackson and Colonel John Hutchings, Colonel Richard Jones, and General Joseph Wheeler.

Today, much of the area of President Andrew Jackson's Muscle Shoals Plantation is now included in the vast General Joe Wheeler Estate. On the riverfront side of Melton's Bluff, the high limestone cliffs, formed during the dawn of time, are a part of the Wheeler Lake Reservoir properties which belongs to the Tennessee Valley Authority. The old bluffs of Melton's home overlook the river and formed the north edge of the old town. These high bluffs of limestone rock are some of the most scenic sites along the Tennessee River.

Now, the area is strangely silent with only the refreshing winds across Wheeler Lake causing lapping waves against the rocky banks that can be heard through the overhanging limbs of old gnarled trees. The likes of Doublehead, John Melton, and the Chickamauga Cherokee settlement are but fading memories to those of us who wonder about the lives of our aboriginal ancestors. Yet, the story of Melton's Bluff ever remains a part of our local history and a flamboyant account of a place on the Tennessee River established by a white Irishman that married the Indian maiden sister of the last Chickamauga Cherokee War Chief.

Lawrence (Colbert) County

On February 6, 1818, Lawrence County, Alabama, was created by the Bureau of Land Management, and approved by the Alabama Territorial Legislature at St. Stephens. In 1818 shortly after the county was created, former Chickasaw and Cherokee territory came open for white settlers. In 1892, the northwestern portion of Lawrence County was annexed into Colbert County. From the present-day northeast corner of Franklin County, the Lawrence County line followed the center of the creek named Town Creek to the Tennessee River. Prior to that, the western border of Lawrence County was a straight line along the old Byler Road, County Line Road or the western fork of Doublehead's Trace and ran through the communities of White Oak, Leighton, Ford City, and to The Shoals (Robert Trent Jones Golf Course) on to the Tennessee River.

Even with Indian trails and roads leading into the area, the rich Indian farmlands along the Muscle Shoals were not considered to be of much value by the government when negotiating treaties with the Cherokee and Chickasaw. On October 8, 1805, Secretary of War Henry Dearborn wrote to Meigs about the price of land, "The average price paid for Indian land in the last four years does not amount to one cent per acre and the highest price we paid for cession of Indian claims to land well suited and of good quality is two cents per acre."

According to Early Settlers of Alabama, "When the public lands were first sold in North Alabama, the United States sold them at public auction, and on credit. Cotton was very high, the rush of immigrants wonderful; and, consequently, lands were bid off at fabulous prices. First-class lands, I think, went off at an average of $20 per acre; and I know of two quarters which were knocked down at more than $100. The purchasers, of course, were not able to pay these rates, and as the installments fell due, they applied their money to a part of what they had bid off at the sales, leaving the rest of their purchases to be relinquished or forfeited. They applied to Congress for relief, and an act was passed, permitting them to apply the money they had paid on the relinquished lands, to the completion of the payments on the land retained. What to do with these relinquished lands became an embarrassing question to Congress, as the purchasers then insisted, that they ought to have the privilege of entering these at their actual value" (Saunders, 1899).

It is ironic that the government paid the Indians one to two cents per acre and sold the same lands at an average of $20.00 per acre just two years later. For all of northwest Alabama, the Chickasaws got $120,000.00, and the Cherokees were paid $60,000.00. In addition to all the broken treaties, this is another classic example of how the United States government ripped off the Native American Indian tribes that lived in North Alabama and across the country.

After the Turkey Town Treaty land cessions of the Cherokees and Chickasaws in 1816, the strong urge by colonial planters to claim the Indian farm lands in northwest Alabama became known as "Alabama Fever." Upon the removal of Indians from the Muscle Shoals area, the cheap Indian land of Lawrence County would become some of the most prized real estate for wealthy cotton planters coming from the eastern colonies.

In large overland wagon trains, many of these wealthy planters and their friends brought their extended families, household goods, farming equipment, livestock, and personal belongings with the help of their black slaves to the Tennessee Valley to increase their fortune and power. Many of these rich planters and their black slaves would settle in Lawrence County. The lands of Lawrence County, Alabama, were purchased at the federal land sale held at Huntsville in 1818. Many white wealthy planters from Virginia and North Carolinas bought most of the large tracts of prime fertile land containing hundreds and sometimes thousands of acres.

On their newly acquired property in Lawrence County, the planters established huge cotton plantations worked by many black slaves. The rich alluvial red soils of the river bottoms, the southeastern hot humid climate, and the well-watered flat valley terrain were ideally suited for growing cotton. Many times, the combination of black slaves and cotton created great wealth for the planters. Some cotton barons built grand plantation mansions with rows of slave cabins. They grew cotton for miles around and made portions of the Tennessee River Valley the appearance of one gigantic cotton plantation.

Migration Routes

Most of the first wealthy cotton planters came into Lawrence County, Alabama, from North Carolina and Virginia by way of Nashville, Tennessee.

Many would follow the Indian route known as the Great South Trail leading to Columbia then splitting toward present-day Florence and Huntsville. Later the route became known as the Old Huntsville Road, leading to Big Spring in Huntsville. Planters arriving in Lawrence County from the Nashville area would fork off the Old Huntsville Road at Columbia, Tennessee, to follow Doublehead's Trace to Loretta, and then to the Muscle Shoals at either Bainbridge or the mouth of Blue Water Creek.

Doublehead's Trace forked at Loretta, Tennessee, with the west fork crossing Shoals Creek then the Tennessee River at Bainbridge, and the eastern fork crossed the Tennessee River at the mouth of Bluewater Creek. Another route was the Sipsie Trail or Lamb's Ferry Road that crossed the Tennessee River south of present-day Rogersville. The Sipsie Trail was an early Indian route from Tuscaloosa to the French Lick (Nashville, Tennessee) on the Cumberland River, and it was known as McCutcheon Trace, Lamb's Ferry Road, and later Cheatham's Road in Lawrence County.

The cotton planter settlers followed old Indian trails many of which that had been upgraded to wagon roads. Beginning with the federal land sales in 1818, these cotton barons begin claiming the fertile lands that lay to the south of the Tennessee River in Lawrence County. Before the arrival of the white cotton planters, these were some of the same lands that the Cherokees and Chickasaws had already been farming cotton with the help of their black slaves.

For the first few years after the Indian land cessions of 1816 and government land sales of 1818, wagon trains regularly rolled along primitive Indian roads and trails of the colonies headed to the northwest Alabama area of the Tennessee Valley to the area of Courtland in Lawrence County, Alabama. Wealthy cotton barons with their families, all their belongings, and sometimes hundreds of black slaves traveled for weeks and months along rough Indian trails to reach the rich flat valley lands along the Muscle Shoals of the Tennessee River.

The Cherokee Indian territory east of Madison and Morgan Counties did not open to white settlement until after Indian removal in 1838. Therefore, before the late 1830's, most of the cotton planters coming to Lawrence County had to avoid passing through Indian territory unless they possessed a passport or permit. After the 1816 Indian land cessions and before 1838, the most direct route without

64

passing through occupied Cherokee Indian Territory was west along Peter Avery's Trace from White's Fort (Knoxville), to Southwest Point (junction of the Clinch and Tennessee Rivers), to Fort Nashborough (Nashville), then south to one of the many Tennessee River ferry crossings.

Courtland

The Town of Courtland would become the hub of the cotton kingdom in Lawrence County, Alabama. Four early Indian roads intersected at Courtland- Gaines' Trace, Upper South River Road (Tuscumbia Road), Sipsie Trail (Cheatham's Road), and Brown's Ferry Road from Huntsville. After crossing the Tennessee River at the Bluewater Ferry, Lamb's Ferry, or Brown's (Cox's or Garner's) Ferry, many of the planters continued on the roads to Courtland in Lawrence County. The town was located somewhat near the center of the flat fertile Tennessee Valley portion of Lawrence County.

Three of the primary Indian trails crossing the Tennessee River to the Courtland area were Doublehead's Trace, Sipsie Trail, and Browns Ferry Road. For many years, John Lamb, a Cherokee Indian, operated his ferry on the Indian path crossing of the Tennessee River which was originally known as the Sipsie Trail. Later in the early 1800's, the route became known as McCutcheon's Trace, Lamb's Ferry Road, or Cheatham's Road. Travelers would leave the Old Huntsville Road at Columbia and head down the Sipsie Trail past Pulaski, Minor Hill, and Rogersville to Lamb's Ferry which was located between Elk River Shoals upstream and Big Muscle Shoals downstream.

The Lamb's Ferry Road would lead planters to Courtland, a major hub for the wealthy cotton barons in Lawrence County, Alabama. According to a February 1829, Lawrence County court record, "a road from Gourd Landing on the Tennessee River to intersect the road from Courtland to Lamb's Ferry at or near Gordon's fence the nearest and best way....Order, 1829, Jury of Review of a road from Courtland to Gourds." The road from Courtland to Lamb's Ferry followed a portion of the Indian path known as the Sipsie Trail (Cheatham's Road).

Also, Brown's Ferry was in use by the time of the Battle of Talladega in 1813. The ferry was used as an early Cherokee Indian ferry crossing of the

Brown's Ferry Road connecting Hunt's Spring (Huntsville) to Gourd's Settlement (Courtland, Alabama). The Brown's Ferry Road crossed the Tennessee River south of Athens and led to Courtland, Alabama. Half-blood Cherokee Captain John Brown ran the ferry prior to moving to Otali which is present-day Attalla. For a short period after John Brown left, his stepdaughter Betsy who married a Cox ran the ferry that was then called Cox's Ferry, and later the ferry was referred to Garner's Ferry; however, the ferry reverted back to the name Brown's Ferry.

Many of the first white planters who came to Lawrence County had already arrived in the northeast half of Madison County which was created in 1806 by the Indian land cession of the Chickasaw Treaty of December 1801. From Madison County, many cotton barons migrated west to claim the new cotton country of Lawrence County by way of the Brown's Ferry Road which led from Hunt's Spring, through Tanner, and then to Courtland.

Courtland was just east of Path Killer's or Big Nance's Creek. The creek was originally named after Cherokee Chief Path Killer, but later took the name of Doublehead's sister, Big Nance. Also near the creek and close proximity to the town, a prehistoric Indian mound indicates thousands of years of aboriginal occupation of the area of the Town of Courtland.

According to Captain Edmund Pendleton Gaines on December 27, 1807, "we proceeded, same course…6th mile…At 116 [chaines] (west of Melton's Bluff) Path Killer's Creek, 3 chains wide from tops of banks" (Stone, 1971). In 1807 when Captain Gaines identified Path Killer's Creek, he was surveying the Gaines Trace which was a road from Melton's Bluff on the Tennessee River to Cotton Gin Port on the Tombigbee River, the heart of the Chickasaw Nation.

In 1816, Major Lewis Dillahunty and his wife Lucinda Johnson Dillahunty became the first white residents of Courtland. Dillahaunty was sent into the territory south of the Tennessee River by President James Monroe to prepare the minds of the Indians for the cession of their lands. In the first election in Lawrence County in 1817, Major Lewis Dillahunty was elected to the House of representatives in the Territorial Legislature, and Green K. Hubbard was his colleague. Dillahunty was appointed postmaster on February 3, 1819.

Planters and Slaves

For several years after Indian removal, a mass influx of wealthy white cotton planters with their black slaves continued to arrive in Lawrence County of the Tennessee Valley after the Indian land cessions. The 1820, 1830, 1840, 1850, and 1860 censuses included many individual slave owners and black slaves that lived in Lawrence County, Alabama, that are not included in this book; those with 10 or more slaves are listed. According to 1860 Lawrence County, Alabama, United States Census, the population included 7,173 whites, 14 free colored, and 6,788 black slaves; therefore, in 1860, black folks made up 48.7 percent of the population of Lawrence County, Alabama.

The following tables are in alphabetical order and cover the 1820 through 1860 census records for Lawrence County, Alabama; the tables include folks in the northeastern portion of Colbert County, Alabama, which was annexed from Lawrence in 1892. Some years of slave ownership were missing or not recorded, and very few planters owned slaves over the span of 40 years of reporting.

After 1860, the Civil War ended the ownership of slaves, and many of the planters lost everything. However, some planter families managed to hold on to vast tracts of land in the Tennessee River Valley. Today, those prior slave owning families that hold hundreds of acres of land still benefit economically from the land by renting to farmers or by farming the land themselves.

Lawrence County Slave Owners	1820	1830	1840	1850	1860
Abernathy, John T		18	41	56	45
Acklin, A.A					22
Adair, Alexander	12				
Aldridge, James	1	4	12	15	7
Alexander, James	0	4	19	1	
Alexander, William			0	9	11
Allen, James		35			
Allen, John Dr	29	1			
Amerson, Charles		44			
Anderson, Hugh A	9	14			
Armstrong, Andrew	1	6	21		
Armstrong, Lucy					17
Armstrong, James	0	5		23	
Ashford, Frederick A					23
Ashford, Thomas	0	10	4	48	23
Baker, John C				4	40
Baker, Wayles			70	1	
Bankhead, William				20	33
Banks, William		14			
Barker, Margaret				10	
Battle, Rachal A				18	
Bean, John				10	
Bean, W. W					11
Berry, Mary					10
Berry, Susan		8	8	12	
Blalock, John C.			30	53	1
Blalock, Thomas				13	19
Blocker, Abner		45			
Body, John E.		37			

Lawrence County Slave Owners	1820	1830	1840	1850	1860
Booth, Harper		27			
Booth, William	45	46			
Bowling (Bolling), Alexander	4	18	34	9	
Bowling (Bolling), William H.				23	47
Brahan, John		26			
Brewer, John J.				21	
Broadnax, John	22				
Broadnax, William	24				
Brown, Eden (Ellen)				22	12
Brown, Samuel	1	8	11		
Burnett, Bolin C.		14			
Burrus, Richard	6	25	4		
Bynum, Drury S.		61			
Bynum, James A.			21	5	
Bynum, Oakley H.				151	124
Byrd, Bolling				19	40
Byrd, Ms. Martha				41	
Byrd, William		20			
Cals, Sand R.		34			
Campbell, Archer			17	22	24
Cannon, David J.					11
Carlock, Thomas V.					16
Carpenter, Sarah		11			
Carter, Joel W. J.		17	19	27	31
Carter, Levi			11	3	4
Carter, M.A.				11	15
Carter, Travis		10			
Chardavoyne, William					26
Clark, Robert		1	8	13	13

Lawrence County Slave Owners	1820	1830	1840	1850	1860
Clay, Frances		64			
Clay, Matthew	50				
Cobb, John B.	18	23			
Cocks, John			24		
Cole, John					12
Coleman, Daniel			27		
Coleman, Ruffin			12		2
Cook, Nathan				30	
Cook, William B.	14				
Cooper, Benjamin		15	31		
Cooper, Wade		6	8	14	
Cox, John		19			
Cox, Mary M.					14
Craddock, John N.			19		
Craddock, Phasant		25			
Crayton (Crawter), Robert				21	24
Critz, George F.	22				
Croom, Jesse Hare	23	41			
Croom, Joshua	20				
Croom, Wiley Jones	29	38			
Dandridge, John Terrell.				9	11
Dandridge, Robert H.	24	15			
Dandridge, William			16		
Daniel, Eliz M.			39		
Davidson, O.S.			12		27
Davis, Owin D.		31			
Dearing, William		164		3	
Degraffenread, A. Maury	7	19	35		
Deloney, Edward			29	30	

Lawrence County Slave Owners	1820	1830	1840	1850	1860
Dillahunty, Harvey		36			
Dinsmore (Dunsmore), David				2	16
Donaian, Obidiah				25	
Donnell, Jas. W. S.				56	85
Dotson, William		7	12		
Douglass, (Douglas) Samuel	11	18			
Doyle, James	11	13			
Drane, Eliza					10
Driver, Bennett				16	19
Dukeminier, Isaac		2	5	8	11
Early, Thomas S.		25	31	39	
Eggleston, J.O.					35
Eggleston, John L.				7	15
Eggleston, Samuel O.		23	36	48	
Elliott, Samuel	6	18	104	55	94
Elliott, Rebecca		13			
Elliott, William	12	14	15	18	19
Epps, Hamlin	23				
Faircloth, Cordial	3	14		38	
Faircloth, John					18
Felton, Mat			27		
Felton, Thadeus W.			21		40
Fennel, Henry			18		
Fennel, Mary				38	54
Fennel, Nelson				18	23
Fenner, Robert			44		
Ferguson, George		14			
Ferris (Farris), Edward			19		
Fitzgerald, Freeman		107			

Lawrence County Slave Owners	1820	1830	1840	1850	1860
Fitzgerald, William		56	3	25	
Foot, Henry		28			
Foster, E. H.					33
Foster, Thomas J.		56	51	95	129
Foster, Washington			54		
Fort, David G.				14	
Fort (Font), Mary			28		
Garrett, William		31			
Garth, George M.					35
Garth, Willis					59
Gewin, C. C.				13	10
Gibson, A. L.				25	
Gibson, Charles				20	34
Gibson, G&C W.M F. Preuitt					12
Gibson, Ira			93		
Gibson, James		5	159		
Gibson, John	15		10		
Gibson, Jordan	16				
Gibson, Mary					14
Gibson, O.D.				21	16
Gibson, R.					31
Gibson, Sylvanus				16	
Gibson, Thomas		22	22		
Gibson, Thomas G.			20		
Gilchrist, Daniel			62	87	
Gilchrist, John					21
Gilchrist, Malcom		9		10	
Gilchrist, Nancy					21
Glass, John		21			

Lawrence County Slave Owners	1820	1830	1840	1850	1860
Glass, Vincent	7	10			
Goode, Freeman		21	84	86	108
Gray, Jonathan		16	23	26	
Gray, Young A.	35	4			
Green, John		6	234		
Green, William	26		13		
Gregg (Gragg), John		5	15		
Gregg (Gragg), Nathan		19		14	
Gregg (Gragg), William			11	17	
Hammon, Dudley			72		
Hampton, Manoah B.		34	56	51	71
Hansell, John				3	15
Harper, Berryman		16			
Harper, Thomas		10			
Harper, William Wilkins		34	40		
Harris, Benjamin	26	33		1	
Harris, John H.		0	13	99	183
Harris, Peter		11			
Harris, Richard		44			
Harris, Stephen W.				62	
Harris, William		0	11	5	12
Harvey, John		10	11		
Hatton (Hatten), F.				26	
Henderson, James	18	0			
Henderson, John	1	13			
Henderson, Martha		15			
Henderson, Samuel		1	11		
Hennegan, Samuel S.			7	31	56
Hickman, John P.	56				

Lawrence County Slave Owners	1820	1830	1840	1850	1860
Hicks, John C.			15		
Hines, William	27				
Hinton, George		20			
Hodges, Asa		11		2	9
Hodges, Daniel			20	18	49
Hodges, Fleming	26		0	6	
Hodges, Henry William		20	15		
Hodges, Nancy			17		
Hodges, William		11			
Holland, Sarah					10
Holland, Thomas	2	15	3	42	
Holland, William F.					13
Holms, Vivian B.	17				
Hook(s), David			17		
Hook(s), Martha			17		
Hook(s), Robert		31			
Hook(s), William				35	
Hopkins, Arthur F.		52	19		
Hubbard, David		10	10	34	31
Hughes (Hughs), Berie			17		
Hughes (Hughs), Eliza				31	
Hughes (Hughs), John		12			
Hughes (Hughs), Ruse		6	21		
Hunter, David		16	7		
Ironsdale, J.					18
Irwin, H.B.					14
Jackson, James			57	11	19
Jackson, John M.		2	4	10	
Jameson (Jemison), Nancy		21			

Lawrence County Slave Owners	1820	1830	1840	1850	1860
Jarmen, Amos		26	42	50	19
Jarmen, Hall		10	13	15	
Jarvin, John				41	
Jarvin, Z. B.				20	
Johnson, James	0	2	37	2	
Johnson, John Sr.	5	22			
Johnson, Nicholas	70	135			
Johnson, William	13	4			
Jones, Alexander S.			10	15	10
Jones, Benjamin B.	51	100			
Jones, Francis	72				
Jones, Frank		100			43
Jones, Judith		56	25		
Jones, Littleberry	57				
Jones, Richard		42		82	107
Jones, Robert			56		
Jones, Tegnal				30	
Jones, Thomas M.				60	108
Jones, Thomas B.			13	26	28
Jones, William		2	20		
Kellum, Thomas R.				17	
Kennedy, Rebecca					14
King, Burchett Curtis				36	15
King, Hartwell N.		60		23	
King, Oswald			18	50	77
King, Paul				16	19
King, Philamon				30	71
King, Robert Sr.			19	63	101
Kingston, Robert					24

Lawrence County Slave Owners	1820	1830	1840	1850	1860
Kinnard, Dell					11
Kitchens, John					13
Knott, David	16				
Lackey, William D.					20
Landers, James E.					171
Landers, Mary		13			
Landers, William				11	1
Landford (Lanford) ?, Nancy			21		
Langston ?, S. C.			19		
Larrier ?, Robert			19		
Leetch (Leitch), William	16	21			
Leigh (Lee), William		38			
Lenoper ?, Noah					10
Lerron ?, Ann H.					25
Lester, Fred		13			
Lewis, David					34
Lightfoot, John F.		2		58	
Lightfoot, Robert M.				14	13
Lightfoot, Thomas	17	22			
Lindsey, Mark		12			
Linthicum (Linticum) Berd	3	11	14		
Livingston, A.A.C.					17
Livingston, Samuel			7	10	10
Louise ?, Mary A.			43		
Luster, Fredrick	26				
Madding, Elisha		17	38	62	
Madding, Eliza					30
Maff, Burwell		20			
Manning, William		15	34	29	

Lawrence County Slave Owners	1820	1830	1840	1850	1860
Martin, George W.		19			
Martin, Hunter			14		
Martin, John				11	
Martin, Joseph	23	27			
Massie (Massey), John M.				17	1
Mayes (Mays), Drewry, Estate		4		20	23
Mayes (Mays), Joshua		12			
Mayes (Mays), Michael W.		9	9	15	9
McAllister, Edward		21			
McCord, Ambrose			25	1	
McCord, Thomas P.				7	11
McCrary, Irwin P.				2	12
McCrary, M.				17	
McCullock, Alexander	18				
McDaniel, Elijah	9	13		21	
McDaniel, P.A.				33	67
McDaniel, Thomas J.				23	59
McDavey, David				36	
McDonald, Wm. A. (M.)				52	58
McGaughey, James P.	0	1	2	5	16
McGaughey, John M.		0	11	15	21
McGaughey, Margaret					10
McGaughey, William			0	11	
McGregor, M.				19	
McGregor, T.					17
McGregor, William		9	28	31	34
McKelvy, William				13	12
McLemore, L.				23	
McMahon, H.C.					11

Lawrence County Slave Owners	1820	1830	1840	1850	1860
McVay, P.				4	13
Meredith, Samuel		25			
Milam, Ben F.				8	16
Moore, Eliz			13		
Moore, John	1		16	23	30
Moore, Joseph	10				
Moore, William		24			
Moschs ?, Elizabeth		24			
Mosely, John	18				
Mosely, John F.	14	28			
Mosely, Robert G.	10	7			
Mosely, William F.	11	29	4	11	33
Mullins, Gabriel				12	
Mullins, James H.	2	19	35	38	45
Mullins, William				13	
Myatt, Aldridge		16			
Napier, John S.			32	25	66
Norment, Nathabiel	19				
Oliver, John		69			
Owen, Isaac N.		7		13	29
Owen/Owens, Estate of J. C.					40
Parham ?, Elizabeth		39			
Parham, H. G.				26	
Patterson, Hamlin		23			
Pearsall, Jeremiah	10				
Pearson, Thomas			11	11	15	
Peebles, Henry W.		59			
Peters, Robert M.				22	
Peters, Samuel		22			

Lawrence County Slave Owners	1820	1830	1840	1850	1860
Peoples, Dudley H.	64				
Petway, Hinchey	27				
Phianizry, John T.				34	
Pickens, Joseph		40			
Pickett, B.O.					14
Pierce, James			67		
Pointer, M.A.					19
Pointer, Phillip (Estate)				39	48
Pointer, Samuel					22
Pointer, Sarah				22	
Pointer, Thomas M.		30		19	
Pointer, William				24	
Pope, John	41				
Preuit (Prewett), Jacob	28				
Preuit, James		2	10		
Preuit, John		5	20	22	10
Preuit, Martha				43	44
Preuit, Richard		8	35	91	163
Preuit, Robert H.				10	
Preuit, T.B.					21
Preuit, William	6	25	63		
Price, Elijah		12			
Price, Robert	44				
Price, William			27		
Priest (Priester), Thomas			22		
Puckett, Richard		6	30		
Puryear, Peter		5		29	34
Rand (Rann), Aldridge			12		
Rand, John W.		21		13	

Lawrence County Slave Owners	1820	1830	1840	1850	1860
Reneau, William	0	5		13	
Reynolds, John	4	17			
Reynolds, Mason	21				
Riggs, John		3	16		
Rooks, William					46
Rose (Ruse), John C.			14		
Rose (Cose) ?, Rachael				15	
Ross, Elizabeth	22				
Rowe, James				13	
Rusts, Caviel		20			
Sale, Alexander		15	16	19	
Saunders (Sanders), Claybourn W.	10	32	45		
Saunders (Sanders), James E.		9	32	41	
Saunders (Sanders), Joseph		18			
Saunders (Sanders), Robert	10				
Saunders (Sanders), Susan			42	1	
Saunders (Sanders), Turner		50			
Savage, Nancy			60		
Scruggs, John				31	43
Shackleford, Jack		24	6	12	
Shackleford, Samuel					86
Shane, Thomas L.		47			
Shaw, Bally		1	13	15	24
Shaw, Ephraim H.			15	10	7
Sheffield, Ed William	0	7	21		
Sherrod, Ben					80
Sherrod, Colonel Benjamin		280	353	394	
Sherrod, Frank					27
Sherrod, N.M.					96

Lawrence County Slave Owners	1820	1830	1840	1850	1860
Simms, David			0	15	
Simms, Thomas D.				18	33
Simpson, Moses	0	9	18	14	
Smith, Allen	13				
Smith, C.G.					12
Smith, John	5	17	19		
Smith, Susan				32	
Spangler, Daniel				14	16
Speake, James B.					13
Speaks, Hansford					11
Stanley, Andrew H.				6	11
Stanley, Edward				34	
Stanley, Ellen			11		
Stanley, James			13		
Stanley, J.H. & E.R.					42
Stanley, Nathaniel		16			
Steenston (Stephenson), Elizabeth					100
Stephens (Stevens), Wiley			47		
Stephenson, Hodge L.		0	8	5	10
Stewart, John		19			
Stone, John	12	6			
Stovall, Archibald		3	4	12	1
Stovall, William	5	11	8	16	11
Stover, Elijah	0		0	16	35
Swoope, C.C.					44
Swoope, Edgar M.			0	142	164
Swoope, I. R.				107	
Swoope, Jacob K. Sr. and Jr.		2	111		48
Swoope, John		5	17	129	117

Lawrence County Slave Owners	1820	1830	1840	1850	1860
Sykes, A.J.					15
Sykes, Frank W.				36	58
Sykes, James Turner			33		
Sykes, William			25		
Taran, Jane S.				35	
Tart, Thomas	23	2			
Tennison, Lemuel	32				
Thomas, Benjamin	12				
Thompson, John			3		18
Thompson, Samuel					1
Thompson, William		7		7	13
Thorn, Harry				9	24
Threldkill (Threlkeld), Phillip	0	8		10	
Tinker, Harris	33	43			
Towns, E. D. (agent J. N. Stanley)				55	
Towns, John L.	17	34			
Truelove ,Breathsett			20		
Tweedy, I. M.				29	
Valient, D. H.		2	21		
Vaughn, Baskerville Estate			20	35	48
Vaughn, Julia					17
Wade, Daniel	20	11			
Walker, Avid H.					24
Walker, Ben F.					36
Walker, David H.		21	51	58	
Walker, John A.	101	24			
Walker, John N.			1	10	
Walker, Sarah W.					15
Wall, James		35			

Lawrence County Slave Owners	1820	1830	1840	1850	1860
Wall, Michael		27			
Wallace, David		25			
Wallace, Elizabeth	24				
Wallace, John	0	3	12	21	
Wallace, Martin		10			
Wallace, Mrs. H. (John's wife)					23
Wallace, William		7	16	11	2
Waller, Obidiah	27				
Walton, George	20	44	4		
Ward, Benjamin		21			
Warden, David			8	17	
Warren, E.T.				2	13
Warren, Henesy W.					15
Warren, Humphry	19				
Warren, Levi		9		50	67
Warren, Robert	0				20
Warren, Thomas J. (W.)				17	18
Warren, William		3	13	26	
Watkins, James L.			37		
Watkins, Paul J.		42		161	148
Watkins, Robert H.			7	140	
Watkins, Samuel	31	96			
Watkins, William (Willis)		28			44
Watt, James			23		
Webb, David			70		
White, John S.		22			
Whitehead, David C.			30		
Whitley, Needham			17		
Wilkinson (Wilkerson), Hildred				10	

Lawrence County Slave Owners	1820	1830	1840	1850	1860
Williams, W. T.			41		
Willichane, Francis		19			
Wilson, Arianna				28	
Wilson, David	2	10	26		
Wilson, Thomas		10	25		
Winston, Isaac (agent John J Ray)				77	82
Wood, Bennett		54			
Wood, Mary			12		
Wood, Obadish		22			
Woolridge, Thomas	17				
Wray, John		21			
Wright, Archibald		3	13	18	
Wright, John		22			
Wright, R.C.					16
Yell, Volvey		16			
Young, Reason			0	4	20

Planters of Lawrence County

The following profiles of some of the planters of Lawrence County, Alabama, are listed in alphabetical order. It is not practical to write profiles of all the planters owning ten or more black slaves.

Alexander, James-Walnut Ford

The Alexander plantation was located in the southeast portion of Lawrence County, Alabama. The upper portion of the West Fork of Flint Creek flowed through the center of the old plantation which butted up against the northern ridge of the Warrior Mountains which is the Tennessee Divide. Indian Tomb Hollow and High House Hill were at one time a part of the vast plantation which encompassed several thousand acres of land. Both the Alexander

Motorway and the old Poplar Log Cove Road passed near the old Alexander plantation house.

Several Indian trails passed in close proximity to the plantation. The east-west Indian trail known as the High Town Path passed to the south of the plantation along the Tennessee Divide. The north-south Black Warriors' Path passed to the east through Poplar Log Cove, and the Coosa Path passed to the north through Oakville and Moulton.

The Poplar Log Cove Road passed a few yards south of the old plantation house. It ran southeast to Poplar Log Cove and joined the Black Warriors Path. To the northwest, the road went to Moulton where it joined the Coosa Path. The old Indian trail and cove road crossed the West Fork of Flint Creek at Walnut Ford just a few yards downstream from its junction with Thompson Creek. The crossing area was the site of a huge passenger pigeon roost, and it was littered with small Mississippi triangle projectile points.

The Alexander Mound was excavated by the Smithsonian in 1924, and the remains of over 100 native Indian people were removed and stored in the museum complex in Washington D. C. Mr. Gerard Fowke (1928) was in charge of the excavation which was reported by the Bureau of American Ethnology. The late Mr. Bruce Dodd told me that when he was a boy he would go to the site and watch the workers digging in the mound. The area around the Alexander Mound site had ancient artifacts that were evidence of paleo-Indian occupation; therefore, the old plantation exhibits some 14,000 years of human habitation.

During the early 1800s, the Alexander Plantation had a cotton gin, lime and brick kilns, tanning yard, black smith shop, several slave and tenant houses, log barns, and at least two large main houses for members of the Alexander family. The main plantation home just west of Walnut Ford was a two storied "L" shaped house with many rooms and chimneys. The bottom of the "L" shape was the front of the house which had top and bottom porches; the inside of the "L" also had top and bottom porches.

James Alexander was born on January 1, 1770, in Chester County, Pennsylvania. He died on August 26, 1851, near Moulton in Lawrence County, Alabama. He was buried in the old Alexander Cemetery at Pinhook. He first

Alexander Plantation House

married Catherine 'Kitty' Walker on January 1, 1798, in Iredell County, North Carolina. Kitty was born about 1782; she died on May 5, 1823. She was buried in the Old Alexander Cemetery near Pinhook in Lawrence County, Alabama. James and Kitty Walker Alexander had ten children:

1) William Wilburn Alexander was born on November 20, 1803;
2) Thomas Walker Alexander was born on January 1, 1804, in Abbeville, South Carolina;
3) David Clay Alexander was born about 1806;
4) Sarah Belle 'Sally' Alexander was born on April 10, 1810, in Kentucky;
5) Elizabeth Alexander was born about 1812 in Kentucky;
6) Catherine 'Kitty' Alexander was born on January 1, 1813, in Lincoln County, Tennessee;
7) Nancy Minerva Alexander was born on January 1, 1814, in Tennessee;
8) James Monroe Alexander was born in 1815 in Lincoln County, Tennessee;
9) Mary Ann Alexander was born on August 11, 1819, in Bedford County, Tennessee; and
10) George Washington Alexander was born June 5, 1821, at Moulton in Lawrence County, Alabama.

After his wife Kitty died, James Alexander married the second time to Elizabeth 'Betsey' Sheffield on July 6, 1823. Betsey was born about 1802 in Virginia; she died on December 5, 1846. She was buried in the Old Alexander Cemetery near Pinhook in Lawrence County, Alabama. James and Betsey had the following children:

1) John Thomas Alexander was born about 1825 at Moulton in Lawrence County, Alabama;
2) Fereby Louisa Alexander was born on January 1, 1830, at Moulton in Lawrence County, Alabama;
3) Malinda (Ellen) Elizabeth Alexander was born on December 14, 1832, at Moulton in Lawrence County, Alabama; and,
4) Riley W. Alexander was born on January 1, 1840, in Lawrence County, Alabama.

According to the 1830 and 1840 Lawrence County, Alabama, census records, James Alexander owned 4 and 19 black slaves, respectively. In 1840, William, the son of James owned 9 black slaves; together, they had a total of 28 slaves in 1840.

William Alexander-High House

William Alexander was born on November 20, 1803, and he died on April 4, 1873. William married Mary Aldridge on May 15, 1823; Mary was born on December 22, 1802, in Abbeville, South Carolina. They had the following children:

1) Jane Caroline Alexander was born on July 24, 1824;
2) Elizabeth Louisa Alexander was born on April 24, 1826;
3) Mary Belinda Alexander was born on August 19, 1828;
4) James W. (Jim Monk) Alexander was born on April 10, 1829;
5) Kitty Elenor Alexander was born on July 23, 1833;
6) Thomas Jefferson Alexander was born on August 7, 1835;
7) William C. Alexander was born on May 18, 1838;
8) David Walker Alexander was born on November 22, 1841;
9) Sarah Ann Alexander was born on March 13, 1844;
10) John Tyler Alexander was born May 25, 1846; and,
11) Henry Clay Alexander was born on January 1, 1848.

High House Hill

The High House Hill home was a large two storied house, and it was covered by four-inch-wide yellow poplar drop siding. The house contained 16 rooms and nine outside doors. Nearly every room had a large brick fireplace with the top of the house having a slave observation deck.

High House Hill was the home of William and Mary Alexander; it is believed that William built the High House plantation home. The High House Hill homesite is now on United States Forest Service property at the point of the south ridge of Indian Tomb Hollow between Gillespie and Lee Creeks. High House Hill was probably used as the mountain home of their plantation which included several thousand acres that encompassed the junctions of the West Fork of Flint Creek and Thompson Creek at Walnut Ford.

According to the 1850 agricultural census of Lawrence County, William Alexander owned 1,560 acres of land. The land included 450 acres of improved crop land and 1,110 acres of unimproved land. The Alexander farm was valued at $350, and the equipment was worth $300. The livestock was valued at $2,128.00. According to the 1850 Lawrence County, Alabama, Slave Schedules, William Alexander owned 11 black slaves; however, it was reported at one time, William owned 34 slaves. Also in the 1850 Lawrence County, Alabama, Argicultural Census, James Alexander, father of William, owned 1,040 acres of land with 600 acres of improved and 440 acres of unimproved worth $3,000.00 and $1,535 worth of livestock; therefore, in 1850, together they owned 2,600 acres of land.

In the 1860 Lawrence County, Alabama, United States Census, Household 202, William Alexander was a 56-year-old male born in North Carolina. His real estate value was $19,000.00, and his personal property value was $65,500.00. Also in his household was Mary a 57-year-old female born in South Carolina, Jane C. a 35-year-old female born in Alabama, Mary B. a 31-year-old female born in Alabama, Kittey a 26-year-old female born in Alabama, David W. an 18-year-old male born in Alabama, Sarah A. a 15-year-old female born in Alabama, John T. a 14-year-old male born in Alabama, Henery C. a 12-year-old male born in Alabama, Sarah A. Fitzgerald a 15-year-old female born in Alabama, Lettice G. a 13-year-old female born in Alabama, Mary E. a 12-year-old female born in

Alabama, William a 10-year-old male born in Alabama, Lucy I. an eight-year-old female born in Alabama, and Henery a six-year-old male born in Alabama.

In the 1860 census next to William in household 203, Thomas Alexander a 24-year-old male born in Alabama was listed as an overseer. This is probably Thomas Jefferson Alexander who was born on August 7, 1835, and died on August 3, 1890. Also in the Thomas Alexander household in 1860, Sarah C. was a 28-year-old female born in Alabama, Morley a three-year-old female born in Alabama, and Mary L. an eleven month old female.

William and Mary Alexander were buried on the old plantation in the new portion of Alexander-Welborn Cemetery. The original cemetery had so many unmarked graves that human bones were being dug up when other members were being buried; therefore, the cemetery was moved about 100 yards to the south. It was in the new portion where William and Mary were buried with small headstones indicating their graves.

Redland Farms

Today in 2019, Mark Yeager lives on the old homesite of the Alexander plantation house which was torn down in the late 1960s; Mark plants cotton and corn on the old plantation. His father Dallas Yeager bought about 2,400 acres from the Alexander descendants in the early 1960's. The farm is now some 1,000 acres and is used as crop and pastureland. Some 1,400 acres of the rough mountainous land of the old plantation was sold to timber companies.

Mark's Redland Farms cultivate about 3,500 acres of cotton each year and picks about 7,000 bales of cotton on his farm and rental properties. He owns the Yeager Gin Company about two miles east of Moulton, Alabama. Each year, he gins only the cotton that Redland Farms produce. Some of his higher-grade cotton is used to make 100% cotton sheets which can be purchased at his retail store on the square in Moulton or at redlandcotton.com. Mark said, "Our highest end cotton is as good as the highest quality Pima cotton of the southwest or Egyptian cotton."

Allen, Captain James M.

Captain James M. Allen was born on May 17, 1782, and died on February 12, 1835. He was buried in the Allen Family Cemetery at Courtland in Lawrence County, Alabama (Find a Grave Memorial Number 38698230). His wife Nancy Allen was born on July 17, 1778, and died on January 7, 1841. Nancy was buried in the Allen Family Cemetery at Courtland in Lawrence County, Alabama (Find a Grave Memorial Number 38698265). Children of Captain James M. and Nancy Allen include:

1) Mary Ann Allen was listed in Lawrence County archives as a daughter of James Allen.
2) Reuben Anthony Allen was listed as a son and executor of James Allen estate in Lawrence County archives.
3) Laurany Allen was listed as a daughter of James Allen in Lawrence County archives.
4) Henry J. M. Allen was a son named in the will of James Allen. Henry was born on December 15, 1810, and died on July 21, 1837.
5) Madison Allen was listed as an executor of the James Allen estate.

According to the 1830 census of Lawrence County, Alabama, James Allen owned 35 black slaves. Also he was head of the household that had one male ten to 15, one male 15 to 20, one male 40 to 50, one female ten to 15, one female 15 to 20, and one female 40 to 50.

According to Lawrence County deed records, James M. Allen owned two lots in the Town of Courtland: In deed book D 222, James M. Allen owned lot 29 in Courtland, Alabama, and in deed book D 454, James M. Allen owned lot 276 in Courtland, Alabama.

According to Old Land Records of Lawrence County, Alabama by Margaret M. Cowart (1991), James Allen entered three tracts of land at Courtland in Township 4 South and Range 8 West. On March 27, 1829, James entered 159 acres in Section 25. On March 10, 1830, he entered 80 acres in Section 25. On July 1, 1831, he entered 160.57 acres in Section 36. The land he entered was adjacent to land owned by Drew S. Bynum.

In addition, James Allen purchased land from Joshua P. Mays. On January 30, 1830, J. P. Mays entered 80 acres in Section 6 of Township 5 South and Range 7 West (Cowart, 1991).

Ashford, Thomas H. Sr.-Free and Easy

The plantation of Major Thomas Harrison Ashford Sr. of Virginia was known as Free and Easy (Jones-Donnell Papers, 1817-1994). Thomas was born about 1791, and he married Jane Sinai Elgin who was born on January 10, 1797, in Maryland; she died on September 11, 1861. Their children included:

1. Thomas H. Ashford Jr. was born about 1820; he married Caroline Tate in 1850.
2. Lucella L. Ashford was born about 1825; she married David Bradenthal in 1850.
3. Fredrick A. Ashford was born about 1830.
4. Dr. Edward Clinton Ashford was born in Alabama on September 24, 1832, and he died on November 17, 1896. Dr. Ashford never married, and he was buried in the family cemetery in Lawrence County, Alabama.
5. Colonel Alva Elgin Ashford was born on July 10, 1834, in Alabama, and died on July 7, 1904. He was a colonel in the Confederate Army, and in 1866, he served in the Alabama House of Representatives. He married Carolyn Fletcher who was born in Alabama on September 27, 1847, and

Ashford Home

she died on March 5, 1897. They are buried in the Ashford Family Cemetery northwest of Courtland in Lawrence County, Alabama.

On September 14, 1818, Thomas Ashford first entered land in Lawrence County, Alabama; on this date, he entered 80 acres in Section 20 and 80 acres in Section 23 of Township 4 South and Range 8 West. From November 24, 1829, through January 9, 1855, Thomas entered another 680 acres in Lawrence County, Alabama (Cowart, 1991).

In the 1850 Lawrence County, Alabama, United States Census, Household 287 is the following: Thomas Ashford, 59, Virginia; Jane S., 53, Kentucky; David Bradenthal, 27, Pennsylvania; Lucella Bradenthal, 25, Alabama; F. A. Ashford, 20, m; Alva E. 17, m; Edward C. 15; Thomas H. 30, Alabama; Caroline, 24, Alabama.

According to the 1850 Lawrence County, Alabama, Slave Schedules, Thomas Ashford owned 48 black slaves. According to the 1850 Lawrence County, Alabama, Agricultural Census, Thomas Ashford owned 1,080 acres of improved land and 315 acres of unimproved land worth $16,640.00. Thomas had $1,090.00 worth of farming equipment and his livestock was worth $3,703.00.

According to the 1860 Lawrence County, Alabama, United States Census, Household 564, Thomas Ashford had a real estate value of $24,000.00, and a personal property value of $25,000.00. In the census, Thomas was listed as being a 69-year-old male farmer born in Virginia, and Jane S. as a 63-year-old female born in Maryland.

Thomas Harrison Ashford Jr.

In 1850, Thomas Harrison Ashford Jr. and Caroline Tate Ashford lived in the household with Thomas Ashford Sr. After he married Caroline Tate in 1850, Thomas H. Ashford Jr. divided his time between his home in Mooresville and his family's Free and Easy Plantation in Lawrence County, Alabama.

Carolina Tate was the daughter of Enos and Nancy McAllister Tate (Jones-Donnell Papers, 1817-1994). On February 7, 1818, Enos, the father-in-law of Thomas, entered 480 acres in Section 14 of Township 5 South and Range 3

West in Limestone County, Alabama; Enos Tate entered a total of 1160 acres in Limestone County (Cowart, 1984).

By 1860, it appears that Thomas Ashford Sr. divided his slaves between two of his sons. In 1860, Thomas Ashford owned 23 slaves, and Frederick A. Ashford owned 23 black slaves.

Bankhead, William Stuart-Albemarle

William Stuart Bankhead was born on January 31, 1826, in Albemarle County, Virginia; his mother was Anne Cary Randolph (January 23, 1791-February 11, 1826). In 1847, he moved to the Courtland area of Lawrence County, Alabama, and purchased the Southdale Plantation home of Littlebury H. Jones. William renamed his estate Albemarle Plantation after his home county in Virginia. According to the 1850 Lawrence County, Alabama, Slave Schedule, William Stuart Bankhead owned 20 black slaves, and by 1860, he owned 33 slaves.

William Stuart Bankhead was a direct descendant of President Thomas Jefferson. He was captain of Company I of 16th Alabama Regiment when he contracted inflammatory rheumatism. After returning home on sick leave, he almost lost the use of a leg from rheumatism. Captain William S. Bankhead resigned his commission when his regiment passed by his Albemarle Plantation near Courtland on its way to Corinth, Mississippi.

On August 6, 1851, William married Martha Jane Watkins, the daughter of Paul J. Watkins and Elizabeth Watt, but she died a year later. On June 20, 1854, he then married Barbara Elizabeth 'Lizzie' Garth (May 29, 1834-December 5, 1867). William and Lizzie had three children:
1. Anne Cary 'Nannie' Bankhead (February 6, 1856-August 25, 1900) married James Harvey Gilchrist; Nannie is buried in the Sykes Cemetery (Find a Grave Memorial Number 49027954).
2. Elizabeth 'Lizzie' Bankhead (August 28, 1865-April 9, 1942) married William Hotchkiss; Elizabeth was buried in the Courtland Cemetery (Find a Grave Memorial Number 43377010). William and Elizabeth Bankhead Hotchkiss lived at the Kolona Plantation home.

Kolona

3. William F. Bankhead (March 18,1858-September 6, 1862) was buried in Sykes Cemetery (Find a Grave Memorial Number 49027879).

On September 21, 1868, William married Catherine "Kate' Mary Gilchrist Garth, the widow of Captain George Martin Garth of the Bonnie Doon Plantation. On January 7, 1870, William and Kate had one son John Stuart Bankhead who died on August 6, 1873; he was buried at the Bonnie Doon Plantation. Catherine Mary Gilchrist Garth Bankhead died on February 19, 1900, at 69 years of age. She was buried at Bonnie Doon in the Garth Cemetery (Find a Grave Memorial Number 39530500).

On November 19, 1898, William Stuart Bankhead died at Courtland in Lawrence County, Alabama. He was buried in the Sykes Cemetery (Find a Grave Memorial Number 47605703).

Booth, William Sr.

William Booth came to Lawrence County, Alabama, from Virginia, with his wife Mary Ann Fitzgerald and her siblings. Mary Ann was born in Virginia about 1781. Mary Ann Fitzgerald's family members who came to Lawrence County, Alabama, included the following siblings:

1. Sarah 'Sally' Fitzgerald Ward who married Benjamin Ward Jr.;
2. Elizabeth Fitzgerald Jones who married Littleberry H. Jones;
3. Reverend Freeman Fitzgerald who married Elizabeth Williams;
4. Anne Roper Williams Fitzgerald who married Mary Ann's brother Thomas Fitzgerald;
5. Martha Fitzgerald Eppes who married Hamlin Eppes; and
6. William Fitzgerald III who married Letty Ann Williams.

On September 10, 1818, William Booth of Madison County and his brother-in-law Littleberry H. Jones of Madison County entered land in Section 31 of Township 4 South and Range 7 West in Lawrence County, Alabama; William entered 160 acres and Littleberry entered 320 acres. Respectively, on September 15, 1818, and October 5, 1818, William Booth and his brother-in-law Hamlin Eppes entered 160 acres in Township 5 South and Range 8 West. Respectively, on February 9, 1830, and February 19, 1830, Benjamin Ward (brother-in-law of William Booth Sr.) and William Booth Jr. entered 320 acres each in Section 6 of Township 5 South and Range 7 West in Lawrence County, Alabama (Cowart, 1991).

According to the 1820 Lawrence County, Alabama Census, William Booth was head of a household that had three white males over 21, one white male under 21, one white female over 21, and eight white females under 21. William Booth also had 45 black slaves in 1820.

William Booth Sr. died before 1824 in Lawrence County, Alabama. According to the Lawrence County Archives records, the 1824 estate of William Booth Sr. was handled by William A. Booth Jr.

According to the 1830 Lawrence County, Alabama Census, William Booth Jr. household had two white males 10-15, two white males 20 to 30, two white females ten to 15, and three white females 15 to 20. In 1830, William Booth Jr. owned 46 black slaves.

According to the 1838-1841 Lawrence County Archives records, William Booth Jr. held the note on the estate of his uncle Hamlin Eppes. Hamlin married Martha Fitzgerald, the sister of his mother Mary Ann Fitzgerald Booth, the wife of William Booth Sr.

According to the Lawrence County Commissioner's Court Minutes, Page 41, June 1818-December 1824, William Booth and others were appointed to contract with the lowest bidder to build a bridge across Big Nance's Creek. In the 1835-1840 Lawrence County will and inventory books, William Booth was the purchaser of the A. C. Young estate. He also held the bond, notes, and accounts on the William Banks estate, and he had the account of the Thomas Pointer estate.

Broadnax, William Edward

In 1794, William Edward Brodnax was justice of Brunswick, Virginia; in 1807, he was the sheriff of Brunswick. William Edward Brodnax died January 12, 1831, aged seventy-six.

William Edward Brodnax married Sarah Jones on December 24, 1787. She was a daughter of Frederick Jones who was the son of Thomas Jones and Elizabeth Cocke. Elizabeth is the eldest daughter of Dr. William Cocke, Secretary of State, and his wife Elizabeth Catesby Cocke, sister of Mark Catesby, the celebrated naturalist. Mrs. Sarah Brodnax died on November 7, 1830, aged about seventy.

William Edward Broadnax (1745-1831) and Sarah Jones (1760-1830) were the parents of three sons: John P. Broadnax, William Fredrick Broadnax, and Thomas Hall Broadnax. By 1818, the following documents indicate that John P. Broadnax and William F. Broadnax came to Lawrence County, Alabama, with each other:

1. In 1818, both John P. Broadnax and William F. Broadnax were listed in the 1818 Circuit Court records of Madison County.

2. On September 10, 1818, both John P. Broadnax and William Fredrick Broadnax entered 160 acres of land each in Lawrence County, Alabama.
3. In the 1820 Lawrence County, Alabama, Circuit Court records, case number 125, both John P. and William F. Broadnax are listed together.
4. In the 1820 Lawrence County, Alabama Census, both John P. Broadnax and William F. Broadnax are listed on the same page and are separated by only three households.
5. By the 1820 Lawrence County, Alabama Census, John P. Broadnax and William F. owned over 20 black slaves each.
6. On May 1, 1821, a summons was issued from Jonathan Burford, Circuit Court clerk, to the sheriff of Lawrence County, Alabama, asking the sheriff to compel John P. Broadnax, William F. Broadnax, and William Faxhall to pay debts.

John P. Broadnax

On September 10, 1818, John P. Broadnax entered 160 acres in both Sections 35, 36 of Township 4 South and Range 7 West. On September 15, 1818, John entered another 160 acres in Section 1 of Township 5 South and Range 8 West (Cowart, 1991).

According to the 1820 Lawrence County, Alabama Census, John Broadnax household had two white males over 21, two white females over 21, four white females under 21, for a total of eight whites. In 1820, John Broadnax owned 22 black slaves which made a total of 30 inhabitants living on his farm.

According to the Lawrence County Archives Records and Deeds, Deed Book C, page 139, Martha Broadnax owned lots 90 and 91 in Courtland, Alabama. Martha Broadnax is listed in the Probate court records of 1824. Martha maybe the wife of John P. Broadnax. According to the Circuit, Orphans, and Probate Court records of Lawrence County, Alabama, John P. Broadnax is listed in the Circuit records of Madison County in 1818 and Circuit records of Lawrence County in 1820.

William Frederick Broadnax

William F. Broadnax was born July 23, 1793; On February 17, 1814, William F. Broadnax entered 161.3 acres in Section 19 of Township 2 South and Range 1 West in Madison County, Alabama (Cowart, 1979). The William F. Broadnax family probably came to Lawrence County, Alabama, in 1818. On September 10, 1818, William F. Broadnax entered 160 acres in Section 27 of Township 4 South and Range 7 West (Cowart, 1991).

According to the 1820 Lawrence County, Alabama Census, William F. Broadnax household had one white male over 21, three white males under 21, one white female over 21, for a total of five whites. William owned 24 black slaves with a total of 29 inhabitants.

According to the records of the Lawrence County Archives, William F. Broadnax was listed in Circuit Court records of 1820 and Orphans Court between 1836-1838. William F. Broadnax was listed in the 1818 Circuit Court of Madison County.

Bynum, Drewry Sugars-Hawkins Springs

Drewry S. Bynum was the son of Drewry Sugars Bynum (Sr.), a son of Turner Bynum and Mary Atherton. Drewry was born about 1786 in Greensville County, Virginia, and raised in Northampton County, North Carolina. The family then moved to Nash County, North Carolina, where Drewry was listed in the 1810 and 1820 censuses. Drewry moved to Lawrence County, Alabama, in the late 1820s after he and his wife Susan sold their land in Nash County, North Carolina. He became a resident of Lawrence County, Alabama, on December 29, 1828. Drewry married Susan Peabody, who survived him. His probate records can be found in Lawrence County court records.

By 1810, Drewry S. Bynum owned 35 black slaves, and in 1820, he owned 38 slaves. By1828, he was living in Lawrence County, Alabama. He owned a large plantation on the county line between Franklin and Lawrence counties (present-day Colbert).

On April 26, 1830, Drewry S. Bynum entered 80 acres, and on April 26, 1831, he entered 120 acres near the south bank of the Tennessee River some five miles west of mouth Town Creek in Section 7 of Township 3 South and Range 9 West in present-day Colbert County (Cowart, 1985). From September 14, 1829, through September 3, 1837, Drewry also entered 800 acres in Townships 4, 5 South and Ranges 7,8, 9 West in Lawrence County, Alabama (Cowart, 1991).

In the 1830 census, he is listed as the owner of 83 black slaves in Franklin County and Lawrence County. Drewry Sugars Bynum left a will in 1837 disposing of his considerable estate. Apart from a life estate to his wife Susan, the estate was distributed among three sons: Frederick W. Bynum, Junias A. Bynum, and Oakley H. Bynum.

Drew S. Bynum died in Lawrence County on October 22, 1837. He was buried in the Bynum Cemetery at Courtland in Lawrence County, Alabama (Find a Grave Memorial Number 313750320).

His wife Susan appears to be in the 1840 household of her son Oakley H. Bynum. Also, Susan was living in the household of Oakley H. Bynum in the 1850 and 1860 census.

Frederick W. Bynum

Frederick W. Bynum was born circa 1815 in Nash County, North Carolina. Before his death on October 22, 1837, Drewry Sugars Bynum left his son Frederick the Hawkins Springs Plantation located in Franklin County, Alabama. He also inherited a parcel of land that bordered his plantation in Lawrence County, Alabama. While in Alabama and Arkansas, Frederick and his wife Cornelia had the following children:
1) Robert (Robin) Bynum was born about 1846,
2) Frederick Bynum was born circa 1849,
3) Harry Bynum was born about 1853,
4) Florence Bynum was born circa 1856, and
5) Belle Bynum was probably born about 1862 in Desha County, Arkansas.

In the 1840 census of Franklin County, Alabama, Fred Bynum is listed as resident and owner of 68 slaves. In the 1850 census, Frederick W. Bynum is listed as a 36-year-old white male, with wife Cornelia and two children less than four years old. According to the 1850 slave census of District 5 in Franklin County, Alabama, F. W. Bynum was listed twice. The first listing shows him owning 77 black slaves, and the second listing, he was shown as owning 56 black slaves with Joseph Askew as manager; therefore, Fredrick owned 133 black slaves.

The 1850 agricultural census of Franklin shows him as the owner of 1,270 acres of improved land and 907 acres of unimproved land for a total of 2,177 acres. The cash value of his plantation home and land was valued at $35,000 with implements and machinery valued at $3,000.00 and livestock valued at $5,000.00 for a net worth of $43,000.00.

Between 1855 and 1860, as did many other plantation owners seeking better and more fertile lands, Frederick W. Bynum moved his family and slaves west in Desha County, Arkansas, which was established in 1838. The county is located on the Mississippi River in the southeastern part of Arkansas. According to the 1860 census of Desha County, Arkansas, Frederick W. Bynum owned 133 slaves, and he was listed as one of largest slave owners in county.

According to the 1870 United States Census of Desha County, Arkansas, Frederick W. Bynum was a 54-year-old white male. His wife Cornelia Bynum is listed as a 43-year-old white female who was born in North Carolina. Living in the household was Robert Bynum a 22 white male, Harry Bynum a 17-year-old male, Florence Bynum a 14-year-old white female, Belle Bynum an eight-year-old white female, and Robert Rice a 21-year-old male born in Arkansas. Between 1870 and 1880, Frederick W. Bynum died. According to the 1880 census of Desha County, Arkansas, Cornelia, his widow, was living in the household with her son Robert Bynum. Robert (1846-1936) and his sister Florence Bynum Grinder (Died 1955) were buried in Memphis, Tennessee.

Junias Antherton Bynum

Junias Atherton Bynum was born about 1814, and he died on May 20, 1853. Junias married in Lawrence County on March 13, 1837, to Margaret J.

Taylor who was born about 1818; she used her middle name "Josephine" in other records. The family Bible of their daughter Margaret Bynum Pointer gives the marriage date as four days later, on March 17, 1837. The Bible record also gives her parents as Robert Taylor and Margaret Saunders. Junias appears in the 1840 and 1850 census of Lawrence County, Alabama, but according to one record, he was killed in a street fight a few years later. According to the family Bible, the children of Junias and Margaret were:

1) Laura Matilda Bynum was born on December 17, 1833; she first married Thomas Bolling Tabb. She later married William McDonald; she died on July 29, 1879. On June 25, 1879, her mother Josephine died at the home of Colonel William McDonald.
2) Junius A. Bynum was born on September 29, 1843.
3) Margaret Josephine Bynum was born on November 9, 1848; she married Philip Pointer.
4) Burt Bynum was born on January 9, 1846.

Oakley H. Bynum

Oakley H. Bynum was the youngest son of Drewry and Susan Bynum; he was born on August 3, 1817. Oakley became a prominent Lawrence County citizen, and he was elected as a state representative in 1839 and 1840, and state senator in 1857 and 1859. Oakley married Effie L. McDonald, and based on census records, they had the following children:

1) Mary Bynum was born about 1844,
2) Oakley H. Bynum was born in 1847,
3) Effie L. Bynum was born about 1848,
4) Ann Bynum was born about 1852,
5) Drury Bynum was born about 1855,
6) Willie Bynum was born about 1857,
7) Susan Bynum was born about 1860, and
8) Henry Bynum was born about 1864.

The 1850 and 1860 census records gave his age as 30 and 40 which suggest his birth year was 1819 rather than 1817. Oakley gave his age as 52 in 1870, and a newspaper death notice gave his age as 61. Oakley inherited the home place from his father.

The 1850 Agricultural Census of Lawrence County, Alabama, indicates that O. H. Bynum owned 2,200 acres of improved land and 3,000 acres of unimproved land valued at $54,000.00. In addition, his farm implements and machinery was worth $1,500.00 with his livestock valued at $8,650.00. According to the 1850 census, Oakley had an overseerer Z. Tomlenson who was a 25-year-old male born in Alabama.

Prior to 1850, Oakley is not listed as owning slaves. He was listed in the 1850 Lawrence County, Alabama, Slave Schedule with 151 black slaves, and in 1860, he is listed as owning 124 black slaves. The 1860 census indicates his real estate was valued at $170,000.00, and his personal property valued at $350,000.00.

According to the 1860 Lawrence County, Alabama Census, household 451, Oakley H. Bynum is listed as a 40-year-old male planter who was born in North Carolina. Also listed is his wife Effie L. who was a 35-year-old female born in Alabama, Mary a 15-year-old female born in Alabama, Oakley a 13-year-old male born in Alabama, Effie a 11-year-old female born in Alabama, Annie a seven-year-old female born in Alabama, Drury a four-year-old male born in Alabama, Willie a two-year-old male born in Alabama, and his mother Susan Bynum a 70-year-old female born in North Carolina.

Oakley and his wife Effie L. McDonald are buried in the Bynum Cemetery at Courtland in Lawrence County, Alabama, along with his father. According to the Moulton Advertiser, Thursday, August, 7, 1879, "Oakley H. Bynum, Born August 3, 1817, Died July 22, 1879-Oakley H Bynum, who died at his residence near Courtland, Alabama, 22nd inst., was born on the 3rd of August 1817, in Nash County, North Carolina, and at four years of age was removed with his father to Lawrence County, Alabama, where he has since resided until his death. He was the son of Drew S Bynum."

From the Moulton Advertiser, Thursday, May 31, 1894, "Effie L. Bynum, Birth: Dec. 9, 1822, Death: May 23, 1894. Effie L. Bynum, Born December 9, 1822, Died May 23,1894, Courtland, Ala, May 26. This community is tinged with deep regret over the loss of one of its excellent matrons, Mrs Effie Bynum, who died at her country seat and was sorrowfully committed to the grave. Her death was peculiarly and extremely sad because the result of an accident. Her carriage overturned a few days previous and she was thrown from it, suffering fatal injuries" (Find a Grave Memorial Number 31375057).

The following is a letter from Courtland written by O. H. Bynum during the Civil War to Honorable Robert Jemison Jr. on April 23, 1864. "Dear Sir: The 29th and 35th Ala regiments have been very much reduced by disease and casualties in battle, indeed so much that they have been sent to this valley to recruit in health and numbers. Col. Jackson of the 29th and Col. Ives of the 27th are exceedingly anxious that their commands should be mounted and assigned to duty in North Alabama. They are of the opinion that they can very soon raise a full size brigade, should the authorities grant them the privilege they so much desire. The 35th and 27th regiments were raised in North Ala and are composed of the very best young men in this part of the state. They have been on duty in Mississippi for the last two years, and have proved themselves on many hard fought battlefields as have the bravest.

We in North Alabama are acting as a break water for Central and South Alabama and defending this part of the state you defend Central Ala also. If you agree with me that these regiments should be mounted, I desire very much that you should use your influence with the Secretary of War to have them mounted and assigned to duty in this part of the country-also to have Col Jackson is a son of your old friend James Jackson of Lauderdale. Col Jackson was a private in the 4th Ala regt and received a serious wound at the first battle of Manassas. He was one of the first to join the army and has been on duty ever since the war commenced. Colonel Jackson is a man of great energy and gallantry. Yours Very Respectfully, O. H. Bynum"

Carter, Ammon

Ammon Carter was the oldest of the Carter Family to move to Lawrence County, Alabama. He was born in Buckingham County, Virginia, in 1765. His parents are probably Joseph Carter and Catherine Ammon.

Ammon was married to Mary "Polly" Burnett who was also born in Virginia, on August 8, 1773. Mary Burnett was the daughter of James Burnett and Frances Hooper; Williamson Burnett and Thomas R. Burnett was listed as her brothers. Ammon Carter and his wife Mary received the amount of inheritance left in the will of James Burnett, May 22, 1821. Ammon and Mary had the following children:

1. Samuel Scott Carter
2. Joel Walker Jones Carter
3. David Burnett Carter
4. Mary Polly Carter Runnels
5. Mahala Carter Minton
6. Levi Carter
7. Elijah Carter
8. Ammon Carter Jr.

Ammon and his family left Virginia, went to Sumner County and Smith County, Tennessee, where Mary's father, brother and possibly mother had gone. After a short stay in Tennessee, Ammon, Mary, and their family moved to Lawrence County, Alabama, except his daughter Mahala Carter Minton who stayed in Smith County, Tennessee.

The 1830 Lawrence County, Alabama Census lists Ammon Carter with one white male 5-10, three white males 15-20, one white male 60-70, one white female 20-30 and one white female 40-50. In 1830, Ammon owned eight black slaves.

In 1840, Ammon lived near Levi and Joel W. J. Carter; his house had five white males with the oldest being 70-80 (Ammon), one white female being 40-50, and no slaves.

According to the 1850 Lawrence County, Alabama, United States Census, House Number 225, Ammon Carter was an 85-year-old white male born in Virginia. Also living in his household was David Morris a 31-year-old male from Tennessee.

The Lawrence County Archives records state that Ammon Carter Sr. was the husband of Mary Carter; the father of Samuel Scott Carter, Levi Carter, and Mary Polly Carter Runnels; and the grandfather of John D. Carter and Mary Carter.

Ammon Carter died on October 20, 1851, in what was then Lawrence County, Alabama, now present-day Colbert. Ammon was buried just to the north of the Jarmon Plantation Home and just a few yards south of the River Road in the Hatton Baptist Cemetery in present-day Colbert County, Alabama.

Ammon Carter's wife Mary Polly Burnett Carter died on October 19, 1837, in Lawrence County, Alabama, present-day Colbert. She was buried in Hatton Baptist Cemetery at Little Hatton in Colbert County, Alabama (Find a Grave Memorial Number 68028931).

Joel Walker Jones Carter

Captain Joel Walker Jones Carter was born on October 23, 1794; he was the son of Ammon Carter and Mary "Polly" Burnett. Joel married Sarah Wallace Carter (1794-1868); she was the daughter of John D. Carter (1819- ____) and Eliza E. Carter McCarley (1837-1899).

The 1830 Lawrence County, Alabama Census gives Joel W. J. Carter as having six white males with the oldest 30-40 and three white females with the oldest 20-30. In 1830, Joel owned 17 black slaves.

According to the 1840 Lawrence County, Alabama Census, Joel J. W. Carter household had five white males with the oldest between 40-50, four white females, and 19 black slaves with eight being males and 11 females.

According to the 1850 Lawrence County, Alabama, United States Census, House Number 241, Joel W. J. Carter was a 56-year-old white male born in Virginia, Sarah Carter a 56-year-old female born in Tennessee, L. H. Carter a 24-year-old male born in Alabama, Carson D. Carter a 22-year-old male born in Alabama, and C. E. Carter a 24-year-old female born in Alabama. According to the 1850 Lawrence County, Alabama Slave Census, Joel J. W. Carter owned 27 slaves.

Joel Walker Jones Carter was listed in the 1860 Census of Lawrence County, Alabama, as being a 65-year-old farmer from Virginia and owning 31 black slaves. His family included Sarah, age 65, from Tennessee; John D., 42-year-old farmer from Tennessee; Nancy, age 42, Tennessee; J. N. McCarley, age

29, merchant from Tennessee; Eliza E., age 30, Tennessee; Lern Carter, 27-year-old male farmer from Alabama; Anna, age 20, Alabama; P. P., 18-year-old male student from Alabama; Alice, age 13, Alabama; J. W., ten-year-old female, Alabama; Mary, age eight, Alabama; Jere, six-year-old male, Alabama; and Marcellus, two-year-old male, Alabama.

According to the 1860 Lawrence County, Alabama, Slave Schedule, J.W. J. Carter owned 31 black slaves. In 1860, Joel W. J. Carter had a real estate value of $6,500.00 and a value of personal property worth of $30,000.

Captain Joel Walker Jones Carter died on March. 20, 1862; he shares a tombstone with his wife Sarah Wallace Carter. He and his wife were buried in the Carter Cemetery, Colbert County, Alabama (Find a Grave Memorial Number 59236484).

The Lawrence County Archives gives the following land records for Joel Walker Jones Carter: Joel W. J. Carter, 78 acres, 60 acres; Joel W. J. Carter to Ammon Carter 213 acres, January 11, 1819; the administrators of Henry Moore to Joel W. Carter 100 acres, January 8, 1817; Joel W. J. Carter to Nancy Wright 100 acres on Hickmans Creek, July 8,1820; and, David Wallis and John Harvey, Jr. to Joel W. J. Carter a tract of land, November 1, 1820.

Other White Carters

According to the 1840 Lawrence County, Alabama Census, Levi Carter household had three white males, no white females, and 11 slaves, with four being males and seven being females. In the 1850 Lawrence County, Alabama Slave Census, M. Carter owned 11 slaves, Levi Carter owned four slaves, and Icabod Carter owned nine slaves. In 1860, Ammon Carter Jr. owned one black slave, Levi Carter owned four black slaves, and M.A. Carter owned 15 black slaves.

Black Slave Carter Family

Members of the black Carter Family in Lawrence and Colbert Counties were the descendants of the slaves of the white Ammon Carter Family who were from Virginia. The Carter Plantation was between the River Road and Tennessee River and was north of the Jarman Plantation and east of present-day Ford City.

After the Civil War, many of the black families stayed on or near the plantation where they were slaves.

The Carter family descendants of the Huston Cobb Jr. family remained in the area Colbert County that was originally Lawrence County. Many of the slaves that were Huston's ancestors stayed near where they lived and worked for their owners prior to the Civil War. Many times some slaves continued to work for their plantation owners after the war.

Cyrus 'Sye' Carter was a slave on the Carter Plantation. Sye was the great grandfather of Huston Cobb Jr. Mr. Huston showed me the tombstone of his great grandfather Sye. Cyrus (Sye) Carter and Mary Alice lived and worked on the Carter Place. They were buried a few miles south of Ford City at Mount Pleasant Cemetery on the County Line Road in present-day Colbert County, Alabama. Cyrus Carter was last listed on the 1880 Census. By the 1900 census, only Cyrus' wife Mary Alice was listed as the head of the household. Therefore, Cyrus must have died between 1880 and 1900; Cyrus and Mary Alice had 16 children.

Tracy Carter, the son of Cyrus Carter, married Fannie Johnson. Tracy and Fannie were the grandparents of Huston Cobb Jr. Tracy Carter was a farmer and fired the boiler for the cotton gin on the River Road about a quarter mile north of Second Street. Tracy C. Carter worked for Will Norman at the cotton gin, and he fired the gin boiler with wood to make steam to run the mill.

Cyrus Carter's daddy lived near the Tennessee River and was a slave of the Carter Family. One day, he just disappeared and no one ever knew what happened to him. Huston Cobb Jr. said, "My great, great grandfather could have been killed, throwed in the Tennessee River, or could have possibly escaped north, but my family always believed the worse. We feel he was killed by his slave holder overseer or owner."

Clay, Matthew-Dixie

Based on land records and written historical references, Matthew Clay, along with several relatives, migrated from Virginia to Madison County, Alabama, by February 1818, and then to Lawrence County, Alabama, by September 1818. It appears that the following family groups migrated to North

Alabama together: Matthew, Thomas, and Clement C. Clay; Arthur F. Hopkins and his first wife Pamelia Moseley Hopkins; John F. Moseley, William F. Moseley, and Thomas Moseley.

In Madison County, Alabama, members of the Clay, Hopkins, and Moseley families entered land on the following first dates: Clement C. Clay, February 2, 1818; Arthur F. Hopkins, February 2, 1818; John Moseley, February 4, 1818; Thomas and William Moseley, February 2, 1818; and Thomas B. Moseley of Tennessee, September 14, 1818 (Cowart, 1979). In Lawrence County, Alabama, land was entered on the following dates: Matthew Clay of Madison County, September 10, 1818; Arthur F. Hopkins of Madison County, September 14, 1818; Pamelia Moseley of Madison County, September 8, 1818; John Moseley of Madison County, September 8, 1818; John F. Moseley of Madison County, September 10, 1818; William F. Moseley, September 10, 1818; and Thomas B. Moseley of Tennessee, September 14, 1818 (Cowart, 1991).

Matthew Clay Jr. was born in 1794 in Amelia County, Virginia; his parents were Matthew Clay (March 25, 1754-May 27, 1815) and Mary Williams Clay (1770-1798). Based on land records, Matthew Clay Jr. and his brother Thomas Clay entered land together. On December 31, 1830, Thomas and Matthew Clay entered 160 acres in Section 1 of Township 5 South and Range 7 West in Lawrence County, Alabama (Cowart, 1991).

According to the 1820 Lawrence County, Alabama Census, the Matthew Clay household had one white male over 21. In 1820, Matthew Clay owned 50 black slaves.

In May 1824, Matthew Jr. married Frances A. Saunders who was born on April 12, 1808. Frances was the daughter of Reverend Turner Saunders (1782-1853) and Frances Dunn. Frances A. Saunders siblings included: Frank Saunders (____-1909), James Edmonds Saunders (1806-1896), Martha Maria Saunders Bradford (1812-1856), William H Saunders (1819-1895), Thomas P. Saunders (1827-1882), and Franklin W Saunders (1833-1886).

Matthew Clay Jr. and Frances Saunders Clay had two sons:
1. Thomas F. was born on February 5, 1825. In 1845, Thomas married Caledonia Anne Oliver, daughter of John Oliver and Ruth

Ann Weedon. John Oliver was the brother of Mrs. Robert H. Watkins of the Oak Grove Plantation in Lawrence County. Thomas and Caledonia lived on the Malcolm Gilchrist Jr. place before moving to Columbus, Mississippi. Thomas F. and Caledonia Clay had the following children: 1) Alice Clay married Wheeler Watson in 1871, and they had five children: Asa W., Caledonia C., Alice, Fanny B. and Thomas C. 2) John Oliver Clay married Fannie Wilson Lawler in 1884, and they had one son Thomas F. 3) Fannie Lou Clay married Henry D. Watson in 1881. Thomas F. Clay died on September 12, 1856, and he was buried in Friendship Cemetery at Columbus in Lowndes County, Mississippi (Find a Grave Memorial Number 12916139).

2. Matthew Clay III was born on February 18, 1827, and he married Mary Harrison, daughter of Isham Harrison. Matthew III died on August 13, 1901, and he was buried in Friendship Cemetery at Columbus in Lowndes County, Mississippi (Find a Grave Memorial Number 12916145).

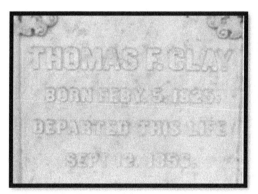 

The following is excerpts from Early Settlers of Alabama by James Edmonds Saunders (1899): "Matthew Clay, of Alabama, second son of Matthew Clay, of Virginia, migrated from Virginia (1816) to Madison County, Alabama, in company with his intimate friends, Arthur F. Hopkins, and John Moseley…In January, 1819, he removed to Lawrence County, Alabama, with the same friends, Hopkins and Moseley, who settled on adjoining places. Clay possessed himself of the magnificent plantation, now owned by Capt. C. C. Swoope (Dixie Plantation)…He built, at once, a double log house, with two stories, hewn neatly, with a broad hall below…His first services were in the House of Representatives of our State Legislature, of which he was a member in 1820, 1821, and 1822…He was a strong public speaker, and very efficient as a member of the Legislature…At Cahaba during the session mentioned, he and Dr. Jack Shackelford, of Texas fame, met for the first time, and they soon found they were congenial spirits…Mr. Clay was elected State Senator in 1825…Early in February, 1827, he left the capital, and traveled home by stage, across the mountain, during a very cold spell. He was seized with pneumonia, and fell its victim at the early age of thirty two years" (Saunders, 1899).

Matthew Clay Jr. died on February 4, 1827, at Courtland in Lawrence County, Alabama. He was buried in Swoope Cemetery Number 4 at Wheeler in Lawrence County, Alabama (Find a Grave Memorial Number 62978273).

After Matthew Clay Jr. died, Frances A. Saunders Clay married Jacob Swoope. After Jacob died, she married Colonel Thomas Carlton Billups (1804-1866). Frances A. Saunders Clay Swoope Billups died on June 1, 1890. She was buried in the Friendship Cemetery at Columbus in Lowndes County, Mississippi (Find a Grave Memorial Number 12916111).

Cobb, John B.

John B. Cobb of Lawrence County, Alabama, was probably the son of Asa Cobb of Franklin County, Alabama. According to Lawrence County, Alabama, marriages records, John B. Cobb married Martha W. Thomas on March 9, 1819.

In the 1820 Lawrence County, Alabama Census, John B. Cobb household had one white male over 21, one white female over 21, and one white female under 21. According to the 1820 census, John B. Cobb owned 18 black slaves.

According to the 1830 Lawrence County, Alabama, United States Census, John B. Cobb household had one white male 20-30, one white male 40-50, two white females under 5, two white females 5-10, and one white female 20-30. Asa Cobb was living in Lawrence County, Alabama, in 1830; he was listed as head of the household with one white male 5 to 10, two white males between 10 to 15, two white males between 20 and 30, one white male between 60 and 70, one white female under five, one white female 10 to 15, and one white female 60 to

70. In 1830, John B. Cobb is between 40-50 years old, and Asa Cobb is between 60-70 years old.

Asa Cobb was found in the 1840 and 1850 census records of Franklin County, Alabama. According to the 1850 agricultural census of Franklin County, Alabama, Asa Cobb had 200 acres of improved land and 300 acres of unimproved land. His property was valued at $5,000 for his land, $500 for his farm equipment, and $2,200 for his livestock.

According to the 1850 Slave Schedule for Franklin County, Alabama, Asa Cobb owned 37 black slaves and had one free person of color living in the household. According to Familysearch.org, Asa Cobb owned 107 black slaves in 1850. Asa's neighbors in the slave schedule were cotton planters James Alexander and William Winston.

The Lawrence County Archives records identify the following members of the Cobb family:
1. James H. Cobb of Georgia owned Courtland Lot number 901.
2. John B. Cobb owned lots 106 and 8 in Courtland.
3. Martha W. Cobb was listed as the wife of John B. Cobb, and she was also listed as the owner of Lot 8 in Courtland.
4. Josiah Cobb was listed as a Lawrence County resident.
5. W. B. W. Cobb was listed as being from Madison County, Alabama.
6. Asa Cobb was in the record from 1825-1830, and in Franklin County.
7. Asa Cobb Jr. was listed in 1830-1834 Lawrence County records.
8. Azariah Cobb was listed in records from 1844-1846.
9. Obidiah Cobb was listed in records from 1844-1846.
10. Polly Cobb was found in records from 1830-1834.
11. Attorney Thomas R. Cobb was listed from 1841-1844.
12. Benjamin Cobb was listed from 1829-1835.
13. John Cobb, Dean of Medical Department of University of Louisville was listed in 1853.

Croom, Wiley Jones

Wiley Jones Croom was born on December 10, 1795, in Wayne County, North Carolina, and he died on August 2, 1849, at Greensboro in Greene County,

111

Alabama. Wiley was the son of Richard G. Croom (1765-6/28/1805). Richard Croom, Big Isaac Croom and Joshua Croom were the sons of Major Croom. Richard G. Croom married Nancy Ann Hare Croom; they had the following children:

1. Jesse Hare Croom died in Alabama age 56.
2. Susan Croom married Dr. Harris Tinker.
3. John Enloe Croom died at age 20, and he was represented by his mother Nancy Croom during the estate division.
4. Ann Hare Croom (1785-1841) married Dr. Richard C. Croom in 1806.
5. Wiley Jones Croom moved to Lawrence County, Alabama, with family members in 1818. Wiley Jones Croom and his brother Jesse Hare Croom of Madison County first entered land in Franklin and Lawrence Counties on September 16, 1818 (Cowart, 1985, 1991).

Wiley Jones Croom married Elizabeth Holliday on December 16, 1817, in Green County, North Carolina. Elizabeth was born in North Carolina on March 13, 1798. She was the daughter of General Thomas Holliday and Elizabeth Hart Holliday. Elizabeth Holliday Croom died on March 12, 1844, in Greene County, Alabama. Wiley Jones Croom and Elizabeth Holliday Croom had the following children:

1) Wiley Jones Croom, Jr. was born in 1817 and died as a child.
2) Richard Croom II was born on October 19, 1818, in Madison County, Alabama, and he married Lucy Huddleston on January 21, 1847, in Greene County, Alabama. Richard died on October 19, 1849, in Greene County, Alabama.
3) Elizabeth Ann Croom was born on March 4, 1820, in Lawrence County, Alabama. On December 9, 1837, Elizabeth married James Levi Tunstall in Greene County, Alabama; she died on October 26, 1911.
4) Thomas Holliday Croom was born on October 31, 1821, in Lawrence County, Alabama. Thomas married Martha W. Hucklebee, and he died on December 3, 1858, in Greene County, Alabama.
5) Jesse Hare Croom was born on August 14, 1823, in Lawrence County, Alabama. On December 2, 1844, Jesse married Emeline 'Emma' Huddleston in Greene County, Alabama, and he was murdered in October 1860 in Fort Bend County, Texas.

6) John LaFayette Croom was born on November 25, 1826, at LaGrange in Franklin County, Alabama. John married Ellen Harriett Davis, and he died on April 26, 1912, at Wharton, Texas.

7) Platt Sylvester Croom, M.D. was born on March 31, 1829. Platt married Sarah May on March 25, 1850, in Greene County, Alabama, and he died in 1889 in Holmes County, Mississippi.

8) Harriett H. Croom was born in 1832. Harriett married George F. Hucklebee on January 15, 1850, in Greene County, Alabama, and she died in 1868.

9) Mary Lousiana Croom was born on December 8, 1833, in Lawrence County, Alabama. Mary married James W. Chadwick, and she died in Texas.

10) Wilie Talamn Croom was born on March 11, 1835, in Lawrence County, Alabama, and she died on May 24, 1841, in Huntsville, Alabama.

11) Susan Jane Croom was born on August 2, 1837, and she died on October 25, 1838.

12) Camilla Dudley Holliday Croom was born on November 8, 1838, in Greene County, Alabama. On August 28, 1858, Camilla married William Blount Rodman in Greene County, Alabama, and she died in 1887 in North Carolina.

13) Laura Sarah Croom was born on November 9, 1840, in Greene County, Alabama. Laura married Reverend Luther Leonidas Hill.

According to the 1820 Lawrence County, Alabama Census, Wiley Jones Croom household had one white male over 21, one white male under 21, one white female over 21, and two white females under 21. In 1820, Wiley Jones Croom owned 29 black slaves. Also in the 1820 Lawrence County, Alabama Census, Wiley's brother Jesse Hare Croom (12/4/1791-4/1/1846) had 23 black slaves, and his uncle Joshua owned 20 slaves.

In the 1830 Lawrence County, Alabama Census, Wiley Jones Croom had 38 slaves and his brother Jesse Hare Croom had 41 slaves. Shortly before the 1830 census, the families of Wiley Jones Croom and Jesse Hare Croom had moved from Lawrence County, Alabama, to Greene County, Alabama, since the census only shows them as head of household with no one else listed. According to other records, Wiley J. Croom moved in 1834 to Greensboro, Alabama.

According to the Lawrence County Archives records, the Croom family owned the following tracts of land in Lawrence County, Alabama.

1. Elizabeth Croom, wife of Wiley owned the south ½ of Section 9, T4S, R9W and the northeast ¼ of Section 26, T3S, R9W.
2. Jesse H. Croom owned the W½ of the NW¼ of Section 15, T4S, R9W; Section 1, T4S, R9W, NW; and, Section 1, T4S, R9W, SE.
3. Joshua Croom of Franklin County, Alabama, owned Section 32, T4S, R9W, SE ¼; Section 5, T5S, R9W, E ½ of NW ¼; and, Section 5, T5S, R9W, W ½ of NW ¼.
4. Richard G. Croom owned Section 7, T3S, R9W, ½ of SE ¼.
5. Wiley J. Croom owned Section 9, T4S, R9W, S ½; and, Section 26, T3S, R9W, NE ¼.

The following are other Croom records in the Lawrence County Archives: Negroes, Joshua & Lewis, paper #9, Thomas Smith Tavern at Courtland, Joshua Croom, Samuel B. Harris, Circuit 1824; Negro Bryant, 7 yrs, Paper #10, Joshua Croom, J.J. Swoope, et. al. 1824; Negroes, Joshua & Lewis, paper #9, Thomas Smith Tavern at Courtland, Wilie J. and Elizabeth Croom, William H. Martin, Orphans 1835; deed Joshua Croom, B. McKiernan, 1824.

Dandridge, Robert Honeyman-Bride's Hill

William Alexander Dandridge and Anne Blair Bolling Dandridge were the parents of Robert Honeyman Dandridge. William and Anne were married on April 21, 1770, at Cobbs in Chesterfield County, Virginia. William was born on April 6, 1750, and died in 1801 in Hanover County, Virginia. Anne was born on February 7, 1752, at West Point in York County, Virginia. The Dandridge family were cousins to Martha Washington, America's First Lady. William and Anne had the following children:

1. Nathaniel West Dandridge (January 14, 1771-July 26, 1847);
2. William Alexander Dandridge (August 30, 1772-September 10, 1842);
3. Elizabeth Blair Dandridge (April 21, 1774-April 1, 1796);
4. Archibald Bolling Dandridge (December 22, 1776- ?);
5. Dorothea Ann Nancy Dandridge (about 1778- ?);
6. John Bolling Dandridge (November 14, 1780-about 1843);
7. Jane Butler Dandridge (about 1783- ?);

8.   Robert Honeyman Dandridge (October 12, 1784-December 3,1838);
9.   George W. Dandridge (February 3, 1787-September 27, 1794);
10. Thomas Bolling Dandridge (February 3, 1789-May 10, 1742);
11. Martha A. Dandridge (January 21, 1790-January 22, 1790);
12. John Marshall Dandridge (May 8, 1793- ?).

Robert Honeyman 'Black Bob' Dandridge was born on October 12, 1784, in York County, Virginia. Robert married his first cousin Elizabeth Terrell Dandridge on December 6, 1808, in Goochland County, Virginia. Elizabeth was born on May 7, 1792, in Virginia; her parents were Robert Ambler Dandridge and Mildred Aylett Allen. Robert and Elizabeth moved to Lawrence County, Alabama, about 1819; they had the following children:

1.   George 'Isham' Washington Dandridge was born about 1812 in Virginia, and he died in 1860. George married Elizabeth Norwood of Tupelo, Mississippi.
2.   Mildred Ann Dandridge was born in Virginia in 1814, and she died about 1870; Mildred married Robert Creilly.
3.   Jane Louise Dandridge was born in September 1816 in Virginia, and she married Reuben Allen, and later married Joseph B. Tardy.
4.   John Terrell Dandridge was born in 1831 at Bride's Hill in Lawrence County, Alabama, and he died in 1870; John married Octavia Banhook.
5.   Robert Honeyman Dandridge Jr. was born in 1832 at Bride's Hill, and he died about 1841 at nine years old.

In the 1820 Lawrence County, Alabama Census at Courtland, Robert Honeyman Dandridge had one white male over 21, two white males under 21, one white female over 21, three white females under 21. In 1820, Robert H. Dandridge owned 24 black slaves.

Robert Honeyman Dandridge, known as Black Bob, was the builder of Bride's Hill which was located in the Courtland vicinity of Lawrence County, Alabama. In the 1820 census, Robert Honeyman Dandridge from Virginia was the only Dandridge living in Lawrence County at that time. Since Bride's Hill was estimated to have been built in the 1820s, Robert Honeyman Dandridge is probably the builder of Bride's Hill house.

According to the 1830 Lawrence County, Alabama Census, the Robert H. Dandridge had two males under 5, one male 15-20, one male 40-50, one female 5-10, one female 10-15, one female 15-20, and one female 30-40. In 1830, Robert Dandridge had only 15 slaves.

In the 1850 Lawrence County Alabama, Slave Schedule, John Terrell Dandridge, the son of Robert H. Dandridge, was listed with nine black slaves. According to the 1850 Lawrence County, Alabama, Agricultural Census, John T. Dandridge had 300 acres of improved land and 200 of unimproved land worth $3,200.00. He had $85.00 worth of farming equipment and his livestock was valued at $325.00.

According to the Lawrence County Archives June 1818-December 1824, Robert Dandridge is mentioned in the court document concerning building a road from the Town of Courtland to the Big Spring in Franklin County, Alabama. Also the Lawrence County Archives mentions William Elliott as a friend of Robert H. Dandridge. The Robert Holmes Dandridge, who was testator of his will, was his wife's nephew who married Margaret Ann Johnson in Itawamba County, Mississippi. The archive records of March 25, 1823 shows Robert H. Dandridge owes C. McClung and Jones $237.88 and owes J. J. Swoope $176.00.

Robert Honeyman Dandridge died on December 3, 1838, in Lawrence County, Alabama. Robert's wife Elizabeth Terrell Dandridge died about 1845 in Lawrence County, Alabama (Find a Grave Memorial Number 127004438).

Bride's Hill

"Bride's Hill, known also as Sunnybrook, is a historic plantation house near Wheeler in Lawrence County, Alabama. It is one of the state's earliest surviving and most significant examples of the Tidewater-type cottage. It was added to the Alabama Register of Landmarks and Heritage on April 16, 1985, and to the National Register of Historic Places on July 9, 1986.

Bride's Hill has a deep cellar, lighted by oblong ground-level windows; the home has a basement kitchen-dining room. On the main floor, a broad central hall, with a graceful reverse-flight of stairway rising to the low half-story above, separates two large rooms. Supposedly, there was a separate brick kitchen structure that stood at the rear of the house. When absorbed into the vast Joseph Wheeler Estate in 1907, the house and surrounding farm became known as Sunnybrook. Located in rural Lawrence County, the house has been unoccupied since the 1980's and is in a state of disrepair.

Bride's Hill

This type of tidewater house is usually a story and a half in height with the design bought to the early northwest Alabama Plantation frontier by settlers from the Tidewater and Piedmont regions of Virginia. The house is characterized by prominent end chimneys flanking a steeply pitched roof often pierced by dormer windows."

"This house (Bride's Hill) was developed according to the double-square formula employed by colonial Virginia house builders. The front elevation of Bride's Hill is almost exactly twice as long as it is high, counting the slope of the roof. Another rare-prehaps unique-feature of this important early Alabama houses is the cantilevered chimney pent, the narrow, shed-roofed projection that abuts the left chimney…another pent [is] to the rear of the right chimney" (Gamble, Robert, 1986).

Donnell, James Webb Smith-Seclusion

James 'Jim' Webb Smith Donnell was born July 13, 1820; he was the son of Reverend Robert Donnell and Ann Eliza Smith, who were married on March 17, 1817. Ann Eliza was the daughter of Revolutionary War Colonel James Webb Smith; Smith County, Tennessee, is named in his honor. Ann Eliza died on November 3, 1828, at age 33 (Find a Grave Memorial Number 39524322). Out of five children, Robert and Ann Eliza of the Pleasant Hill Plantation at Athens had only one son James 'Jim' Webb Smith Donnell to live to adulthood.

On July 10, 1839, James 'Jim' Webb Smith Donnell married Sarah Maria Louisa Jones at her home at Druid Grove Plantation in Madison County, Alabama. Sarah Maria was born on April 6, 1824, to John Nelson Spotswood 'Spot' Jones and Elizabeth 'Eliza' Ann Haywood. Eliza Haywood was the daughter of the early Tennessee Judge John Haywood who stated that Doublehead had more blood on his hands than anyone at that time in history.

According to the Jones-Donnell Papers, 1817-1994, the Seclusion Plantation was 2,400 acres in an isolated area of flat fertile land west of the Town of Town Creek in Lawrence County, Alabama. The plantation was originally owned by Captain Llewellen Jones and inherited by his son John Nelson Spottswood 'Spot' Jones; then given to Spot's daughter Frances Anna Mariah Jones Perkins who probably lived there with her husband Benjamin and their children. Later the plantation was owned by Sarah Maria Jones Donnell and her husband James W. S. Donnell.

After James W. S. Donnell and his wife Sarah Maria Jones Donnell moved there, James built the fine plantation house at Seclusion around 1850 with slaves and skilled workmen. Seclusion was once a beautiful two story 13 room plantation home, but it was demolished in the 1950s. The Seclusion Plantation was adjacent to the plantation of Benjamin B. Jones who was from Nashville, Tennessee.

The following description of the plantation mansion was given by Wendell Givens in the Birmingham News-Age Herald in December 1949 as follows, "One approached it by cedar lined avenue; its servant's quarters, cabins, were located several hundred feet to the west…the land was level and when cleared and planted in vast rows of cotton, one could see long distances, to the front of the building, over a mile in distant, was a range of high hills, then called the mountain…The mansion structure was…a large

Maria Louisa Jones Donnell (1824-1894)
James Webb Smith Donnell (1820-1876)
Seclusion

frame two-story…a long porch extended across the front, supported by small pine columns. The two front rooms measured 22 by 24 feet, the back rooms at 16 by 22 feet, as recorded by one Birmingham reporter, before it was demolished. The double parlors, to the left of the entrance hall, were lavishly furnished with massive furniture, pier mirrows, fine drapery, huge mantles…It must be noted that the stairway…was ornately carved; there were four large bedrooms in the upper floor and a small apartment as well. Judge Richard Lowe has two mantels and two doors from Seclusion in his house near Hartselle, Alabama" (Jones-Donnell Papers, 1817-1994).

James and Sarah Maria Donnell initially settled in Athens in Limestone County before coming to Town Creek in Lawrence County to the 2,400-acre Seclusion Plantation. James W. S. Donnell's family is listed in the 1850 Lawrence County, Alabama, United States Census, Household 160 as follows: J.

W. S. Donnell, 30, AL; Sarah L., 26; Clara A., 10; Robt., 8; Nannie, 14; Spotswood, 2; John H. 6/12; and, M. A. A. D. Kinsen, 28, f, NY.

According to the 1850 Lawrence County, Alabama Slave Schedules, James Webb Smith Donnell owned 56 black slaves. In the 1860 Lawrence County, Alabama Slave Schedule, James Webb Smith Donnell owned 85 slaves.

In April of 1862, Maria, the pregnant wife of J. W. S. Donnell, took some of the couple's children to stay at the Pleasant Hill Plantation home in Athens, Alabama. Maria would be closer to medical help should she need assistance in delivering her baby. The Pleasant Hill home belonged to Reverend Robert Donnell which was inherited by his son James Webb Smith Donnell. The reverend was a prominent member of the Cumberland Presbyterian clergy and a respected citizen. This was just prior to the first Union Army troops occupying the area of North Alabama during the Civil War.

The Civil War would divide the family between Seclusion Plantation near Town Creek in Lawrence County and the Pleasant Hill Plantation at Athens in Limestone County, Alabama. After the Union troops arrived, Jim Donnell and his oldest daughter were stranded at Seclusion. They were unable to join the rest of the family in Athens because, Jim would have been arrested as a Confederate sympathizer.

In May 1862, Union forces under the command of General John Basil Turchin entered Limestone County. The General and his troops took up residence at Pleasant Hill and surrounding grounds. Maria and her children were terrified of the Union encampment. The Union soldiers stole everything of any value including the family silver. The Union forces would occupy and loot the entire town which became known as the 'Sack of Athens.'

At the Seclusion Plantation, Jim Donnell donated the Confederate troops 70 bales of cotton to create fortifications, and they confiscated another 15 bales of cotton. The Confederates abandoned the cotton because they were unable to transport the bales to their next encampment. Then, Donnell ran into a more serious problem when Union soldiers burned some 700 bales of his cotton.

On November 20, 1865, James W. S. Donnell wrote to Colonel Abel D. Straight as follows, "I have seen General Wagner on his return South. He says that you are under the impression that the stock taken from me 28th April 1863 by your command for use of the U. S. Government was restored…I did not have the stock which your command took (43 mules and 7 horses) returned…The heavy cannonading and approach of General Dodge towards Town Creek induced Mr. Weems to move back across the mountains when he unwittingly fell in with your command who took all his mules and horses. The heavy forces engaged at Town Creek, General Dodge from the west and General Forrest and Roddy on the east of my plantation. The latter being all cavalry subsisted upon me several days…Being on the front these occurrences often took place on or near some of my plantation…Now I need not be at the trouble to place the claims referred to in hands of claim agents…General Thomas…advised me individually and has also made a general order advising everyone who had property taken for use of the U.S. Government to present them to the proper authorities…I am your obt. svt. J. W. S. Donnell" (Jones-Donnell Papers, 1817-1994).

After the war, many of the planters including James 'Jim' Webb Smith Donnell and his family succumbed to loss of their property and slave labor which eventually brought about their financial ruin. By the end of the war, Jim Donnell's wealth was gone. In 1867, Seclusion and Pleasant Hill were auctioned to pay debts and taxes.

James 'Jim' Webb Smith Donnell died on January 8, 1876, at the age of 55 (Find a Grave Memorial Number 39524014). His wife Maria died on August 16, 1894 (Find a Grave Memorial Number 39524060). Also, a daughter and son are buried in the Athens City Cemetery in Limestone County, Alabama. Their tombstone is inscribed with a quote found in an 1867 letter from Donnell to his son Robert, "Let the family circle be unbroken and its bonds and integrity intact."

Today, the Seclusion Plantation home is gone with very few remnants of the once splendid antebellum mansion still visible. However, the Pleasant Hill Plantation home of the Donnell family still stands on the campus of Athens Middle School on Clinton Street. The old planter home was preserved as The Donnell House and is open for tours and events.

Fortune

Fortune was a black slave who lived on the Seclusion Plantation near Town Creek (Jonesboro) in Lawrence County, Alabama. A set of lonely tombstones that marks the grave site of Fortune was placed there by his owner James 'Jim' Webb Smith Donnell. The grave of Fortune is the only one with inscribed tombstones in the Seclusion Plantation slave cemetery.

When Wendell Givens wrote his article "An Ancient Landmark Dies" in the Birmingham-News-Age-Herald in December 1949, he stated, "I have gone to the site of Seclusion and into a graveyard, perhaps for the slaves, where some unmarked stones were still visible, and in the center an eight foot granite slab was inscribed: "Fortune…died February 1859…To the virtues and excellencies of a faithful servant this testimony is erected by his master J.W.S. Donnell" (Jones-Donnell Papers, 1817-1994).

It is obvious that Jim Donnell thought the world of his faithful servant and placed the tombstones for Fortune in his honor and out of respect for him. The large eight-foot marker as the head stone with a smaller stone marker at the foot identifies the grave of Fortune. Both tombstones are inscribed with the same words of his master J. W. S. Donnell.

Jim Donnell even referred to his slave Fortune in his correspondence to Maria on May 6, 1855, and called him 'Fort' as a nickname. Fortune held an esteemed position at Seclusion, and he was the most beloved slave of Donnell who gave him a prominent position on the plantation. It is said that Fortune lived in a brick home, and the other slaves lived in wooden cabins.

Posey Farms

Today in 2019, Steve Posey and his family own and farm much of the Seclusion Plantation in addition to other rental properties. The main Posey farming operation, which is within a short distance to the Seclusion Mansion site, is approximately one mile east of the stream of Town Creek and one mile south of Highway 20 in Lawrence County, Alabama.

Steve Posey said, "We typically plant and harvest almost 10,000 acres of grain each year." His farming operation has some 3,250 acres of winter wheat which they harvest in June then plant back in soybeans. The wheat averages about 70 bushels/acre and the soybeans average about 50 bushels/acre. He said, "You may see soybean planters in the same fields as the wheat combines." They also plant about 3,250 acres of corn which averages 140 bushels/acre on unirrigated dry land. The harvested soybeans, wheat, and corn are stored in several grain silos which are located on Highway 101 about one mile north of the Town of Town Creek.

According to Steve Posey, "My great grandfather George Young purchased the old plantation homeplace and surrounding area of Seclusion. George Young had several children and intended to sell part of his estate to each child. Cole Young Sr. was the only child wanting the land bad enough to pay his father's asking price of $13.00/acre for a 360-acre tract which was split between Cole's two daughters. The family formed a limited partnership company of all the land of Annie Laura Young Posey called the Donnell Quarter Limited Partnership in order to keep the James Webb Smith Donnell memory alive." Steve Posey is the son of Annie who was one of the daughters of Cole Young Sr.

Eggleston, Samuel O.

Samuel Overton Eggleston was born on April 24, 1797, in Hanover County, Virginia. He was the son of Matthew Jaquelin Eggleston and Anne Cary Eggleston. The Lawrence County Archives also lists the children of Matthew Jaquelin Eggleston family as follows:
1. Charles D. Eggleston,
2. Edward M. Eggleston,
3. Eliza Judith Cary Eggleston Baptist,

4. Everard M. Eggleston,
5. George Payton Eggleston,
6. Hugh Blair Eggleston,
7. John Lucius Eggleston,
8. Miles C. Eggleston,
9. Samuel O. Eggleston,
10. William C. Eggleston.

The first wife of Samuel Overton Eggleston was Caroline Woolridge Elam Eggleston. According to the 1825 Madison County, Alabama, Marriage Records, Samuel O. Eggleston married Caroline Elam on February 22, 1825. Based on Lawrence County Archives records, it appears that Caroline Elam Eggleston died before 1835 since she is listed as deceased. The second wife of Samuel Overton Eggleston was Eliza Flemington Stannard Eggleston; Eliza died in 1871.

The children of Samuel Overton Eggleston were: Matthew Overton Eggleston, Miles Lucerne Eggleston, Virginia Caroline Eggleston Thomson, Marcellus Archer Eggleston, Robert Stannard Eggleston, W. F. Eggleston. In the 1850 Lawrence County Archives Orphans court records, Samuel O. Eggleston, guardian Matt O. Eggleston, was to collect in gold ward.

In the 1830 Lawrence County, Alabama Census, Samuel O. Eggleston household had one white male 0-5, one white male 10-15, one white male 15-20, one white male 30-40, one white female 0-5, one white female 30-40. Also listed was 23 black slaves with seven being males and 16 being females.

According to the 1840 Lawrence County, Alabama Census, Samuel O. Eggleston home had two white males 0-5, one white male 5-10, one white male 10-15, one white male 15-20, one white male 20-30, one white male 40-50, one white female 5-10, one white female 30-40.

In 1840, Samuel owned 36 black slaves with 22 being males and 14 being females. In the 1840 Lawrence County Archives records, the names of some of the Eggleston slaves are Peter, William, Abner, Dick, Kate, Henry, Tessa, Clarissa, Anna, Amanda, Archer, and Jerry.

The 1850 Lawrence County, Alabama, United States Census, House Number 218 listed the following: Samuel O. Eggleston M 53 Virginia; Eliza J. F. Eggleston F 49 Virginia; M. O. Eggleston M 21 Alabama; M. L. Eggleston M 18 Alabama; Caroline V. Eggleston F 16 Alabama; Marcellus A. Eggleston M 13 Alabama; and, Wm. F. Eggleston M 9 Alabama. According to the 1850 Lawrence County, Alabama Slave Census, Samuel O. Eggleston owned 48 black slaves.

Eggleston Home

According to the 1850 Lawrence County, Alabama, Agricultural Census, Samuel O. Eggleston owned 700 acres of improved land and 490 acres of unimproved land worth $6,000.00. Samuel's farming equipment was valued at $355.00 with his livestock valued at $1,238.00.

The 1860 Northern Division, Lawrence County, Alabama, United States Census gives Samuel O. Eggleston M 63 Va; Eliza Eggleston F 59 Va; W. F. Eggleston M 19 Ala; Mary Foster F 77 Va; and, James H. Nelms M 30 Ala. In 1860, the real estate of Samuel O. Eggleston was valued at $5,850.00, and his personal property value was $31,520.00.

In the 1870 Lawrence County, Alabama, United States Census, Courtland, Samuel O. Eggleston was a 74-year-old male born in Virginia, and Eliza Eggleston was a 70-year-old female born in Virginia. In 1870, Samuel O. Eggleston was listed as farmer with a real estate value of $5,000.00 and a personal estate value of $500.00.

Samuel Overton Eggleston died on August 8, 1874, at the home of his son W. C. Eggleston in Limestone County, Alabama. He was buried at his old homeplace at Leighton in Colbert County, Alabama.

According to Lawrence County Archives records, Samuel Eggleston owned 160 acres in the south ½ of the southwest ¼ of Section 17, T3S, R9W. From September 16, 1818, through December 16, 1839, Samuel O. Eggleston entered 760 acres in Township 3 South and Ranges 9, 10 West; at that time, the area was either Franklin County or Lawrence County (Cowart, 1985). In 1857, Lawrence County Archives records indicate that M.L. Eggleston owned Sections 31 and 32 of Township 3 South and Range 9 West.

Elliott, Samuel-Boxwood

Samuel Elliott Sr. was born August 26, 1767, in Antrim County, Ireland. He emigrated to the United States in 1787, and originally settled in Middle Tennessee. In September 1818, Samuel Elliott Sr. came to the Tennessee Valley area of Fox's Creek from Wilson County, Tennessee.

Samuel first entered land in Lawrence County, Alabama, in the drainage of Fox's Creek. One of the main roads that passed through his plantation was Burleson's Trace. Joseph Burleson of Moulton was authorized by the Alabama Legislature in the early 1820s to upgrade an Indian trail from Mouse Town at the mouth of Fox's Creek, to Moulton, and then to the Byler Road which continued to Tuscaloosa. Burleson's Trace passed through Samuel Elliott's Boxwood Plantation from Mouse Town located at the east mouth of Fox's Creek. At Mouse Town, members of the Burleson family operated a ferry to Cow Ford Landing in Limestone County on the north side of the Tennessee River. By state law on the Byler Road portion, Joseph Burleson was not allowed to collect a toll.

Just northeast of Samuel Elliott plantation, George Peck established Peck's Landing near Mouse Town on an island on the south side of the river at the Morgan-Lawrence County line near the north beginning of Burleson's Trace. In order to avoid the dangerous Muscle Shoals, goods coming down the Tennessee River were often transferred to wagons at Peck's Landing to be transferred by way of Burleson's Trace, to Byler's Old Turnpike, and then to Tuscaloosa. George Peck, who operated the landing, was married Celia Fennel; therefore, George was a son-in-law to Wylie Fennel and a brother-in-law to James Fennel of the Walnut Grove Plantation. The Fennel plantation was to the southeast of the Boxwood Plantation of Samuel Elliott.

The wife of Samuel Elliott Sr. was Sarah Elliott who was born on March 25, 1770. Samuel and Sarah had the following children:

1. Samuel Elliott Jr. was born on November 15, 1809, in Tennessee; he first married Frances Rather in 1833. After Frances died, he married Elizabeth Pearsall in 1844. Samuel Elliott Jr. died on July 16, 1870; he was buried in the Elliott Jackson Cemetery at Hillsboro in Lawrence County, Alabama (Find a Grave Memorial Number 47449164).
2. Randolph Elliott Sr. was born on December 25, 1812; he married Elvira A. Brown on December 25, 1837, in Carroll County, Mississippi. Randolph died on April 27, 1844, at 31 years old; he was buried in the Elliott Cemetery in Grenada County, Mississippi (Find a Grave Memorial Number 68604253).

 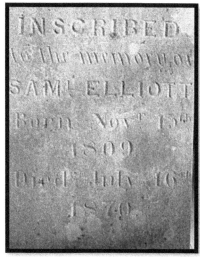

Most of the land of Boxwood Plantation was entered in September 1818 by Samuel Elliot Sr. From September 7, 1818, through November 20, 1834, Samuel Elliott Sr. entered some 3,000 acres of land in Lawrence County, Alabama; of which, about1600 acres were entered in September 1818 in Townships 4, 5 South and Range 6 West (Cowart, 1991). Samuel Elliott Jr. also entered several hundred acres in Lawrence County; together, father and son built Boxwood into one of the largest plantations in the county.

In the 1820 Lawrence County, Alabama Census, Samuel Elliott had one white male over 21, two white males under 21, one white female over 21, and three white females under 21. In 1820, Samuel Elliott owned six black slaves.

In 1830 Lawrence County, Alabama Census, Samuel Elliott Sr. had one white male 15-20, one white male 20-30, one white male 50-60. In the 1840 Lawrence County, Alabama Census, Samuel Elliott Sr. had one white male 70-80. Samuel Elliott Jr. had two white males under 5, one white male 5-10, one white male 20-30, one white male 40-50, one white female 5-10, and one white female 20-30. Probably in 1830 both Samuel Sr. and Jr. were living in the same household.

Samuel Elliott Sr. died May 10, 1844, at 76 years old. He was buried in a box tomb in the Elliott-Jackson Cemetery at Hillsboro in Lawrence County, Alabama (Find a Grave Memorial Number 109683361). The Elliott Cemetery is located on the land once owned by Samuel Elliott Sr. The earliest burial in the cemetery was his wife Sarah who died on October 19, 1824; her box tomb still exists. She was buried in the Elliott-Jackson Cemetery at Hillsboro in Lawrence County, Alabama (Find a Grave Memorial Number 109683475).

In the 1850 Lawrence County, Alabama, Slave Schedule, Samuel Elliott Jr. owned 55 black slaves. According to the 1850 Lawrence County, Alabama, Agricultural Census, Samuel Elliott owned 700 acres of improved land and 1,600 acres of unimproved land valued at $12,000.00. His farm equipment and implements were valued at $940.00 while his livestock was valued at $3,225.00.

Boxwood

By 1860, Samuel Elliott Jr. owned $36,000.00 in real estate, $96,500.00 in personal property, and 92 black slaves. Both the original two story brick Boxwood Plantation Mansion and the plantation slave quarters were built by Samuel Elliott Jr. around 1855, some eleven years after the death of his father.

The Boxwood Plantation Mansion was destroyed by the Alabama Highway Department during the widening of Alabama Highway 20 in the 1950's. Although the main house was demolished, the slave quarters were remodeled and continued to serve as a dwelling. The surrounding area continued to operate as a farm until 2010, when some of the plantation property was purchased to construct an industrial park.

Today in 2019, the only known surviving brick slave home in the Tennessee Valley is located on the old Boxwood Plantation site situated on the south side of Highway 20 at the entrance of the Jack Daniels plant in Lawrence County, Alabama. The neat slave cabin is on the west side of the entrance road to Mallard Fox West Industrial Complex near the Lawrence-Morgan County line.

Boxwood Plantation-brick slave cabin

The slave quarters are being preserved, and the later alterations have been removed to reveal the buildings original form. The Lawrence County Historical Commission provides money for maintenance and upkeep of the historic building.

The house was originally built as living quarters for Boxwood Plantation Mansion servants. It was constructed of slave made brick and located just a few yards southwest of the site of the Boxwood Plantation Mansion. The Boxwood Plantation servant/slave quarters home is on the Alabama register as a historic building. In 2013, this rare brick remnant of an early plantation slave home in the Tennessee Valley was listed on the National Register of Historic Places.

Elliott, William

There were two William Elliotts living in Lawrence County, Alabama; they were probably father and son since the archives lists a William and William Elliott Jr. William Elliott was listed as a slave owner in Lawrence County from

1820 through 1860. According to the Lawrence County Marriages Records, William Elliott married Sarah Ann Mitchel on January 13 or 15, 1829; both dates are listed on the marriage record.

In addition, Old Land Records of Lawrence County, Alabama includes a William Elliott and William Elliott Jr. William Elliott of Tennessee first entered 160 acres of land in Section 6 of Township 4 South and Range 8 West in Lawrence County, Alabama. On September 14, 1818, this tract of land was assigned to Rebecca Elliott. William Elliott Jr. entered 80 acres on November 20, 1834. From February 22, 1830, through May 21, 1851, an additional 640 acres were entered by one of the William Elliotts in Townships 4, 5 South and Range 7 West (Cowart, 1991).

On July 15, 1818, William and Richard Elliott entered 160.48 acres of land in Section 17 of Township 5 South and Range 5 West in Morgan County, Alabama. William entered an adjoining 80 acres on the same day (Cowart, 1981). In the 1820 Lawrence County, Alabama Census, William Elliott had one white male over 21, one white female over 21, and one white female under 21. In 1820, William Elliott owned 12 black slaves.

According to the 1830 Lawrence County, Alabama Census, one William Elliott household had two white males 20-30, and one white female 20-30. The other William Elliott had one white male under 5, two white males 5-10, one white male 30-40, two white females 15-20, and one white female 20-30. In 1830, William Elliott owned 14 black slaves.

The 1840 Lawrence County, Alabama Census gives one William Elliott household with two white males under 5, one white male 20-30, one white male 30-40, one white female under 5, and two white females 20-30. The other William Elliott household had one white male under 5, two white males 5-10, one white male 30-40, and one white female 20-30. In 1840, William Elliott owned 15 black slaves.

In the 1850 Lawrence County, Alabama Census, William Elliott is listed as a 47-year-old male born in Virginia. Also listed in his household is Theophalus a 14-year-old born in Alabama, Julia A. a 12-year-old born in Alabama, Lettitia Quarles a 35-year-old born in Virginia, and Thomas a 15-year-old born in

Virginia. According to the 1850 Lawrence County, Alabama Slave Schedules, William Elliott owned 18 black slaves.

According to the 1860 Northern Division, Lawrence County, Alabama, United States Census, Household 220, William Elliott is a 58-year-old male farmer born in Virginia, with a real estate value of $18,000.00 and a personal value of $12,700.00. Also living in his household is a 24-year-old male born in Virginia, Julia a 21-year-old female born in Virginia, and Lutitia Qualls a 46-year-old female born in Virginia. In 1860, William Elliott owned 19 black slaves.

According to the Lawrence County Archives records, William Elliott owned the following tracts of land: Section 27, T4S, R7W, NE; Section 18, T7S, R6W, N½ of W½ of SW¼; Section 18, T7S, R6W, N½ of W½ of SW¼; Section 13, T7S, R7W, SE¼; Section 13, T7S, R7W, SE¼; Section 18, T7S, R7W, W½ of SW¼; Section 18, T7S, R7W, N½ of W½ of SW¼; Section 13, T7S, R7W, SE¼; Section 13, T7S, R7W, SE¼; Section 18, T7S, R7W, N½ of W¼ of SW¼; Section 13, T7S, R7W, SE¼; and an Oakville lot and house. Township 7 South and Range 6 West is centered in the Speake and Oakville area with its eastern boundary being Morgan County. Township 7 South and Range 7 West is basically south and southeast of Moulton to the edge of Bankhead Forest.

Findagrave.com has a handmade marker for William Elliott at Campground Cemetery in Morgan County, Alabama. This marker may or may not be the same William Elliott.

Epps, Hamlin

Hamlin Epps married Martha Fitzgerald who was a daughter of William Fitzgerald II and Sarah Epps Fitzgerald of Virginia. Hamlin came to Lawrence County, Alabama, with seven of the families of the children of William Fitzgerald II. After 1818, the following children of William II and Sarah Epps Fitzgerald moved to Lawrence County, Alabama.
1. Sarah 'Sally' Fitzgerald married Benjamin Ward II.
2. Elizabeth Fitzgerald married Littleberry Hardyman Jones.
3. Mary Ann Fitzgerald married William Booth.
4. William Fitzgerald III married Letty Williams.
5. Martha Fitzgerald married Hamlin Epes.

6. Reverend Freeman Fitzgerald married Elizabeth Williams Irby.
7. Thomas Fitzgerald married Ann Roper Williams; he died in Virginia, but, Ann Roper Williams Fitzgerald and her children came to Lawrence County, Alabama. Ann and Letty were sisters and aunts of Elizabeth Williams Irby.

Hamlin Epps and the Fitzgerald families moved from Virginia, to Madison County, Alabama. Around 1818, the related families moved to the Wheeler area near Courtland, Alabama. In September 1818, Hamlin Epps of Madison County, Alabama, entered a total of 600 acres of land in Lawrence County, Alabama, with an additional 80 acres on October 5, 1825. On September 14, 1818, Hamlin Epps entered 320 acres of land in Section 14 of Township 4 South and Range 8 West in Lawrence County, Alabama (Cowart, 1991). Most of the land Hamlin entered was north to northeast of Courtland, Alabama.

In the 1820 Lawrence County, Alabama Census, Hamlin Epps had three white males over 21, one white female over 21, and one white female under 21. In 1820, Hamlin Epps owned 23 black slaves. Based on Lawrence County Archives records, it appears that Hamlin Epps died before 1830. In 1830, Hamlin Epps is not listed as owning any slaves; however, his brother-in-law Freeman Fitzgerald owned 107 black slaves. Freeman probably got the slaves of Hamlin. Much of the land Hamlin Epps entered was assigned to Freeman Fitzgerald. Freeman Fitzgerald entered several tracts of land on September 14, 1818, in Lawrence County, Alabama. Freeman went back to Virginia before 1840 where he died shortly thereafter.

After ten to twelve years, Hamlin Epps was dead and most of the Fitzgerald children he came with were gone from Lawrence County except William III and Letty Fitzgerald, the owners Ingleside Plantation. William and Letty lived on their plantation which was just north of the Brown's Ferry Road about halfway between Courtland and Brown's Ferry on the Tennessee River.

Faircloth, Cordial

Cordial Faircloth was born in Virginia on March 31, 1786; his father was Ephraim Faircloth, and his mother was Phereba Jones. In 1816, Cordial first married Sarah 'Sally' Reynolds (1792-1822) in Williamson County, Tennessee, and they moved to Lawrence County, Alabama.

After Sally died, Cordial Faircloth married Meredian Cornelia Johnson on February 28, 1824, in Lawrence County, Alabama. Meredian was born on November 23, 1806, in Virginia. She was the daughter of John Johnson of the nearby Green Onion Plantation near the mouth of Town Creek in present-day Colbert County, Alabama. Cordial Faircloth had the following children:

1. George R. Faircloth, son of Sally, was born on June 24, 1818, and he died on October 24, 1845. He was buried in the Faircloth Cemetery in Colbert County, Alabama (Find a Grave 102703879).
2. Richard Benjamin Faircloth, son of Sally, was born on May 8, 1820, and he died in 1850.
3. Daughter of Meredian Faircloth was born on March 17, 1825, and died on August 24, 1834. She was buried in the Faircloth Cemetery in Colbert County, Alabama (Find a Grave Memorial Number 17409136).
4. John W. Faircloth, son of Meredian, was a 21-year-old male born in Alabama, according to the 1850 census. He was listed in the household of Cordial Faircloth and was born in 1829.
5. Thomas Faircloth, son of Meredian, was born on June 8, 1833, and lived only seven days; he died on June 15, 1833 (Find a Grave Memorial Number 17409209).
6. Haley J. Faircloth, son of Meredian, was born in 1834, and died on April 10, 1890, in Mississippi. He served in Company D, 23rd Mississippi Infantry, Confederate States of America. According to the 1900 census, Haley left his widow Mary with eight children: M. A. Faircloth (Daughter), Cornelia, Endora, Joseph, Kate, Inez, Jesse, and Belle. He is buried in the Wheeler Grove Baptist Church Cemetery in the Wheeler Grove Community in Alcorn County, Mississippi (Find a Grave Memorial Number 87776099).

In the 1820 Lawrence County, Alabama Census, Cordial Faircloth had one white male over 21, two white males under 21, and one white female over 21. In 1820, Cordial owned only three black slaves.

According to the 1830 Lawrence County, Alabama Census, Cordial Faircloth had one white male 0-5, one white male 5-10, one white male 10-15, one white male 20-30, one white male 40-50, one white female 0-5, one white female 5-10, and one white female 20-30. In 1830, Cordial owned 14 black slaves.

In the 1840 Lawrence County, Alabama Census, Cordial Faircloth had one white male 5-10, one white male 10-15 one white male 20-30, one white male 50-60, one white female 0-5, one white female 10-15, one white female 30-40.

For some reason, there were no slaves listed in 1840, but in 1850, Cordial had 38 black slaves. The 1850 Lawrence County, Alabama, United States Census, House Number 236 listed the following: Cordial Faircloth, male, 63, Virginia; Maredian Faircloth, female, 44 Virginia; John W. Faircloth, Male, 21, Alabama; Haley Faircloth, male, 16, Alabama; J. M. Faircloth, male, 8, Alabama; Martha Faircloth, female, 6, Alabama; Robert H. Leonard, male, 11, Alabama; Malcum Leonard, male, 9, Alabama; Sarah F. Leonard, female, 8, Alabama; George Herse, male, 16, Alabama.

According to the Lawrence County Archives records, Cordial Faircloth was the husband of Meredian Johnson (the daughter of John Johnson) and heir of John Johnson. Cordial received the Johnson estate of Hog Island on the Tennessee River. Cordial was a school commissioner and builder of a road from Marathon to Bainbridge. According to the record, Cordial Faircloth owned Section 16, T3S, R9W about a mile and half south of the Tennessee River in Lawrence County (present-day Colbert County). Some of the Faircloth slaves were Martin, Hoss, Little Sophia, Sophia, and Coleman.

Cordial Faircloth died on October 18, 1853, at 67 years old. The inscription on his tombstone says, "SACRED to the memory of Cordial Faircloth; who was born March 31, 1786; Professed faith in Christ August 1847, died in blessed hope of a glorious immortality October 18th 1853; Blessed are the dead which die in the Lord." He was buried in the Faircloth Cemetery in present-day Colbert County, Alabama (Find a Grave Memorial Number 17409156).

Meredian Cornelia Johnson died on February 3, 1855, in Lawrence County, Alabama. She was buried in the Faircloth Cemetery in present-day Colbert County, Alabama (Find a Grave Memorial Number 102703298).

Fitzgerald, William-Ingleside

According to the The Heritage of Lawrence County, Alabama Book (1998), "The family of William Fitzgerald II…built the Leinster Plantation in Virginia." William II married Sarah Eppes who was born on November 7, 1757; she was the daughter of Francis and Mary Eppes. William II married a second time to Catherine 'Queen' Cralle Ward Jones; the former wife of Benjamin Ward Sr. and Daniel Jones (1747-1795). William Fitzgerald had the following children:

1. Sarah 'Sally' Fitzgerald was born about May 6, 1778; she married Benjamin Ward Jr. (April 2, 1778-November 8, 1840), son of Benjamin Ward Sr. and Catherine Cralle Ward Jones Fitzgerald (Find a Grave Memorial Number 174630935).

2. Dr. John Henry Fitzgerald was born on July 24, 1779, and died on June 30, 1816; he married Louisa Catherine Jones who was the daughter of Daniel Jones and Catherine Cralle Ward Jones Fitzgerald.

3. Elizabeth Fitzgerald Jones was born March 26, 1781; she married Littleberry Hardman Jones, the son of Daniel Jones and Catherine Cralle Ward Jones Fitzgerald.

4. Mary Ann Fitzgerald Booth was born about 1781; she married William Booth.

5. Dr. Francis Fitzgerald was born March 1783, and he died September 1860. He married Frances 'Fannie' Jones (1789-1823) the daughter of Daniel Jones and Catherine Cralle Ward Jones Fitzgerald.

6. Robert Fitzgerald was born about 1786; he died in Virginia around 1838.

7. Major Thomas Fitzgerald was born January 14, 1787. On December 20, 1810, in Nottoway, Virginia, Thomas married Anne Roper Williams who was born on September 1, 1793. Ann was the daughter if Catherine Greenhill and Thomas Roper Williams. After her first husband Thomas died in May 1816, Ann married Samuel Savage. She died on October 7, 1840, in Courtland, Alabama, at age 47, and is buried at Ingleside (Find a Grave Memorial Number 187665313).

8. William Fitzgerald III was born about 1788 in Virginia; he married Lettice 'Letty' G. Williams, the sister of Ann Roper Williams.

9. Martha Fitzgerald Eppes was born in Virginia, she married Hamlin Eppes.

10. Freeman Fitzgerald was born September 29, 1792. On September 30, 1813, he married Elizabeth Irby, the daughter of William Irby and Elizabeth Williams. Elizabeth Williams was the sister to Ann Roper

Williams Fitzgerald and Letty Williams Fitzgerald. Elizabeth Williams Irby Fitzgerald was born December 9, 1795; she died on January 10,1842. Freeman died on March 25, 1845 (Find a Grave Memorial Number 175140295).

Around 1817, the families of seven children of Major William Fitzgerald II departed Virginia, and came to Madison County, Alabama. Their uncle James Fitzgerald had entered land in Madison County on November 12, 1811 (Cowart, 1979). James was born in 1760 at Amelia, Virginia, and died in Madison County, Alabama. Prior to coming to Lawrence County, Littleberry H. Jones, Hamlin Eppes, and other family members lived in Madison County, Alabama. By September 1818, most of the Fitzgerald siblings and their family had settled near Wheeler and Courtland, Alabama.

The seven families of William Fitzgerald II's children ended up in Lawrence County, Alabama, but many moved back to their Virginia home. The ones that lived in Lawrence County included: 1) Sarah 'Sally' Fitzgerald Ward, 2) Elizabeth Fitzgerald Jones, 3) Mary Ann Fitzgerald Booth, 4) William Fitzgerald III, 5) Martha Fitzgerald Epes, 6) Reverend Freeman Fitzgerald, and 7) Ann Roper Williams Fitzgerald.

According to the Lawrence County, Alabama census records, the members of the extended Fitzgerald family had the following number of black slaves: Benjamin Ward owned 21 slaves in 1830, William Booth owned 45 slaves in 1820 and 46 in 1830, Hamlin Epps owned 23 slaves in 1820, Freeman Fitzgerald owned 107 slaves in 1830, William Fitzgerald III owned 56 slaves in 1830, Littleberry H. Jones owned 57 slaves in 1820, and Nancy Savage owned 60 black slaves in 1840. If these families came together from Virginia to Lawrence County, Alabama, with all their slaves, they had some 370 black slaves to help them along the way.

William Fitzgerald III

After the Turkey Town Treaty of 1816, William III and Letty Fitzgerald and other wealthy slave owning cotton planters settled from Huntsville to Courtland along the Indian trail that became the old Brown's Ferry Road. William III and Letty Fitzgerald probably built the plantation home known as

Ingleside in Lawrence County. The Brown's Ferry Road was an early Indian trail leading from Hunt's Spring (Huntsville) to Gourd's Settlement (Courtland). The road passed through present-day Tanner and crossed the Tennessee River at Brown's Ferry which was just east of the upstream end of Brown's Island. Captain John Brown, who was one half Cherokee, operated the ferry until the Turkey Town Treaty of 1816, and then, he moved to Otali, present-day Attala, Alabama. The Fitzgerald family probably came from Madison County along the Brown's Ferry Road and crossed the Tennessee River at Brown's Ferry. At various times, the ferry was also known as Cox's Ferry and Garner's Ferry.

The Ingleside Plantation Mansion of Lawrence County was the home of William III and Letty Fitzgerald. The home was just north of the Brown's Ferry Road approximately halfway between the Brown's Ferry crossing of the Tennessee River and Courtland, Alabama. Ingleside was nearly opposite the Dixie Plantation of Captain Charles C. Swoope.

According to the 1830 Lawrence County, Alabama Census, Reverend Freeman Fitzgerald, the brother of William, owned 107 black slaves, and William Fitzgerald owned 56 slaves. In 1840 only three slaves are recorded for William, and Freeman is not listed; Freeman Fitzgerald probably moved back home to Virginia where he died in 1845. Obviously, for some census years, slave counts were missed or wrong. In the 1850 Lawrence County, Alabama Slave Schedule, William Fitzgerald owned 25 black slaves.

Ann Roper Williams Fitzgerald Savage, the sister of Letty Williams Fitzgerald died in 1840, and she was buried in Letty's garden at Ingleside. In the 1840 census, Nancy Savage owned 60 black slaves; Nancy was probably the sister-in-law to Ann Williams Fitzgerald Savage, since her household is listed next to William Fitzgerald III and Letty, the sister Ann. In the 1840 census, the household of Nancy Savage had one white female under five and one female between 40 and 50 years of age which was Nancy.

The following is the will of William Fitzgerald III given on September 22, 1840: "Known to all men by these presents that I, William Fitzgerald Sr., of Lawrence County...I leave to my nephew Willliam Fitzgerald my silver watch and stock buckle with a request that should he ever marry and have a son to be called William that the said watch and stock buckle shall descend to him, they being old family peiced handed down to me through my father, William Fitzgerald. Item I. After the payment of all my just debts, I leave to my affectionate wife, Lettice G. Fitzgerald all the property that I may died possessed of every description whatsoever with a request that she shall give and secure to my nephew William Fitzgerald a negro woman named Matilda together with her and their increase from this fate (the wife of Preston). The balance of said property so left to my affectionate wife shall be at her free will and disposal. Item II. I leave my affectionate wife L.G. Fitzgerald whole and sole exectrix of this my will with a positive request that she sall not be held and bound to give security for her administration on my estate. Item III. And lastly, that it is my request that there shall be no inventory of my estate whatsoever. Signed, sealed and acknowledged 22 of September 1840, Test: Richard H. Bur"

The nephew of William Fitzgerald III listed as William Fitzgerald was the son of Major Thomas Fitzgerald and Ann Roper Williams Fitzgerald Savage. He was known as Colonel William Fitzgerald who was born in Virginia on September 30, 1811.

In the 1850 Lawrence County, Alabama, United States Census, Household 519, William Fitzgerald III was listed as 63 years old born in Virginia, and Lettie G. was a 59-year-old born in Virginia. In the 1850 Lawrence County, Alabama, United States Census, Household 520, William Fitzgerald Jr. was a 38-year-old born in Virginia, Mary was a 23-year-old born in Alabama, Thomas was seven, Sarah A. R. was five, Lettice G. Jr. was four, Mary E. was two, and William was two months old. William Fitzgerald III died at Ingleside in 1852, and Colonel William Fitzgerald died on October 1, 1854, and he was also buried at Ingleside near his mother (Find a Grave Memorial Number 150856040).

Barclay Family

Dr. James T. Barclay, who was a missionary, purchased Monticello after the death of his family friend President Thomas Jefferson. In 1868, James moved to Lawrence County, Alabama, and lived with his oldest son, Dr. Robert Gutzloff Barclay at Ingleside Plantation. Robert was born on July 15, 1832, and died on November 19, 1876, and was buried at Ingleside (Find a Grave Memorial Number 31375362).

Dr. James T. Barclay died in 1874, and he was buried in an unmarked grave in the Barclay family plot at Ingleside. Emma Bakenall Barclay, the wife of Dr. Robert G. Barclay, and James T. Barclay Jr.(1/8/1868-7/2/1945), son of Robert and Emma, were buried in the Ingleside Plantation Cemetery. Other Barclay family members were also buried at Ingleside in Lawrence County, Alabama.

In 1863, John Judson Barclay (November 12, 1834-January 9, 1910), brother of Robert G. Barclay, married Decima Hermans Campbell (October 12,1840-May 4, 1920). Decima was the daughter of Dr. Alexander Campbell who founded and organized of the present-day Church of Christ. John Judson and Decima Campbell Barclay lived in the Ingleside Plantation Mansion for some five years. They had a son born on September 16, 1870, and a daughter born on November 12, 1875, while living at Ingleside near Wheeler Community in Lawrence County, Alabama.

Years ago, the Ingleside Plantation mansion fell into ruin and has long since vanished from the landscape. All that remains of the Ingleside cotton plantation is the family cemetery of less than a dozen graves that memorialize the distinguished people buried in the cemetery.

Foster, Thomas Jefferson-Green Onion

Colonel Thomas Jefferson Foster of Lawrence County, Alabama, was born in Nashville, Tennessee, in 1813; he was the son of Robert Coleman Foster, Sr. and Ann Slaughter Foster. Thomas Jefferson Foster was the youngest of seven sons, and became a large cotton planter in North Alabama. He amassed a fortune from his own successful cotton farming operations.

On October 30, 1833, Thomas Jefferson Foster married Virginia Prudence Watkins; she was born on October 22, 1816, in Georgia. Virginia was the daughter of Robert H. Watkins (1782-1855) and Prudence Thompson Watkins

140

(___-1867). Virginia Prudence Watkins Foster died on May 12, 1837, in Lawrence County, Alabama. The grave of Virginia was unmarked and no tombstone was found. She had an infant son Foster; they were buried in the Foster Graveyard at Brickhouse Ford in Lawrence County, Alabama (Find a Grave Memorial Numbers 104417576 and 104146702). Virginia Prudence Watkins was only 21 when she died.

Colonel Thomas J. Foster married a second time in 1844 to Ann Hood of Florence, Alabama. Thomas and Ann had the following children:
1. James Foster of Lawrence County, Alabama, married Tillie Toney.
2. Coleman unmarried, and educated, with his brother, at Edinburgh, Scotland. Coleman Foster was a planter on the Tennessee River, Lawrence County, Alabama
3. Annie married Lieutenant Longshaw of the U. S. Army in 1872.

After Ann died, Colonel Thomas Jefferson Foster married a third time to a Mrs. Longshaw. According to the 1850 Lawrence County, Alabama, Agricultural Census of the Green Onion Plantation, Thomas Jefferson Foster owned 1,200 acres of improved land and 600 acres of unimproved land valued at $12,000. He also had $810.00 worth of farm equipment and implements with his livestock valued at $3,325.00.

According to the 1850 Lawrence County, Alabama Slave Schedule, Thomas Jefferson Foster owned the Green Onion Plantation with 95 slaves. In the 1860 Lawrence County, Alabama Slave Schedule, Thomas Jefferson Foster owned 128 black slaves.

According to Wikipedia.org, "Thomas Jefferson Foster (July 11, 1809-February 24, 1887) was a soldier and prominent politician serving the Confederate States of America during the American Civil War. He served two terms in the Confederate Congress and was later elected to the United States Congress but was denied his seat.

Thomas Jefferson Foster was a member of the Confederate States Congress in 1861. With the secession of Alabama, he raised the 27th Alabama, an infantry regiment in the Confederate States Army and served as its first colonel. Colonel Thomas Jefferson Foster, CSA, was instrumental in urging the construction of Fort Henry to defend the vital Tennessee River, serving in the fort under General Lloyd Tilghman until its forces surrendered to Union General Ulysses S. Grant.

In 1865, he was elected to the United States House of Representatives, but as a result of the policies of the Radical Republicans and Reconstruction, former Confederates such as Foster were denied their congressional seats."

From Footprints in Time by Myra Borden (1993), "United States viz: NW quarter of Section 20, North half of Section19, SW quarter of Section 17, a little over half of Section 18, S half of Section 18, all in Township 3, Range 8 West, and NE quarter of Section 24 in Township 3 Range 9 West and known as the plantation on which said John F. Lightfoot died, and as the plantation now in the occupancy and possession of Petitioner as the legal representatives of said John F. Lightfoot, and cultivated as such, by the slaves of said Estate, during the present year; bounded by Big Nance Creek on the East; Tennessee River on the North; Town Creek on the West, and the plantations of Thomas J. Foster and Robert Lightfoot on the South."

Some historians state that the burial place of Thomas Jefferson Foster was unknown; however, a death record says that he died in Florence, Alabama. Foster's obituary was printed in the Moulton Advertiser on February 24, 1887. Colonel Thomas Jefferson Foster died on February 12, 1887, at Beat Number 3 in Lawrence County, Alabama, at the age of 78; he was a widowed white male planter.

Thomas Foster-Former Black Slave

The 1870 Lawrence County, Alabama, United States Census, Household number 126 lists the following: Thomas Foster, male, 60, black, Virginia; Kitty Foster, female, 55, Virginia; Crady Foster, female, 20 Alabama; and, Sarah Foster, female, 11, Alabama.

Spotswood "Spot" Foster-Black Slave of Foster Family

The following is the story of a black slave probably from Thomas Jefferson Foster's Green Onion Plantation. About 1834, Spotswood "Spot" Foster was born into slavery in Tennessee; the same place that the cotton planter Thomas Jefferson Foster was born. Since he was a slave of the Foster Family in Tennessee, Spot Foster took the last name of his slave owner. Colonel Thomas Jefferson Foster and his black slaves worked the Green Onion Plantation near the mouth of Town Creek in Lawrence County, Alabama.

The United States Government hired William Mosely, another local runaway slave, to recruit slaves to help build forts; Mosely probably recruited Spotswood. After the Union Army announced plans to fortify Decatur, Spotswood Foster ran away from the Lawrence County plantation of his owner and joined the Union Army on March 15, 1864.

Spotswood "Spot" Foster enlisted in Company K of the 111th United States Colored Troops. His military records showed him as being five feet and six inches tall. Spot, along with others of the 111th Infantry, were entrenched in Athens when Confederate General Nathan Bedford Forrest arrived in Limestone County, Alabama. The Union had constructed forts along the Alabama Central Railroad to protect supply lines feeding the Union.

After the end of the Civil War, Spotswood 'Spot' Foster was back in Lawrence County, Alabama. He filed for a military pension, and his pension application described his service during the Civil War. Spotswood Foster stated in his Application for Pension that he contracted fever and smallpox. He was in the hospital in Murfreesboro, Tennessee, for some time.

In Spot's petition, Monroe Lile stated he joined the Union Army in Courtland, Alabama, with Spotswood and that he shared a tent with him during the war. Lile saw him as a prisoner in Cherokee before he escaped. Lile stated people in camp talked about Spot Foster having smallpox, and that Foster was sent to the small pox hospital at Stone's River in Murfreesboro, Tennessee.

Spotswood's great, great, granddaughter, Emma Foster, who was the oldest of four children born to John and Emma Foster Hollaway, lived with and worked in the fields with Foster's son until his death. After this, she married William Leroy Torain. Emma stated, "Things were hard in them days, but everybody worked. We cleared fields so we could plant a cotton crop. We worked like Spotswood and all of the slaves."

Spotswood "Spot" Foster was not only a Union soldier who fought for his freedom, but he was also a remarkable farmer. Spot's descendants are extremely proud of him and of their other ancestors. Spotswood's family moved from slavery to become successful farmers, educators, business owners, and professional people.

The thing Foster's family was most proud of was the fact that Spot signed his pension application which let them know he was an educated man. Spotswood "Spot" Foster was a brave man who fought to preserve our country. Spot died on September 12, 1896, in Lawrence County, Alabama. He was buried in the Foster-Davis Cemetery at Moulton where he has a grave marker. (Find a Grave Memorial Number 37324400).

Garth, George Martin-Bonnie Doon

George Martin Garth was born on August 12, 1832, at Charlottesville in Albemarle County, Virginia. He was the son of William Durrett Garth (8/22/1794-11/27/1860) and Elizabeth Lewis Woods Martin (died 1868). On November 11, 1851, George married Catherine 'Kate' Mary Gilchrist who was born on June 4, 1830. Catherine Mary Gilchrist Garth was the fourth child of Daniel Gilchrist and his wife, Nancy Philips. George Martin Garth and Catherine Mary Gilchrist Garth had the following children:
1. Annie Philips Garth (10/20/1852-10/12/1853).
2. Lizzie M Garth (5/18/1854-3/28/1861).
3. Sarah Ellen Garth (7/8/1856-9/26/1857).
4. William E. Garth (6/13/1859-2/8/1860).
5. Catherine Garth (1/18/1858-1/11/1906) married Robert M. DuBose.
6. George Martin Garth Jr. (2/28/1862-5/30/1941) married Kate Burt.

Bonnie Doone

Captain George Martin Garth and Kate Gilchrist Garth lived on a plantation called Bonnie Doone. In 1860, George M. Garth was household 215, and William Elliott was household 220. There was another cotton plantation called Bonnie Doone just south of Athens, Alabama.

In the 1860 Lawrence County, Alabama, United States Census, Household 215, George Martin Garth was a 27-year-old male planter from Virginia. Also in his house was Catherine a 30-year-old female born in Alabama, Lizzy a six-year-old female born in Alabama, and Kate a 2-year-old female born in Alabama. In 1860, George Garth had a real estate value of $86,440.00 and the value of his personal property was $48,000.00

According to the 1860 Lawrence County, Alabama, Slave Schedule, George Martin Garth owed 35 black slaves, and Willis Garth owned 59 slaves. Willis, who born about 1827, is probably a cousin of George.

Shortly after making the rank of Captain, George Martin Garth died on April 30, 1862, at Courtland in Lawrence County, Alabama. He was buried in the Garth Cemetery at Bonnie Doon (Find a Grave Memorial Number 39530645).

On September 21, 1868, Katherine married a second time to Captain William Stuart Bankhead from Virginia. Catherine 'Kate' Mary Gilchrist Garth

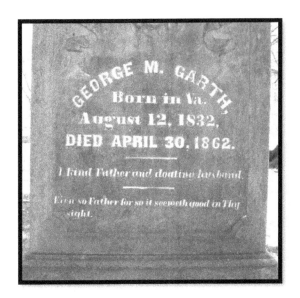

GEORGE M. GARTH,
Born in Va.
August 12, 1832,
DIED APRIL 30, 1862.

Bankhead moved to Courtland from Bonnie Doone Plantation, her Federal-style plantation home. She lived in the Garth-Shackelford House which was built for her about 1880. Bonnie Doone burned down in 1935.

Katherine Mary Gilchrist Garth Bankhead died on February 19, 1900, at 69 years of age. She was buried in the Garth Cemetery in Lawrence County, Alabama (Find a Grave Memorial Number 39530500).

According to the Moulton Advertiser on Thursday March 1, 1900, "Mrs. Katherine M. Bankhead died at her home in this city Monday morning and was buried Wednesday at the family burial ground at Bonnie Doon. She was the mother of George M. Garth Jr. and Mrs. R. M. DuBose and sister of Mr. John A. Gilchrist."

Gibson, John

John Gibson was born on May 11, 1784, in North Carolina. John was the son of Sylvanus Gibson and Eleanor Taylor. John married Nancy Ann Orr who was born on December 11, 1782, in Georgia; she died on September 2, 1823, in Lawrence County, Alabama. Nancy Ann was the daughter of Christopher Orr and Martha 'Patty' Watkins. John Gibson died on August 8, 1838, in Lawrence County. The children of John and Nancy Ann were:
1) Judge Charles Gibson married Clarissa McDowell
2) William Gibson
3) Martha Gibson married Richard C. Perkins
4) Christopher Gibson
5) Olive 'Olley' Gibson married James C. McDaniel
6) Sylvanus Gibson
7) Nancy Orr Gibson married John H. Tabor

8) John Gibson married Martha Ann Boyce

9) Reece Watkins Gibson married Martha D. Johnson

In the 1820 Lawrence County, Alabama Census, John Gibson had one white male over 21, five white males under 21, one white female over 21, and three white females under 21, and 15 slaves. The 1830 Lawrence County, Alabama Census listed John Gibson and John Gibson Jr.

According to the Lawrence County Archives, John Gibson owned the following land: Section 29, T7S, R6W, N½ of W½ of NE¼; Section 20, T7S, R6W, E½ of SE¼; Section 20, T7S, R6W, E½ of SE¼; and, Section 29, T7S, R6W, N½ of W½ of NE¼. Township 7 South and Range 6 West is centered in the Speake and Oakville area with its eastern boundary being Morgan County and southern boundary the northeast edge on Bankhead Forest.

Sylvanus Gibson

Sylvanus Gibson was born in 1785 and died in 1851. Sylvanus was probably a brother of John Gibson who was born in 1784 died in 1838, and an uncle of Charles Gibson who was born in 1802.

In 1850 Sylvanus owned 825 acres of land and his farm valued was at $5,000.00. Sylvanus was born in 1785 and died in 1851. According to the 1850 Lawrence County, Alabama, Agricultural Census, Sylvanus Gibson owned 400 acres of improved land and 425 acres of unimproved land worth $5,000.00. He had $400.00 worth of farming equipment and $300.00 worth of livestock.

According to Lawrence County Archives records in 1853, Sylvanus Gibson was appointed to oversee a road from Sommerville to Centerville. He was also appointed commissioner of the road to Poplar Log Cove Road at Centerville to Moulton and Somerville.

Sylvanus Gibson is buried in Gibson Cemetery Number 1 with tombstone records as follows: Mary Gibson, 3/11/1785-12/20/1874, w/o Sylvanus Gibson, Sylvanus Gibson, 11/24/1785-7/25/1851.

Charles Gibson

Judge Charles Gibson was born on March 15, 1802; he married Clarissa McDowell Gibson (1802-1864). Clarissa was the daughter of Private John McDowell who was born on August 10, 1758, and died on January 1, 1841; John was a private in the Continental Line during the Revolutionary War.

The following about Charles Gibson is from Early Settlers of Alabama by James Saunders (1899), "Charles Gibson was our fourth Probate Judge. He was the son of John Gibson, who had moved his family from Georgia and settled them in Lawrence County, near Oakville, in 1818. Charles was then about 17 years of age. He had been reared to work on a farm, with only such opportunities for an education as were afforded by the common schools of Georgia, which he attended at intervals when he could be spared from the business of the farm.

In 1823 he married Clarissa, a daughter of John McDowell, an Irishman, and Revolutionary war soldier….Their married life was a very happy and busy one, and continued about forty years, during which they made a good estate, and, moreover, reared (to be grown) six sons and four daughters. During the first years of his married life, he amused himself with military affairs. He was captain, then adjutant, then major and colonel…In 1858 he was elected Probate Judge….Charles Gibson…was reelected Probate Judge in 1864, and was disfranchised before two years of this term had expired…in 1875, he was elected a member of the Constitutional Convention, and then retired from public life. He was a farmer for fifty years, and was very successful. He boasts that, in all that time, he never bought a bushel of meal, or a pound of meat or lard, but, on the contrary, has sold a good deal.

When the judge was about sixty-five years of age he married a second time…a Mrs. McCulloch.…Judge Gibson's children were:
1) John C.…a wealthy farmer in Ellis County, Texas…
2) J. J. (commonly called Mack), who is farming near Moulton.
3) Sylvanus, who died at 21 years of age.
4) William, who was killed at the battle of Murfreesboro, and belonged to the Sixteenth Alabama Regiment.

5) James S., who was in the Sixth Arkansas Regiment, and at the battle of Shiloh was wounded in the head three times, but not severely. He is a Baptist preacher and a merchant at Landersville.

6) Charles, the youngest, who studied law, went to Texas and married a Miss Ellis. He was clerk of the District Court in Ellis County, and a member of the Legislature in 1878. He was a member of the Sixteenth Alabama Regiment at Shiloh; had a bone in his leg broken at the battle of Murfreesboro, and afterward, at the battle of Chickamauga, was wounded in the same place.

Of Judge Gibson's daughters, one married Darius Lynch, Esq., of Moulton, and had been dead many years; another married J. T. Adair, of Trinity, and never had any children; the third married Robert Prewitt, brother of J. W., who now lives east of Moulton. They are both dead, but have left a son named Talbot; the fourth daughter married W. L. Kirk, of Texas" (Saunders, 1899).

According to the <u>Moulton Advertiser</u>, on August 21, 1856, Horatio Lynch, born in 1822, was buried on top of the Copena Burial Mound in the Old Settler's Cemetery at Oakville Indian Mounds Education Center. He died at the home of Darius Lynch (1809-1898) and Nancy O. Gibson Lynch, who was the daughter of Colonel Charles and Clarissa McDowell Gibson. John McDowell, Clarissa's father, was a Revolutionary War soldier that was buried in the Preuit-Gipson Cemetery at Oakville.

In the 1837 Lawrence County Archives records, Charles Gibson was appointed to a road from Oakville to McDaniel's Horse Mill. The mill was located on the West Fork of Flint Creek about a mile east of Five Points and the Old Moulton Road which originally followed a portion of the Chickasaw Trail.

The 1850 Lawrence County, Alabama Census, House Number 65 listed the following: Charles Gibson, male, 48, Georgia; Clarisa Gibson, female, 47, North Carolina; Silvanus Gibson, male, 18, Alabama; Martha Gibson, female, 14, Alabama; William Gibson, male, 11, Alabama; James Gibson, male, nine, Alabama; and Charles Gibson, male, seven, Alabama.

In 1850, Charles owned 800 acres, and his farm was valued at $2,500.00. His farm equipment was worth $1,000.00 and his livestock was valued at

$1,190.00. In the 1850 Lawrence County, Alabama, Slave Schedules, Charles Gibson owned 20 slaves. Charles Gibson owned and farmed the land where the Indian mounds are located in the present-day Oakville Indian Mounds Park.

The 1860 Southern Division, Lawrence County, Alabama, United States Census listed the following: Charles Gibson, male, 58, Georgia; Claricy Gibson, female, 57, South Carolina; Charles R. Gibson, male, 17, Alabama; Sarah McDowell, female, 88, North Carolina; and Charles W. Gibson, male, 11, Alabama. According to the 1860 Lawrence County, Alabama Slave Schedules, Charles Gibson owned 34 black slaves.

In the 1880, Beat 7, Lawrence County, Alabama, United States Census listed Charles Gibson as a 78-year-old male farmer born in Georgia, William Anderson a 27-year-old male born in Alabama, Jane Almon a 30-year-old female born in Alabama, and Phoeba Gibson the 71-year-old wife of Charles Gibson born in Tennessee.

Judge Charles Gibson died on May 16, 1883; he was buried in Preuit Cemetery Number 2, in Lawrence County, Alabama (Find a Grave Memorial Number 30855529). According to the Moulton Advertiser, Thursday May 24, 1883, "The large funeral procession that followed the remains of the late Honorable Charles Gibson to his grave was a beautiful tribute to his memory. But he now sleeps by the side of his early companion and the mother of all his children, on whose tombstone is the following inscription: 'In memory of Clarrissa, wife of Hon. Charles Gibson, born June 24, 1802, died June 5, 1864; aged near 62 years.'

Honorable Charles Gibson departed this life, at his residence, in Moulton, on Wednesday the 16th inst., at 9 o'clock p.m. in the 82nd year of his age. Thursday May 31, 1883, Tribute of Respect, The Enon Church has been called to mourn the loss of one of its most useful and influential members, Charles Gibson, who was born in the State of Georgia, March 15th, 1802, and died at his home in the town of Moulton, Alabama, May 16th, 1883, aged 81 years, 2 months and one day…He leaves a wife, five children, many grand children and great grand children. In his last hours he was comforted by the presence of all his children except one, and many of his grand children. Two of his sons from Texas, John C.

Gibson and Hon. Charles R. Gibson, arrived a day or two before their father's death."

Gilchrist, Malcolm-Old Homestead

Malcolm Gilchrist was born in Cantire, Scotland, and first came to North Carolina where he married Catherine Buie. He moved to Maury County, Tennessee, in 1809 (Saunders, 1899). Malcolm and Catherine had Malcolm Jr. and Daniel who eventually made their home in Lawrence County, Alabama, near Melton's Bluff. Malcolm Jr. was born in 1786, and Daniel was born on December 22, 1788.

Daniel Gilchrist-Arcadia and Summerwood

Daniel was born December 22, 1788, and in 1819 married Nancy Philips near Nashville, Tennessee. She was born January 21, 1793; they had seven children. Daniel and Nancy made their home in Lawrence County, Alabama, where they built a large plantation home called the Old Homestead near Courtland, Alabama; later, Daniel Gilchrist's family built Arcadia.

Arcadia

Along with his brother Malcolm, Daniel became recognized as one of the best surveyors in the area doing much work for the government. The brothers received numerous land grants from the government for their services. The family was very actively involved in the Presbyterian Church where Daniel served as elder.

According to the Lawrence County Heritage Book (1998), "Courtland Presbyterian Church: Prior to the Civil War, the bricks for the buildings were made by slave labor from the slaves of Daniel Gilchrist's plantation. They were made on his plantation." Slave labor was used to make the bricks for many of the homes in the area. The northwest portion of Lawrence County became known as Brick Community because of all the building constructed of slave made brick; in the 1890's, the community was annexed into Colbert County.

The family of Daniel Gilchrist built a mountain top home some two miles south of Courtland near a place known as the Devil's Den. The unique feature on the mountain is a large circular hole that rounds out toward the bottom like a huge bell, and it is very deep and dangerous. The Devil's Den is still owned by the descendants of the Daniel Gilchrist family, and their Summerwood home was not far to the west of the huge hole. The Gilchrist's probably used Summerwood during the hot season when mosquitoes were prevalent to avoid malaria or yellow fever. The last Gilchrist family members known to live at Summerwood were Joseph P. and Alice Gilchrist.

Summerwood

According to the 1850 Lawrence County, Alabama, Agricultural Census, Daniel Gilchrist owned 900 acres of improved land and 2,100 acres of unimproved of land worth $22,500.00. His farm equipment was worth $400.00 and his livestock was valued at $4,250.00. According to the 1850 Lawrence County, Alabama, Slave Schedule, Daniel Gilchrist owned 87 black slaves.

In the 1850 Lawrence County, Alabama Cenus, household 302, Daniel Gilchrist was a 61-year-old male planter born in North Carolina worth $11,000.00, Nancy was a 57-year-old female born in Kentucky, CME was a 20-year-old female born in Tennessee, John A. was a 16-year-old male student born in Alabama, and M.F. was a 19-year-old male student born in Tennessee.

According to the 1860 Northern Division, Lawrence County, Alabama, United States Census, Nancy Gilchrist was a 67-year-old female born in Kentucky. In the 1860 Lawrence County, Alabama, Slave Schedule, Nancy Gilchrist (wife of Daniel) owned 21 black slaves, John Gilchrist (son of Daniel) owned 21 slaves, and William Bankhead (son-in-law of Daniel) owned 33 slaves.

Daniel Gilchrist died on July 24, 1855, at Courtland in Lawrence County, Alabama. The inscription on his tombstone is as follows, "He was affectionate to his family, faithful to friends, energetic in business, and earnest in religion." He was buried in the Gilchrist section of the old Courtland Cemetery at Courtland in Lawrence County, Alabama (Find a Grave Memorial Number 33422475).

Nancy A. Philips Gilchrist died in May 1863, at Courtland in Lawrence County, Alabama. She was the daughter of Philip Philips and Susannah Friend of Kentucky and Davidson County, Tennessee. Her middle name could be Ashcraft after her mother's sister, Nancy Friend Ashcraft. Her children were: Philip Philips Gilchrist (1825-1888); Catherine Mary Gilchrist Garth Bankhead (1830-1900); John A Gilchrist (1834-1915). Nancy was buried in the Courtland Cemetery at Courtland, Alabama.

Malcolm Gilchrist

Malcolm Gilchrist Jr. was never married and accumulated a fortune as a cotton merchant and surveyor. He left a large inheritance of lands to the family of his brother Daniel Gilchrist. Malcolm Gilchrist Jr. was a land speculator, and he made a fortune by shipping cotton over the dangerous shoals of the Tennessee River, to the Mississippi River, and on to New Orleans. Most of his income was built on transporting cotton, and he owned his own fleet of boats.

When the Indian lands in North Alabama were sold at public auction in 1818, Malcolm Gilchrist Jr. bought large tracts of land as investments, then he resold these land to cotton planters reaping large profits. Gilchrist personally surveyed every parcel of land before he purchased it; therefore, valley planters knew that they were getting good cotton lands when Gilchrist offered it to them.

In addition to buying and selling cotton land, Malcolm Gilchrist was a cotton freighter. The planters who lived east of the Muscle Shoals were at a disadvantage in transporting their cotton to the markets. Many times the cotton was off loaded on wagons at Peck's Landing east of Elk River Shoals and transported by way of Burleson's Trace, Blyer's Old Turnpike, to Tuscaloosa, then by water to Mobile ports.

Malcolm Gilchrist came to the rescue of planters east of the shoals by building large fleets of flatboats. Gilchrist had the confidence of the cotton planters and enough capital to purchase a large number of boats. He would employ a steersman for each boat and four more to work the oars.

As fast as the boats were loaded with cotton, they passed through the Muscle Shoals under the care of an experienced pilot. The first pilot was an Indian named James Melton of Melton's Bluff. James Melton was the half-blood Lower Cherokee son of Irishman John Melton and his wife Cherokee Ocuma, the sister of Doublehead.

Gilchrist's pilots would take control of the flatboats as they entered the upper region of the Muscle Shoals near Melton's Bluff. There were four groups of dangerous obstructions in the river between Brown's Ferry and Waterloo. These included Elk River Shoals, Big Muscle Shoals, Little Shoals, and Colbert Shoals. The first three formed an almost continuous line of treacherous impediments to the river for about seventeen miles. As the boats proceeded down river from the Elk River Shoals, they had to pass over rapids just above Blue Water Creek that were called "Galloping Water." Between Galloping Water and Campbell's Ferry at Bainbridge was the most dreaded obstacle known as the "Big

Jump." It was a ledge of rocks about four feet high which stretched from shore to shore. Only the skilled pilots knew how to head for a thirty-foot gap in this wall where the gushing waters created a tremendous force. After clearing these and other hazards, some of Gilchrist's hired pilots would disembark at Campbell's Ferry at Bainbridge and walk back to Melton's Bluff for another trip. Other pilots would go all the way to New Orleans where they would spend nearly all their wages. After completing the trip, the pilots would walk back to Melton's Bluff through the Choctaw and Chickasaw Nations.

The price of freight to New Orleans was one dollar per hundred pounds, and the cotton freighter reaped a rich harvest. Gilchrist would require his pilots to write to him at several points on the Mississippi River. When his last boat was loaded, Malcolm would board it to New Orleans. By the time his fleet of boats reached New Orleans, he had gathered information along the way that helped him obtain the best possible prices for his clients who had trusted him with their cotton. Malcolm would collect his money from the commission merchants, and return by steamer to Memphis, and thence home by stagecoach.

Prior to the coming of the Tuscumbia-Decatur Railroad in the early 1830's, Gilchrist's mode of transporting the cotton crop was by flatboats through the tortuous and dangerous channels of the Muscle Shoals. After the completing the railway, some cotton was transported around the shoals by rail to Tuscumbia Landing where it was sent down the Tennessee, Ohio, and Mississippi Rivers to New Orleans. From New Orleans, the cotton was shipped to England or northeastern ports. Prior to the Civil War planters were getting seven to ten cents per pound, but shortly after the war, cotton prices jumped to $1.80 to $2.00 per pound. In addition to the blockade during the war, the loss of slave labor brought demise to the large cotton plantations.

Malcolm Gilchrist Jr. had a Midas Touch. By shipping cotton and land speculation, Malcolm amassed a great fortune when "Cotton Was King." His cotton boats successfully challenged the almost impassable barriers in the Tennessee River at the Muscle Shoals. Some of the above information on Malcolm Gilchrist Jr. came from Early Settlers of Alabama (1899).

Goode, Freeman

In 1828, Colonel Freeman Goode moved to Courtland in Lawrence County, Alabama. He was born about 1796 in South Carolina. Freeman was the son of John Goode and Ann Freeman. John was born about 1765, and he died in 1853 at Edgefield, South Carolina. Besides Freeman, John and Ann Freeman Goode had six other children:

1) Frances was born in 1780 and married a Brooks.
2) Elizabeth was born in 1783, and she married a Burt from Edgefield County, South Carolina.
3) Ann was born in 1785, and she married Dionysius Oliver.
4) John Goode was born in 1788.
5) Talitha Goode was born on April 22, 1792. She first married Coleman Watkins (1786-1819), and in 1821, she married Colonel Benjamin Sherrod. Tabitha and Coleman had two sons Willis Watkins and Goode Watkins. Colonel Benjamin Sherrod and Talitha had four children: Eliza died young; Susan Adelaide married Samuel W. Shackelford; C. Charles Fox married Susan Billups of Columbus, Mississippi; and William Crawford married Amanda Morgan. Talitha Goode Watkins Sherrod died on May 14, 1873, at the residence of her son-in-law, Colonel Samuel W. Shackelford, near Courtland, Alabama. She was originally buried in the Sherrod Cemetery but was moved to the Courtland Cemetery (Find a Grave Memorial Number 45692758).
6) Lucinda Goode (1799-February 25, 1847) married a McLemore of Edgefield, South Carolina, and moved to Courtland, Alabama. Lucinda was buried in Swoope Cemetery Number 1 near Courtland, Alabama (Find a Grave Memorial Number 47671383).

On February 23, 1830, Freeman Goode entered 79 acres in Section 2 of Township 5 South and Range 7 West in Lawrence County, Alabama. On February 24, 1830, Freeman Goode entered 235 acres in Section 34 of Township 4 South and Range 7 West in Lawrence County, Alabama (Cowart, 1991).

According to the 1830 Lawrence County, Alabama Census, the Freeman Goode household had two white males between 20-30 years old. In 1830, Freeman Goode owned 21 black slaves.

In the 1840 Lawrence County, Alabama Census, Freeman Goode was listed with two white males between 40-50 years old in his household. He was listed in the 1840 census between Turner Saunders and John Hunter Harris of Rosemont Plantation. In 1840, Freeman Goode owned 84 black slaves.

On February 12, 1844, Freeman Goode bought a plantation house that was built by Turner Saunders of Tennessee in the early 1800's. On September 10 and 14, 1818, Turner Saunders entered several tracts of land in the area (Cowart, 1991). Turner was a Methodist preacher that came to Lawrence County from Tennessee; he was originally from Brunswick County, Virginia.

Rickey Butch Walker at Saunders-Hall-Goode Mansion

According to the1850 Lawrence County, Alabama, United States Census, Household 559, Freeman Goode was a 50-year-old male farmer from South Carolina worth $55,000.00. Also in his household was Phillip Goode a 31-year-old male and James Burt a 25-year-old male born in South Carolina. In 1850 census, James Edmonds Saunders of Rocky Hill Plantation was Household 557, and Robert Watkins of Oak Grove Plantation was Household 556.

In the 1850 Lawrence County, Alabama, Agricultural Census, Freeman Goode had 1,800 acres of improved land and 1,700 acres of unimproved land worth $35,000. He also had $1,260.00 worth of farm equipment and $6,013.00 worth of livestock. According to the 1850 Lawrence County, Alabama Slave Schedule, Freeman Goode owned 86 black slaves.

In the 1860 Lawrence County, Alabama, United States Census, Household 246, Willis Watkins, the nephew of Freeman Goode, was a 50-year-old male planter from South Carolina with a real estate value of $32,000.00 and a personal property value of $63,500.00. Also in the household was Martha a 35-year-old female born in North Carolina, Adalaid an 18-year-old female born in Alabama, Caroline a 16-year-old female born in Alabama, William a 14-year-old male born in Alabama, Frank a 12-year-old male born in Alabama, Goode a five-year-old male born in Alabama, Thomas a three-year-old male born in Alabama, and Freeman Goode a 60-year-old male planter born in South Carolina. In 1860, Freeman Goode had a real estate value of $72,500.00 and a personal property value of $107,725.00.

According to the 1860 Lawrence County, Alabama, Slave Schedule, Freeman Goode owned 108 black slaves, and his nephew Willis Watkins owned 44 black slaves. It is believed that Willis Watkins family was living with Freeman Goode at the Saunders-Goode-Hall plantation house in 1860.

The Freeman Goode family sold the plantation house to the Hall family who sold it to the Mauldin family in the 1940's. The Mauldins still own the old plantation home with a 1,000-acre farm; however, they have never lived in the two story brick house. Because of its architectural significance, the house was placed on the National Register of Historic Places on October 1, 1974, and is still standing today December 2018.

At age 60, it was said that Freeman Goode married a young girl who caused him to die of a broken heart. According to Footprints in Time by Myra Borden(1993), "Friday September 17, 1875: Colonel Freeman Goode was born in Edgefield District, South Carolina, in January 1796, and died at the residence of Honorable W. C. Sherrod, near Courtland, September 4th, 1875, aged 79 years and 8 months. He removed from South Carolina to Alabama in 1828, and settled near Courtland. William Crawford Sherrod was the nephew of Colonel Freeman Goode."

Gray, Dr. Young A.

Dr. Young A. Gray was born on April 13, 1786. He and his wife probably had five children:

1. Calphurnia C. Gray Keenon was born on December 23, 1807, and she died on May 31, 1833 (Find a Grave Memorial Number 74984245).
2. Susan M. Gray McClung was born on January 20, 1812; she died on September 10, 1833 (Find a Grave Memorial Number 74983874). Susan married John A. McClung who was born in 1795 in Rockbridge County, Virginia, and he died in Florence, Alabama, on September 13, 1832 (Find a Grave Memorial Number 74984131).
3. Elizabeth F. Gray was born on July 30, 1823, and she died on August 4, 1844 (Find a Grave Memorial Number 74984779).
4. Martha W. Gray was born on June 11, 1829, and she died in September 1834 at five years old (Find a Grave Memorial Number 74984554).
5. Robert H. Gray was born on September 9, 1833, and he died on July 3, 1835 (Find a Grave Memorial Number 74984629).

According to the 1820 Lawrence County, Alabama Census, the Young A. Gray household had two white males over 21, one white male under 21, one white female over 21, and five white females under 21. In 1820, Dr. Young A. Gray owned 35 black slaves.

In the 1830 Lawrence County, Alabama Census, the Young A. Gray household had one white male under five, one white male 5-10, one white male 40-50, one white female under 5, one white female 5-10, one white female 10-15, and one white female 15-20, one white female 40-50.

The following article from Footprints in Time by Myra Borden as found in the Courtland Herald on Friday, August 30, 1830, "DR. YOUNG A. GRAY-From Circumstances over which he had neither knowledge or control has for the present abandoned his contemplated removed with his family to Florida, he therefore offers his professional services to the public and that share of patronage from the community generally and particularly, from his old friends which they think his merit entitles him to, he pledges himself that his charges shall be regulated by the general custom of the country. Courtland, February 12th, 1830. P.S. He has a general assortment of medicine and Surgeon's instruments and will be always prepared to perform any operation."

Young A.Gray died on February 12, 1834. He was buried in the Oakwood Cemetery at Tuscumbia in Colbert County, Alabama (Find a Grave Memorial Number 74984477). One large monument in the cemetery has eight inscriptions which are: Susan McClung, January 20, 1812-September 10,1832; John A. McClung died September 13, 1832; Calphurnia C. Keenon, December 23, 1807-May 31, 1833; James Y. McClung, September 3, 1831-September 1, 1833; Y. A. Gray, April 13, 1786-February 12, 1834; Martha W. Gray, June 11, 1829-September 1834; Robert H. Gray, September 9, 1833-July 3, 1835, and Elizabeth F. Gray, July 30, 1823-August 1844.

Hampton, Manoah Bostick Sr.

The father of Manoah Bostick Hampton Sr. was Samuel Hampton who served in the Revolutionary War. Samuel Hampton was one of his father's executors in 1794. On November 4, 1800, he had a Fairfax grant of 70½ acres of land. Samuel married Bethenia Bostick, and they had the following children: Manoah Bostick Hampton, James, Samuel, John B., Mary, and Susannah.

Manoah Bostick Hampton Sr. was born on June 25, 1799, in Stokes County, North Carolina. His wife Cynthia Mitchell was born on June 24, 1795, in Iredell County, North Carolina. He married Cynthia Mitchell on February 28, 1822, in Stokes County; she was the daughter of Andrew Mitchell and Sarah "Sally" Snoddy. Manoah and Cynthia had the following children:
1. Mary Mitchell Hampton was born.about 1823 in North Carolina. She died February 1, 1899, in Lincoln County, Missouri. She married Thomas Franklin Houston who was born on July 30, 1818, at Hunting Creek in Iredell County, North Carolina.
2. Dr. John Placibo Hampton was born on January 22, 1825, in Lawrence County, Alabama. John Hampton died on June 8, 1907, in Madison County, Alabama, and buried in Maple Hill Cemetery, Huntsville. He first married Amanda Evans who was born on September 6, 1831. They were married on November 16, 1848, and she died on December

20, 1851. John then married on June 6, 1854, to Susan Ann Burt who was born on January 30, 1836, and died on August 8, 1867. John then married in 1868 to Mary Thomas Battle who was born on February 21, 1844, and died May 1884, in Madison County.

3. Cynthia Amanda Hampton was born on May 10, 1827, and she died on September 18, 1843, at Athens in Limestone County, Alabama.

4. Susan E. Hampton was born about 1830 in Alabama, and she died in Missouri. She married Van T. Chilton who was born in Virginia about 1818.

5. Matilda Hampton was born about 1833 in Alabama, and probably died Montana. She married Dr. William Parberry who was born in Kentucky about 1833.

6. Manoah Bostick Hampton, Jr. was born April 16, 1835, at Leighton in Colbert County, Alabama. He died at the age of 79 years on March 2, 1915, in Leighton. Manoah, Jr. married on May 31, 1860, to Emma Jane Battle who was born on August 17, 1840, at Meridianville in Madison County, Alabama; Emma died on June 7, 1882, in Lawrence County, Alabama. He then married Lida who was born in Illinois in November 1875. C.S.A.

7. Thomas F. Hampton died as a child on August 1, 1835, at Leighton in Colbert County, Alabama.

According to birth records, Manoah and Cynthia were in Lawrence County, Alabama, prior to the birth of their son John Placibo Hampton on January 22, 1825. Manoah Sr. was assigned 80.2 acres in Section 21 of Township 6 South and Range 7 West just north of Moulton which he released in 1829. On August 30, 1833, he entered 39.865 acres in Section 6 of Township 5 South and Range 8 West in Lawrence County, Alabama, west of Courtland near the banks of Town Creek (Cowart, 1991).

According to the 1850 Lawrence County, Alabama, Slave Schedule, Manoah B. Hampton owned 51 black slaves. In the 1850 Lawrence County, Alabama Census, Household 181, Manoah Bostick Hampton was a 55year old male farmer from North Carolina. His wife Cynthia was listed as a 55 female from North Carolina. Also living in the household was Susan E. a 19-year-old female born in Alabama, Metilda B. a 17-year-old female born in Alabama, and Manoah Bostick Hampton Jr. a 15-year-old male farmer born in Alabama.

Manoah Bostick Hampton II home in Leighton, AL

According to the 1850 Lawrence County, Alabama, Agricultural Census, Manoah's farm was 1,200 acres of improved land and 840 acres of unimproved land worth $20,000.00. He had $600.00 worth of implements and machinery with his livestock valued at $3,225.00.

Manoah Sr. died on February 16, 1858, in Lawrence County, Alabama. Cynthia died on May 21, 1853, at Murfreesboro in Rutherford County, Tennessee, at the age of 57 years. The following inscriptions are on their tombstones:

1. "M. B. H. In Memory of MANOAH BOSTIC HAMPTON, Born in Stokes County, N.C. June 25, 1799, Married Cynthia Mitchell, The 28th of February, 1822 Departed this life at his home In Lawrence County, Ala. The 16th of February, 1858."
2. "In Memory of Cynthia Hampton, Daughter of Andrew and Sarah Mitchell, Born in Iredell County, N.C., June 24th, 1795, Married M. B.

Manoah Bostick Hampton

Cynthia Mitchell Hampton

Hampton, The 28th of February, 1822, Departed this life atMurfreesboro, Tenn the 21st of May, 1853. She lived and died a Christian and was beloved By all who knew her."

Manoah Bostick Hampton, Jr.

On May 31, 1860, Manoah Bostick Hampton Jr. married 19-year-old Emma Jane Battle at Meridianville in Madison County, Alabama. Based on census records, Manoah Jr. and Emma lived in Lawrence County, Alabama.

Manoah Bostick Hampton Jr. and Emma Jane Battle, daughter of Josiah and Eliza Battle, lived at their home in Leighton in present-day Colbert County, Alabama. They had seven children before Emma died at the age of 41. Their children were:

1. Cynthia Mitchell Hampton was born on May 12, 1861, at Huntsville in Madison County, Alabama, and she died on May 5, 1937, at Pasadena in Los Angeles, California. Cynthia married on October 30, 1907, to Arthur Wallace Sias who was born on June 7, 1855, and he died on August 2, 1928, in Pasadena, California.
2. Mary Elizabeth "Lilie" Hampton was born on September 6, 1863, at Leighton, and died on June 23, 1925, in Nashville, Tennessee. She married on August 11, 1885, to Walter Flavis McClure Sr. who was born on March 1, 1856, at Cornersville, Tennessee. He died on July 24, 1915, in Birmingham, Alabama.
3. Dr. Thomas McCrary Hampton was born on June 9, 1865, in Leighton. He married Anne Mackintosh Cameron on October 7, 1895; she was born on February 1, 1875.
4. Emma Battle Hampton was born on July 14, 1869, in Leighton. She married James Theodore Wood who was born on February 4, 1865, in Illinois, and he died in March 1935, in Meagher County, Montana.
5. Matilda Parberry Hampton was born on July 26, 1873, and she died on January 30, 1953, in Helena, Montana. She married Gideon Kennedy Spencer on October 16, 1902; he was born on October 21, 1873, at Canyon Ferry and died after 1953.
6. Manoah Bostick Hampton III was born on August 14, 1877, in Alabama, and he died on December 1, 1957, in Los Angeles, California. He married Eva Hartfield on November 16, 1911; she was

born on December 23, 1884, in Minnesota, and died on July 2, 1974, in Los Angeles, California.

7. Brock Chilton Hampton was born on September 15, 1880, and probably died in Washington, D.C. He married July 31, 1918, to Anna Edith Boitano who was born on November 24, 1886, in Mayfield, California.

According to the 1860 Lawrence County, Alabama, Slave Schedule on page 168B, Manoah Bostick Hampton Jr. owned 71 black slaves. In 1860, Manoah Jr. had a real estate of $25,000.00 and personal value of $89,530.00.

According to the 1860 Lawrence County, Alabama Census, Manoah Bostick Hampton Jr. was a 25-year-old male planter from Alabama. Also living in his household was Emma a 19-year-old female born in Alabama, Matilda a 27-year-old female born in Alabama, and Lucy Martin a 40-year-old female born in North Carolina.

Manoah Bostick Hampton Jr., W. M. Hampton, and J. G. Hampton served in the same Company B, 11th Alabama Cavalry of the army of the Confederate States of America. Manoah Jr. attended the University of North Carolina. Manoah Jr. joined the Confederate States Army in 1862, and he was commissioned 1st Lieutenant, Company H, 35th Alabama Infantry. Subsequently, he was commissioned captain and raised a company of cavalry which became Company B, 11th Alabama Cavalry, Confederate States of America (CSA). Though badly wounded at the Battle of Corinth, he recovered and rejoined his regiment, in which he served until the end of the war. He resided in Leighton, Alabama, until his death where he was active in Camp Fred A. Ashford, UCV.

On March 2, 1915, Manoah Bostick Hampton, Jr. died at the age of 79 years in Leighton. He lived 33 years after his beloved Emma died. Emma's gravestone reads: "EMMA JANE HAMPTON, Born in Madison County, Alabama Aug 17, 1840, Married M. B. Hampton, Jr., May 31st, 1860, Departed this life in Lawrence County, Alabama June 7, 1882, Homeplace of Manoah B. Hampton II, Leighton, Alabama."

Harris, Benjamin

Benjamin Harris was born on September 9, 1788, in Goochland County, Virginia. His parents were William Wager Harris (1773-1820) and Mary Ann Farrar (-1827). Benjamin Harris served in the War of 1812; he testified in support of Samuel Meredith's application for bounty land, stating that he served in the same unit of the Tennessee Militia as Samuel Meredith.

According to Lawrence County Archives records, Benjamin Harris married Minerva Tazewell Jones on December 18, 1821, in Lawrence County, Alabama. Minerva Tazewell Jones Harris was born on August 17, 1801, in North Carolina. Benjamin and Minerva had the following children: William Wager Harris (1822-1822); Mary Ann Harris (1823-1896); Amanda Melvina Harris (1826-1829); Benjamin Royal Harris (1828-1870); Minerva Amanda Harris (1835-1867); and Lucy mentioned by Saunders (1899).

According to the 1820 Lawrence County, Alabama Census, Benjamin Harris owned 26 black slaves; no whites were listed. In the 1830 Lawrence County, Alabama Census, Benjamin Harris had one white male under 5, one white male 20-30, one white male 40-50, one white female 5-10, and one white female 20-30. In 1830, Benjamin Harris owned 33 black slaves.

"Frank Caleb Owen was the third son of Caleb and Mary Owen. He was born 1817 in Madison County, Alabama. Frank was a merchant for many years in Moulton…In 1850, he married Lucy, daughter of Colonel Benjamin Harris, of Russell's Valley (Russellville), one of the first setters there. Colonel Benjamin Harris surveyed and speculated in lands with the Gilchrists of Lawrence County, Alabama, forming a partnership from which he became quite wealthy. Colonel Benjamin Harris was the brother of Nehemiah Harris of Lawrence County, Alabama. Frank Caleb Owen died in Moulton, Lawrence County, Alabama, in 1857…Benjamin lived a few miles southwest of Moulton and later moved to Mississippi" (Saunders, 1899).

The Lawrence County Archives records indicate that Benjamin Harris owned Section 17, T4S, R8W, SW¼ and E½ of NW¼. Also in the records, Benjamin Harris was listed with several others to view and mark out road from Lamb's Ferry to Courtland. He along with other men was appointed by court to mark out a road from Town of Courtland leading from McDaniel's Ferry in Cotaco at county line.

Benjamin Harris died on July 29, 1847, at Cherokee in Franklin (present-day Colbert) County, Alabama. The inscription on his tombstone reads, "IN MEMORY OF BENJAMIN HARRIS, Born in Goochland County VA. Sept. the 9th, 1788, Departed this life in Franklin County, Alabama July the 29th, 1847, Aged 58 years 10 months & 20 days An Honest Man The Noblest Work of God." Colonel Benjamin Harris was buried in the Cross Cemetery at Cherokee in Colbert County, Alabama (Find a Grave Memorial Number 102044873). On November 1, 1859, his wife Minerva Tazewell Jones Harris died in Panola County, Texas.

Harris, John Hunter-Rosemont and Egypt

John Hunter Harris of Rosemont Plantation in Lawrence County, Alabama, was born about 1801. According to Early Settlers of Alabama, "John Hunter Harris, son of Norfleet Harris and Mary Hunter, married Susan Smith of Limestone County, daughter of Gabriel and Mary Smith…Mr. Harris was one of our most respectable and successful planters, and would have left a large estate to his children but for the results of the war. He and his wife both died acceptable members of the Methodist Church, South." John and Susan lived at Rosemont Plantation in Lawrence County, Alabama.

The children of John Hunter Harris and Susan Smith Harris were:

1. Mary Harris married Frank Sherrod, son of Felix Sherrod, and grandson of Colonel Benjamin Sherrod. Their sons were Frank and Harris.
2. Elizabeth Harris was never married.
3. Susan Harris married Captain E. F. Comegys.
4. Ida Harris married Colonel Alexander Allison.
5. John H. Harris Jr. married Susan M. Jackson.
6. Richard N. Harris married Lizzie Hood, daughter of John and Caroline Hood of Lauderdale County.
7. Lucy Harris married to Mr. Joseph Brewer of New Orleans.

Rosemont

The John Hunter Harris family also had another plantation known as Egypt in Lawrence County, Alabama. The Egypt Plantation was located between Egypt Ford of Big Nance's Creek and the present-day site of the International Papermill north of Courtland. As part of the Wheeler Basin studies prior to the impoundment of Wheeler Reservoir, the Hood Harris Indian mound at Egypt was excavated. The conical Copena Indian burial mound, 70 feet in diameter and nine feet high, was located 100 yards east of Big Nance's Creek and about four miles from the mouth of the creek on the Tennessee River. Besides human skeletons, unique artifacts removed included two copper reels, strings of copper beads, large balls of worked galena, and stalactite effigy pipes, one of which represented a dog.

Rosemont

According to the 1850 Lawrence County, Alabama, United States Census, Household 301, John H. Harris was a 49-year-old white male born in North Carolina. Also listed in his household was Susan P. Harris a 39-year-old female born in Tennessee, Mary A. Harris a 15-year-old female born in Alabama, E. C. Harris a 13-year-old female born in Alabama, Susan P. Harris an eight-year-old female born in Alabama, Virginia W. Harris a six-year-old female born in Alabama, Ida Harris a five-year-old female born in Alabama, Jack Harris a four-year-old male born in Alabama, and Richard Harris a two-year-old male born in Alabama. In the 1850 Lawrence County, Alabama, Slave Schedule, John Hunter Harris owned 99 black slaves.

In the 1860 Northern Division, Lawrence County, Alabama, United States Census listed John Hunter Harris a 59-year-old white male born in North Carolina, Susan Harris a 45-year-old female born in Virginia, Lizzie Harris a 20-year-old female born in Alabama, Susan Harris a 17-year-old female born in Alabama, Ida Harris a 15-year-old female born in Alabama, Jack H. Harris a 14-year-old male born in Alabama, Richard Harris a 11-year-old male born in Alabama, and Lucy Harris a two-year-old female born in Alabama.

In the 1860 census, John Hunter Harris had a real estate value of $181,237.00 and a personal property value of $211,240.00. In the 1860 Lawrence County, Alabama, Slave Schedules, John Hunter Harris owned 176 black slaves.

John Hunter Harris Sr. died on April 14, 1866; he was 66 years old (Find a Grave Memorial Number 37502470). His wife Susan P. Smith Harris died on August 12, 1866; she was 56 years old (Find A Grave Memorial Number

37502411). They were buried in the Harris Cemetery in Section 11 of Township 4 South and Range 8 West in Lawrence County, Alabama.

John Hunter Harris Jr.

Harris-Simpson House

John Hunter Harris Jr., son of John Hunter Harris and Susan P. Smith Harris of Rosemont Plantation, was born on August 9, 1846. John Hunter Harris Jr. married Susan McKiernan Jackson (December 1, 1852-January 2, 1930). Susan was the daughter of William Jackson and the granddaughter of James Jackson of the Forks of Cypress Plantation in Lauderdale County, Alabama.

In 1895, Susan Jackson Harris, wife of John Hunter Harris Jr. of Rosemont Plantation, moved to Courtland, Alabama. She purchased the Harris-Simpson House to spend her final days. The Harris-Simpson house was built around 1820 and faces north to an Indian trail known as the Upper River Road or Tuscumbia Road. It is one of the oldest houses in Courtland and sets on a lot surveyed by the Courtland Land Company in 1818.

Susan McKiernan Jackson Harris died January 2, 1930, and she was buried in the Courtland Cemetery at Courtland in Lawrence County, Alabama (Find a Grave Memorial Number 43375412). According to the <u>Times Daily</u> on January 3, 1930, "Mrs. Susie Jackson Harris, aged 80, of Courtland, died at the family residence there

yesterday about noon following an illness of pneumonia of several weeks. Mrs. Harris has been a resident of Courtland for almost 60 years and is widely known throughout the district, where she has a wide circle of friends and acquaintances. Surviving are four sons, R. N. Harris of Decatur, James J. Harris of Courtland, and Thomas J. and Frank Harris of New Orleans; and two daughters, Mrs. Kate Link, of New Orleans, and Mrs. Carrie Simpson, of Oklahoma. Three sisters, Miss Jennie Jackson, Miss Ellen Hunt Jackson, and Miss McCullough Jackson, all of Florence, and one brother James Jackson, of Memphis. Among cousins surviving are Judge J. J. Mitchell, Mrs. Kate Lassiter and Alex Jackson, of Florence, and James Jackson Jr., a nephew, also of Memphis."

John Hunter Harris Jr. died on October 25, 1915, at Courtland in Lawrence County, Alabama. He was buried in the Courtland Cemetery at Courtland in Lawrence County, Alabama (Find a Grave Memorial Number 43375207).

Henderson, James Henry

Colonel James Henry Henderson was born on February 12, 1787, in Elbert County, Georgia; he married Martha Patsy Woolridge about 1804. James died in Lawrence County, Alabama, in 1830. Martha Woolridge Henderson appears to have died sometime after 1830, but before 1840, probably also in Lawrence County.

The children of James Henry Henderson and Martha Patsy Woolridge are as follows:
1) Mary Woolridge Henderson, born in 1805 in Georgia, married Michael Warren Mayes about 1825. Martha died in 1864 at Courtland in Lawrence County, Alabama. Their son Joshua Pritchard Mayes went to Texas. He was buried in the Colorado County Cemetery at Clear Creek with his uncle Thomas Jordan Henderson. The obituary of Joshua was published on July 9, 1925, in the Colorado Citizen which states, "He was the son of Michael and Mary Woolridge Mayes, and he came to Texas from Alabama as very young boy."
2) Sarah Florence Henderson, born in 1807 in Georgia, married Joshua Bloomer Ashmore about 1832. Sarah died between 1843-1848 in Tennessee.

3) Loucinthia Henderson, born in 1809 in Georgia, married Joshua Pritchard Mayes in Lawrence County, Alabama, on June 3, 1824. Joshua was the brother of Michael Warren Mayes. On January 30, 1830, Joshua P. Mayes entered 80 acres of land in Section 6 of Township 5 South and Range 7 West in Lawrence County, Alabama; the land was near a later entry by his brother Michael W. Mayes (Cowart, 1991). On August 22, 1839, Loucinthia later married Caleb Joiner in Noxubee County, Mississippi. Loucinthia died in Texas sometime after 1860. Loucinthia's two sons were Joshua P Mayes Jr. and John Joiner.
4) Thomas Jordan Henderson, born in 1814 in Georgia, married Martha Hendricks in Lawrence County, Alabama. On February 9, 1878, Thomas died in Colorado County, Texas, and he was buried in the Clear Creek Cemetery.
5) Penina Henderson married Dr. John Perry Brown on December 4, 1836, in Noxubee County, Mississippi. Penina died in Fayette County, Texas, between 1870 and 1880. Dr. John P. Brown died in 1884 in Fayette County, Texas.
6) William Henderson was the son of James and Martha Henderson.

According to Lawrence County Archives records, James Henderson owned the SE¼ of the NW¼ of Section 23, T6S, R8W. On September 15, 1818, James Henderson entered 159.5 acres of land in Section 12 of Township 5 South and Range 8 West in Lawrence County, Alabama. On July 18, 1833, William Henderson entered 39.875 acres of land near his daddy in Section 12 of Township 5 South and Range 8 West in Lawrence County, Alabama. On February 21, 1837, Micheal W. Mayes entered 40 acres adjacent to his father-in-law James Henderson and brother-in-law William Henderson. From February 11, 1851, through December 7, 1859, Michael and Drewry Mayes entered another 480 acres in Township 5 South and Ranges 7, 8 West in Lawrence County, Alabama. Drewry entered several additional tracts of land by himself (Cowart, 1991).

In the 1820 Lawrence County, Alabama Census, James Henderson household had one white male over 21, two white males under 21, one white female over 21, and three white females under 21. In 1820, James Henderson owned 18 black slaves. According to the 1830 Lawrence County, Alabama

Census, Martha Henderson, wife of James, owned 15 black slaves; Martha also served as a midwife.

After the death of their parents, several of the children from the James Henry Henderson family moved to Noxubee County, Mississippi. Thomas Jordan Henderson, Penina Henderson Brown, and Loucinthia Henderson Joiner moved to Mississippi. These families eventually also moved to Fayette County and/or Colorado County in Texas together, where they all lived until their deaths.

Hickman, John Pryor-Pond Spring

Major John Pryor Hickman was born on September 9, 1788, in Davidson County, Tennessee. He was the son of Edwin Hickman and Elizabeth Pryor Hickman. John Pryor Hickman married Narcissa Weakley who was born on June 4, 1798, in Davidson County, Tennessee. Narcissa was the daughter of Colonel Robert Weakley Jr. (1764-1845) and Jane Locke Weakley (1769-1838).

Since Major John Pryor Hickman was an important military figure in Tennessee history, there are some letters online that can be found about Hickman's interactions with Andrew Jackson. After problems with authorities in Tennessee, Major Hickman was dismissed from the army about 1813. His dismissal aroused his anger, prompting Hickman to write the President.

Major Hickman's dismissal might explain why he came to Madison County, Alabama, and eventually to Lawrence County to begin a new life. According to the Lawrence County land records, John P. Hickman is noted as being from Madison County. He only stayed in Lawrence County, Alabama, from September 1818 to around 1827 before moving back to Davidson County, Tennessee.

Major John P. Hickman settled in Lawrence County, Alabama, at Hickman's Spring which is now known as Wheeler. From September 10, 1818, through August 13, 1825, John P. Hickman entered some 556 acres of land in Townships 4, 5, 6, South and Range 7 West in Lawrence County, Alabama; two tracts of 316.76 acres were entered with Colonel Benjamin Sherrod. Some of the land Hickman entered was adjacent to the Dixie Plantation of Matthew Clay and later Captain Charles C. Swoope.

According to the Lawrence County Archives records, the Hickman burying ground was the W ½ of the SW ¼ of Section 34, T4S and R7W. Hickman also owned the W ½ of SE ¼ of Section 34, T4S and R7W. John P. and Narcissa Hickman were the original owners of Pond Spring Place that became Pond Spring Plantation. The Pond Spring was located on an old Indian trail known as Upper South River Road. The trail eventually became the Tuscumbia Road and later Highway 20 or alternate Highway 72.

About 1818, John and his black slaves refurbished a one room house of hewn logs; later, a second room and a dogtrot were added. Eventually, several log structures were erected including a dog trot slave cabin. The roofs of the cabins had wooden shingles and board floors with a fireplace at each end.

Hickman dog-trot slave cabin

In the1820 Lawrence County, Alabama Census, the John P. Hickman household had four white males over 21, two white males under 21, three white females over 21, and two white females under 21. According to the 1820 Lawrence County, Alabama Census, John Pryor Hickman owned 56 black slaves.

With the help of his black slaves, John Hickman had the land cleared and planted cotton.

According to the Lawrence County Archives records, John P. Hickman was appointed to build a road to McDaniel's Ferry. In the June 1818-December 1824 records, John P. Hickman was mentioned concerning building a road from the Town of Courtland to the eastern edge of Lawrence County toward Decatur.

Major John Pryor Hickman died on February 4, 1840, in Davidson County, Tennessee. He was buried in the Mount Olivet Cemetery at Nashville in Davidson County, Tennessee (Find a Grave Memorial Number 26618699). Narcissa Weakley Hickman died on January 4, 1849, in Davidson County, Tennessee; in 1947, her remains were moved next to her husband Major John Pryor Hickman in Mt. Olivet Cemetery (Find a Grave Memorial Number 26618653).

Colonel Benjamin Sherrod

In 1827, Colonel Benjamin Sherrod purchased Pond Spring Plantation from Major John Pryor Hickman. With the land purchases and an 1818 land grant, the Pond Spring Plantation of Colonel Sherrod eventually consisted of 1,760 acres. The plantation passed to Felix Sherrod, the son of Colonel Benjamin Sherrod; Felix lived at Pond Spring. The Sherrod family expanded the largest dogtrot log cabin into a clapboard covered Federal style house.

The Pond Spring Plantation passed from Felix Sherrod to his son Benjamin Sherrod, who married Daniella Jones. After the death of the young Benjamin, ownership of Pond Spring passed to his widow Daniella Jones Sherrod; she was the daughter of Colonel Richard Jones. Daniella also inherited the Caldonia Plantation from her parents. The plantations eventually passed to General Joseph "Joe" Wheeler after his marriage to Daniella Jones Sherrod. At one time, the land holdings of Joe Wheeler included some 18,000 acres adjacent to Pond Spring Plantation.

Today in 2019, the 1818 Hickman log cabin, the Sherrod house, and the Joseph Wheeler home still stand. The Alabama Historical Commission owns, protects, and manages the Pond Spring homes of Hickman, Sherrod, and Wheeler.

Hines, William

In the 1820 Lawrence County, Alabama Census, William Hines had one white male over 21, one white male under 21, one white female over 21, three white females under 21. In 1820, William Hines owned 27 black slaves. According to the Lawrence County Archives records, William Hines was the husband of Nancy. In 1819, William Hines was appointed for specific task in building road from Town of Courtland in the direction of the Big Spring in Franklin County, Alabama. Hines was appointed to a road that was to run to the west side of Town Creek in the direction to the Town of Bainbridge in Franklin County until it intersects with the county line.

Hodges, William-Oakville

William Hodges Sr., who served in Revolutionary War, was born about 1753 in Virginia. William first married Elizabeth Kerby of South Carolina; she died 1824 in Monroe County, Alabama. William then married the second time to Sarah Walker, widow of Thomas Thompson. Sarah Walker was a sister to Dr. Tandy W. Walker of Oakville, Alabama. William Hodges died April 18, 1843.

The William Hodges Family was among the first prominent wealthy white settlers who owned black slaves in the Oakville area of Lawrence County, Alabama. Some of the Hodges Family members are buried under large stone crypts on top of the Copena Indian burial mound at the Oakville Indian Mounds Park. William and Elizabeth Hodges had the following children:
1) Colonel Fleming Hodges Sr. was born in1792, and he died in 1827. Fleming Sr. fought in the War of 1812.
2) Colonel William Mason Hodges Jr. was born about 1793, and he died in 1835.
3) John Hodges
4) Moses Hodges
5) Jane Hodges married Jonathan Fuller.
6) Elizabeth Hodges married David Wiget.
7) Frances Hodges married Samuel W. Wallace on April 2, 1818, in Shelby County, Alabama; she was born in 1798 in Warren County, Georgia. In 1840, Frances and Samuel moved from Oakville to Wolf

175

Springs in Lawrence County, Alabama (Find a Grave Memorial Numbers 115159677 and 36549815).

According to Lawrence County Archives records, the family of William Hodges from South Carolina applied for a Revolutionary War Pension, Lawrence County, Alabama Records Number 5090. On August 4, 1851, Samuel W. Wallace, who was administrator of the estate of William Hodges, personally appeared for the deceased before Henry A. Mcgee, Judge Probate Court. The following declaration for benefit of surviving children of said William Hodges to wit: John Hodges, Moses Hodges, Jane Hodges who married Jonathan Fuller, Elizabeth Hodges who married David Wiget, Frances Hodges who married Samuel W. Wallace. The application was made by Samuel W. Wallace in order to obtain benefits of the Act of May 15, 1828.

The pension application stated that William Hodges, a private in the Revolutionary War, served in the state troops and Militia of South Carolina, for upward of two years tours in different direction in Colonel Brandon's Regiment, and in tours not known to declarant. Wife of said William Hodges died in Morgan County, Alabama, several years prior to his death. On August 4, 1851, Samuel W. Wallace of Lawrence County, Alabama, filed the pension application. Daniel Hodges appeared and made oath that he believed William Hodges served in the Revolutionary War. The rejected claim did not mean that William Hodges was not in Revolutionary War, but that conditions of papers did not meet requirements to receive pensions.

Colonel Fleming Hodges, Sr.

According to land records, two sons of William and Elizabeth Kerby Hodges were in Lawrence County by September 9, 1818. Colonel Fleming Hodges Sr., the eldest of two brothers, and Colonel William Mason Hodges Jr., the younger brother, came together to Lawrence County in 1818.

Colonel Fleming Hodges Sr. (1792-1827) first married Elizabeth Martha Johnston of Madison. On January 19, 1816, Fleming married a second time to Martha Looney or Lowery (1797-1869). According to the Morgan County, Alabama, Marriage Records, Fleming Hodges was married to Martha Lowery with no date given. Fleming and Martha had the following known children:

1) Elizabeth Hodges married Benjamin Cooper and moved to Cass County, Texas, during 1850. Benjamin and Elizabeth Cooper had a daughter who married Fleming T. Jones.
2) Eliza Hodges married Lewis Boalt in Lawrence County.
3) Sarah Hodges married Edmund Waddell in Lawrence County.
4) Maria Hodges married Richard Pruitt of Lawrence County, Alabama.
5) Fleming Hodges, Jr. was born on January 2, 1826, in Lawrence County, Alabama, and he died about 1845. He was buried in Old Settlers's Cemetery on the Copena burial mound at Oakville Indian Mounds Park in Lawrence County, Alabama.
6) Asa Hodges
7) William Hodges
8) Martha Hodges
9) Frances Hodges

Colonel Fleming Hodges Sr. first entered land in Madison County, Alabama, prior to entering land in Lawrence County. From September 7, 1809, through December 22, 1810, Fleming entered some 640 acres in Township 3 South and Range 2 West in Madison County, Alabama (Cowart, 1979). On September 9, 1818, Fleming Hodges of Madison County entered some 1,520 acres at Oakville in Township 7 south and Range 6 West in Lawrence County, Alabama (Cowart, 1991).

According to the 1820 Lawrence County, Alabama Census, Fleming Hodges had one white male over 21, two white males under 21, one white female over 21, and four white females under 21 for a total of eight white inhabitants. In 1820, Fleming was reported having 26 black slaves.

According to Chancery Records of Madison County, Alabama, Circuit Court, April 25, 1831, Fall Term, 1836, "William Hodges and Asa Hodges, executors of the last will and testament of Fleming Hodges Sr., deceased, and Martha Hodges, widow of said decedent, late of Lawrence County, Alabama, January 19, 1816. William Howson mortgaged land and slaves to said Fleming Hodges as surety on a note to John Camp which was not recorded until 1820. The slaves were really Mrs. Howson's patrimony. Howson conveyed the SE ¼ of Section 6, Township 4 South, Range 2 West. Fleming Hodges' executory qualified December 24, 1827. The slaves in question were sold to his widow,

Martha Hodges, who has little or no property save them. Bond signed by William Pruitt and William Hodges. William Pruitt is the present husband of Martha, the late widow of Fleming Hodges. An amended bill showing the widow of Fleming Hodges has married William Pruitt, and resides in Lawrence County. Heirs of said decedent as follows: Elizabeth (Hodges) Cooper and husband, Benjamine Cooper. She a daughter of decedent, Lawrence County, Alabama. Asa Hodges, son of decedent, Lawrence County, Alabama. Lewis Boalt, in right of late wife, Eliza (Hodges) Boalt, Lawrence County, Ala. Edmund Waddell in right of late wife Sarah (Hodges) Waddell Lawrence County, Ala. Maria (Hodges) Pruitt and husband Richard Pruitt, she a daughter of decedent of Lawrence County, Alabama. Fleming Hodges, Jr., infant son of decedent, of whom Benjamine Cooper is guardian. William Hodges, infant son of decedent, of whom Martha Pruitt is guardian. Martha Hodges infant daughter of decedent of whom Martha Pruitt is guardian. Frances Hodges, infant daughter of decedent, of whom Martha Pruitt is guardian."

According to the Lawrence County Archives records, Fleming Hodges owned the tracts of land as follows: Section 21, T7S, R7W, N ½ of E ½, NE ¼, S ½ of W ½, E ½ of SE ¼; Section 33, T7S, R7W, NW ¼; Section 22, T6S, R9W, W ½ of NW ¼; Section 18, T7S, R6W, NW ¼ of NW ¼; and Section 13, T7S, R7W, NE ¼. The deceased Fleming Hodges owned 564 acres and Oakville Lot number 12.

Colonel Fleming Hodges was a member of the General Assembly (Senate) in 1819, 1820, and 1821. He died about 1827, and his wife Martha survived him.

After Fleming died, Martha married William Pruitt. On November 28, 1837, William Pruitt sold land to John Nelson Spotswood Jones as follows, "Whereas I, William Pruitt of Lawrence County and State of Alabama, have this day bargained and sold a certain tract or parcel of land containing 114 acres, being land which was laid off as the part or portion of land belonging to Martha Hodges, relict of Fleming Hodges, now wife of William Pruitt, situated in Limestone County, Alabama, adjoining the land of John N. S. Jones in said county on the waters of Beaverdam Creek for the sum of $1,000.00 payable as follows: $500.00 on the 1st of March next and $500.00 twelve months afterward…"

Colonel William Mason Hodges

According to Saunders (1899), Colonel William Mason Hodges Jr. was a member of the House of Representatives in 1828-1829. Colonel William Hodges married Virginia Janet Daugherty around 1814; she was a native of Smith County, Tennessee. Janet Daugherty Hodges died on October 19, 1839; she was buried on the Copena burial mound at Oakville Indian Mounds Park. William Mason and Janet Hodges had five sons and four daughters as follows:

1) Captain William Hodges was a captain of a company organized in Moulton, Alabama. He was in Tennessee before being killed at Fishing Creek in Kentucky.

2) Captain Thomas Pope Hodges was a First Lieutenant in Captain LaFayette Hodges' company of Prairie Mount, Mississippi. Soon after he made captain, Thomas was killed at the Battle of Atlanta in 1864.

3) Colonel Fleming Hodges was born on February 26, 1815, in Smith County, Tennessee. Fleming had considerable talent for trade, and moved to Mississippi. He first married Katherine Whitaker, and after her death, he married a second time to Margaret Crayton on November 15, 1838, at Mt. Hope in Lawrence County, Alabama. Margaret was the daughter of Thomas and Elizabeth (McDaniel) Creighton who was born August 9, 1821, at Courtland in Lawrence County, Alabama. Fleming died July 27, 1893, at Lonoke, Arkansas, and he was buried in Elmwood Cemetery in Shelby County, Tennessee. Fleming's son William (Buck) Hodges was the captain of Company F of the Sixteenth Alabama Regiment, who made so much reputation in the Civil War. He was wounded several times and terribly mangled at the Battle of Chickamauga, and afterwards placed upon the retired list. After the war, he was a member of the Mississippi Legislature and lived at Aberdeen, Mississippi (Saunders, 1899). According to the 1850 Lawrence County, Alabama, United States Census, Fleming Hodges was 34 years old and born in Alabama. Others listed were his wife Margaret, age 28; William, age ten; Thomas P. age seven; James F. age five; Alis a female age three; and, Margaret, age one. In 1850, Fleming Hodges owned six black slaves.

4) James Hodges was born in 1820, and the date of his death is unknown; he married Jane Shackelford and moved to Mississippi.

5) Moses Hodges was born in 1822, and he died in 1886 in Tennessee. On October 10, 1850, he married Abigail Price in Lawrence County, Alabama; they moved to Mississippi.
6) Docia Hodges married a Patterson.
7) Asa M. Hodges, born about 1820, was a lawyer. He was a deputy sheriff to William Reneaum, second sheriff of Lawrence County. Asa eventually moved to Arkansas. In 1860, Asa Hodges owned nine black slaves.
8) Elizabeth Hodges first married a Johnson, and second marriage was to a Townsend.
9) Mary Hodges.

According to the 1830 Lawrence County, Alabama Census, William Hodges owned 11 black slaves. Also listed in his household was one white male under five years old, two white males between 5-10, one white male between 10-15, one white male between 15-20, one white male between 30-40, two white females under 5, one white female between 5-10, one white female between 10-15, and one white female between 30-40.

Colonel William Mason Hodges married a second time to Jane. She was buried in Old Settlers's Cemetery in Lawrence County, Alabama.

Colonel John Hodges

Colonel John Hodges (1748-1819) was probably a brother to Revolutionary War Private William Hodges Sr. John and his wife Sarah Frances Merritt (1779-1871) of Greenville County, South Carolina, had the following children:
1. Fleming Hodges, born in 1805, married Sarah Kimzey. Fleming Hodges died on August 26, 1839, at Oakville in Lawrence County, Alabama (Find a Grave Memorial Number 36549600). According to the Moulton Banner of September 4, 1839, "Died, at his residence, at Oakville, Lawrence County, Alabama, on the 26th August, Fleming Hodges, Sen. in the 34th year of his age. In the death of Mr. Hodges, society has lost one of its most valuable and useful members in the various relations of Husband, Father, Citizen and Friend. He has left a disconsolate wife and three small

children upon the boisterous ocean of life, to sail admidst its tempests unguided and unprotected by him."

2. Charlotte Hodges (1803-1882) married a Hightower.
3. Daniel Merritt Hodges died in Greenville County, South Carolina, in 1883.

Also, other Hodges are listed as black slave owners in Lawrence County, Alabama, and include the following: Henry William Hodges owned 20 slaves in 1830; Nancy Hodges owned 17 slaves in 1840; and Daniel Hodges owned 49 slaves in 1860.

Hodges buried in Lawrence County

Hodges Cemetery
Asa M. Hodges11/13/1816-8/27/1881
Daniel M. Hodges 2/14/1809-5/27/1883
Fannie E. Hodges 4/28/1861-10/11/1867 d/o D.M. & Martha Hodges
Infant son Hodges 3/22/1878 s/o A. M. & M. J. Hodges
Dr. J. P. Hodges 2/24/1850-9/25/1900
Katie I. Hodges10/12/1853-8/8/1886 w/o Dr. J. P. Hodges
Lena R. Hodges 9/10/1863-9/22/1878 d/o DM & Martha Hodges
Martha Pruit Hodges 1/27/1828-6/18/1898 w/o D. M. Hodges, Sr.
Nancy Ann Hodges 1811-3/21/???? d/o William Preuit Hodges
Robert Clinton Hodges 9/14/1896-2/22/1901 s/o TF & Nettie Hodges
Oakville Indian Mound Cemetery
Eliza Hodges 8/20/1818 w/o Daniel M. Hodges
Fleming Hodges 8/26/1839 s/o Col. John & Sarah Hodges of S. C.
Elisa H. Hodges 3/28/1829-10/6/1837 d/o Fleming & Sarah Hodges
Eliza Hodges 9/17/1845 d/o BM & Elvira E. Hodges
Jane Hodges 10/19/1832 w/o Col. Wm. Hodges
Louise Haseltine Hodges 8/5/1839 d/o Fleming & Sarah Hodges
Margaret Hodges 8/9/1821-7/28/1850 w/o Fleming Hodges
William Hodges 3/25/1835
William B. Hodges 3/31/1828-11/5/1859
Masterson Cemetery
William Hodges 1754-4/18/1843, PVT SC Militia, Rev. War
Moulton Memory Gardens

Claudie Hodges 6/19/1900-6/17/1976 w/o Jim Hodges
Jim Hodges 7/29/1899-5/23/1988
Preuit Cemetery #1
F. J. Hodges, 1823-1847 s/o Flemnon & Martha Hodges
W. P. Hodges, 1826-1847 s/o Flemnon & Martha Hodges

Oakville Indian Mounds

Today in 2019, the Oakville Indian Mound Cemetery is protected in the Oakville Indian Mounds Education Center in Lawrence County, Alabama. I, Rickey Butch Walker, was honored to help establish the park which opened to the public in 1995. I retired in 2009 from the Lawrence County Board of Education, after some 35 years with the school system including 24 years with the Indian program as director of Lawrence County Schools' Indian Education Program and Oakville Indian Mounds Park and Museum.

Prior to my retirement, some 120 acres of property containing two ancient Indian mounds were purchased and protected. At one time, the land was part of the Hodges estate that came under the ownership of the late P. B. Lowery and late John Wiley. I helped purchase the property from Joyce Lowery Hames and the late Mr. and Mrs. Travis Clark. In addition, the following things were completed: 8,000 square feet Indian museum and offices, paved roads, festival area with dance arena, amphitheater with stage, picnic pavilions, large maintenance shop, restroom facilities, trees planted, fencing around the property boundary, walking bridges, and underground electrical and water supplies.

Thomas Holland

Thomas Holland was born in Laurens County, South Carolina, about 1793; his parents were Rezin Holland (1764-1802) and Mary Lowe (1759-1836). Rezin and Mary Holland had at least two other children: Jeremiah Holland Sr. (August 22, 1796-August 17, 1840) and Mary Offutt Holland McCrary (September 26, 1798-February 23, 1875).

Thomas married Sarah who was born in North Carolina about 1796. From September 8, 1818, through December 27, 1846, Thomas Holland entered some 803 acres in Township 5 South and Ranges 6, 7 West in Lawrence County,

Alabama. According to the 1820 Lawrence County, Alabama Census, Thomas Holland had one white male over 21 years of age, one white female over 21 years of age, two white females under 21 years of age, and two black slaves.

According to the 1830 Lawrence County, Alabama Census, Thomas Holland had two males under five years old, two males from five to ten years old, one male 30 to 40 years old, one female from five to ten years old, three females ten to 15 years old, one female 30 to 40 years old, and one female 60 to 70 years old. According to the 1830 Lawrence County, Alabama, slave schedule, Thomas Holland owned 15 black slaves.

By 1850, Thomas Holland owned 42 black slaves. According to the 1850 Lawrence County, Alabama Census, household 432, Thomas was listed as being 57 years old born in South Carolina. Also in his household was Sarah a 54-year-old born in North Carolina, Sarah L. a 13-year-old born in Alabama, and William F. a 17-year-old. Living next door in household 433 was Richard Holland a 20-year-old born in Alabama, Mildred a 26-year-old, Thomas A. a two-year-old, and John P. six months old. In 1850, another Thomas Holland lived in household 264; he was a 16-year-old and Jane was 12-year-old.

According to the 1850 Lawrence County, Alabama, Agricultural Census, Thomas Holland owned 950 acres of improved land and 1,190 acres of unimproved land valued at $6,000.00. He owned $1,069.00 worth of farming implements and machinery with $5,000.00 worth of livestock. In the 1860 Lawrence County, Alabama, Slave Schedule, Sarah Holland, Thomas' wife, owned 10 slaves, and his son William F. Holland owned 13 slaves. Since Thomas was not listed in the 1860 records, he probably died between 1850 and 1860.

According to Wikipedia online, "The Thomas Holland House is a historic residence near Hillsboro, Alabama. The house was built around 1836 by Thomas Holland, a South Carolinian who had come to Lawrence County, Alabama, in 1823. Holland began his plantation with 40 acres and built it to over 2100 acres by 1849. The house is a full two-story dogtrot house constructed of logs, one of the only of its type in Alabama. The exterior has since been covered in clapboard, and the breezeway has been finished with vertical boards and a chair rail. Enclosed stairways in each lower room give access to the upper floor; the central room over the dogtrot is only accessible from the eastern room. The house was listed on the Alabama Register of Landmarks and Heritage and the National Register of Historic Places in 1991. The house was destroyed by fire in 1997."

Thomas Holland House

Hopkins, Arthur Francis

Arthur F. Hopkins came to Lawrence County, Alabama, with his friends Matthew Clay and John Moseley. Both Arthur and his wife Pamelia Moseley Hopkins entered land in Lawrence County. On September 8, 1818, Pamelia Moseley Hopkins of Madison County entered 320 acres of land in Section 17 of Township 5 South and Range 6 West in Lawrence County, Alabama. On September 14, 1818, Arthur F. Hopkins of Madison County entered 160 acres of land in Section 36 of Township 4 South and Range 8 West in Lawrence County, Alabama (Cowart, 1991). Both husband and wife entered additional tracts, but these two were the first that they entered in Lawrence County.

According to the 1820 Lawrence County census records, Pamelia Moseley Hopkins owned nine black slaves. In the 1830 and 1840 Lawrence County census records, Arthur F. Hopkins owned 56 and 19 black slaves respectfully.

The following is from the First Families of Lawrence County, Alabama by Donna R. Causey (2011), "Arthur Francis Hopkins was born October 18, 1794, in Virginia, to James and Frances (Carter) Hopkins. He came to Alabama in 1814 after growing up in Virginia and attending several academies in North Carolina and Virginia. Arthur's father, born February 22, 1765, fought in the Revolution.... Judge (Arthur) Hopkins was educated in the common schools, in an Academy at New London, Virginia, an Academy in Caswell County, North Carolina and attended the University of North Carolina, at Chapel Hill, but did not graduate. He studied law with Judge William Leigh of Halifax County, Virginia, and began the practice of law in Huntsville, Madison County, 1816. With the exception of one or two years in St. Louis, Missouri, he practiced his profession entirely in Alabama.

Settling in Huntsville, he also became a successful businessman, and a large landholder, operating plantations in Mississippi and Alabama and ending his career as president of the Mobile and Ohio Railroad. He moved from Huntsville to Lawrence County in January 1819....He was elected to the State Senate from Lawrence County in 1822....In 1825, he returned to Huntsville....He was elected to the State legislature as a representative from Madison County in 1833 and was elected a justice of the supreme court of the state, January 1836. He was elected to the U. S. Senate in 1837, and in the same year was made chief justice of the Alabama supreme court...in 1844...he was again elected to the U. S. Senate...returned to that body in 1847 and 1849.

Arthur moved to Missouri in 1845, and a year later located in Mobile.... He retired from the practice of law in 1856, and in the following year became president of the Mobile and Ohio railroad.... He was a Presbyterian. Married. (1) in 1815, in Bedford County, Virginia, to Pamelia Moseley who died in 1852, daughter of Arthur and Pamelia (Thorpe) Moseley...Bedford County, Virginia...(2) to Mrs. Julia Aan Opie Gordon, who was known as 'the Florence Nightingale of the Confederacy,'...who was buried in Arlington Cemetery....Children, by first marriage:
1. Arthur Moseley Hopkins...married Eliza Bibb daughter of Governor Thomas Bibb...;
2. Marie Malinda Hopkins married Major John James Walker...son of John Walker, first U. S. Senator from Alabama;
3. Louisa Hopkins, m. George P. Blevins...;

4. Cornelia Carter Hopkins married Henry Allen Lowe…cotton merchant…;
5. Augusta Hopkins married Captain John Washington Rice…;
6. Mary Moseley Hopkins m. Major William Barnewall…;
7. Catherine Erskine Hopkins married Colonel Starke H. Oliver…;
8. William Leigh Hopkins…unmarried;
9. six other children who died in infancy or very young;
10. Juliet Butcher by adoption, married General Romaine B. Ayres…

Arthur Francis Hopkins died in Mobile Nov. 10, 1865. He was buried in Magnolia Cemetery in Mobile, Alabama, along with his wives and many children" (Causey, 2011).

Hubbard, David-Kinlock

Major David Hubbard was born in 1792 in Bedford County, Virginia. He was the son of Thomas Mortimer Hubbard (November 26, 1754-July 31, 1841) and Mary Blakely Swann Hubbard (October 17,1756-1838). Major Thomas Hubbard, an officer in the Revolutionary War from Virginia, was the Regimental Quartermaster, First Virginia, from 1777 to May 1778. The following were the children of Thomas and Mary Hubbard:
1. Green Kirk Hubbard (July 7, 1786-1876)
2. David Hubbard (1792-January 20, 1874)
3. Vincent Hubbard
4. Stephen Decatur Hubbard (1800-1844)
5. James Hubbard (1803-1865)
6. Thomas Hubbard Jr.
7. Elizabeth Hubbard Wilson
8. Margaret Hubbard Hewlett
9. Catherine Hubbard Morris (1805-1896)

David Hubbard married Eliza Campbell Hubbard (1788-1841) and Rebecca Stoddert Hubbard (1797-1872). David's children include Dona Hubbard Henderson (1834-1909), Emily Hubbard Young (1838-1901), George C Hubbard (1839-1863).

David Hubbard moved from Virginia to Rutherford County, Tennessee. On November 19, 1813, David Hubbard entered 160 acres in Section 25 of

Township 3 South and Range 1 East in Madison County, Alabama; he paid $16.00 as a down payment which was reverted and returned on November 3, 1828 (Cowart, 1979).

David became a volunteer under General Andrew Jackson and fought the British at the Battle of New Orleans. On December 23, 1814, in a midnight attack on the British, he was a wounded in the hip. He became a prisoner of war of the British until January 8, 1815.

From February 5, 1818, through July 15, 1818, David Hubbard entered 560 acres in Townships 5, 6, 8 South and Ranges 2, 4, 5 West in Morgan (Cotaco) County, Alabama. On July 11, 1818, David and his father Thomas jointly entered 160 acres in Section 28 of Township 5 South and Range 4 West in Morgan County. David's father Thomas died in Morgan County on July 31, 1841.

Prior to his death, Thomas Hubbard filed the following last will and testament: "The State of Alabama, Morgan County, August 18, 1840, I Thomas Hubbard, Senior…Item 1st….I hereby give and bequeath unto Vincent Hubbard, David Hubbard, Stephen Hubbard, and James Hubbard my four son's in equal parts all of my property…Item 2nd. I hereby appoint my son David Hubbard as executor …will by selling all of the property at public sale for cash…pay to Green K. Hubbard, Thomas Hubbard, Elizabeth Wilson, Margaret Hewlett, and Catherine Morris, One Silver Dollar each and nothing more. And the residuum of the proceeds shall be divided…Vincent, David, Stephen and James…I give to Cynthia Calledonia Hubbard my largest bed…I give to Laura Emily Hubbard my remaining bed and furniture...Witness my hand and seal this nineteenth day of August in the year eighteen hundred and forty in the presence of W.C. Roberts, M.K. Murphy and Alexander McCartney. Thomas Hubbard"

Beginning on March 30, 1818, Samuel P. Black and David Hubbard entered 560 acres in Lauderdale County, Alabama. From October 8, 1820, through December 7, 1850, David Hubbard of Cotaco County entered another 400 acres on his own in Lauderdale County (Cowart, 1996). In 1823, David moved to Florence, Alabama, where he practiced law and was elected Solicitor.

David Hubbard spent many of his years as a resident of Lawrence County, Alabama. From September 18, 1818, through January 9, 1859, David Hubbard entered some 3,800 acres across Lawrence County, Alabama (Cowart, 1991). He lived at various times in Courtland, Moulton, Mount Hope, and the famous Kinlock Mill Tract of southwest Lawrence County.

In Lawrence County, Alabama, David Hubbard was a large land holder and owned black slaves for some 40 years. According to the census records, in 1830 and 1840, he had 10 slaves; in 1850, he owned 34 slaves, and in 1860, David owned 31 black slaves.

The following are excerpts about David Hubbard are from Early Settlers of Alabama, by James Edmonds Saunders (1899), "Major Hubbard held his office (Solicitor for the Huntsville circuit) for four years, during that time he moved his family to Moulton, Alabama…in 1827, he commenced a mercantile business…and was elected to the State Senate….In 1829, he moved to

David Hubbard

Courtland….He was a member of the House of Representatives in 1831-32…he was engaged in buying and selling Chickasaw Indian land….In 1839 he was elected to Congress….In 1841, in his canvass for Congress….The next year (1842), Major Hubbard was elected member of the House in the General Assembly, and served in 1843 and also in 1845….In 1849 Major Hubbard…served during the Thirty-first Congress….In 1859 Major Hubbard again became a member….In April, 1859, he was appointed by the Governor a State delegate to the Southern Commercial Convention….When the Confederate Government was formed, Major Hubbard was appointed "Commissioner of Indian Affairs,"….His appointment as Commissioner occurred on the 12th of April, 1861, and on the 25th of the succeeding month the Cherokees seceded from the Union and declared themselves an independent nation…While these operations were progressing, he made his home in Nashville. His losses by the war were considerable. He lived at Spring Hill, Tennessee, near General Ewell (who was a relative), some six or eight years, and died at the house of his son Duncan, in Louisiana, at the age of 82 years."

Major David Hubbard was a black slave owner, planter, merchant, lawyer, land speculator, factory and mill owner, famed orator, politician, veteran of the War of 1812, surveyor with his brother Green K. Hubbard, and cousin to Sam Houston. David and brother Greene Kirk Hubbard worked on the original surveys of Lawrence County, Alabama. On March 16, 1861, Jefferson Davis appointed David Hubbard to the Indian Affairs Commission for the Confederate States of America.

David Hubbard's political career included United States House of Representatives from 1839 to 1841 and 1849 to 1851; Alabama State Senate from 1827 to 1828; Alabama State House of Representatives in 1831, 1842 to 1845, and 1853; and Presidential Elector from Alabama in 1860.

David Hubbard died January 20, 1874, at his son Ducan's home in Pointe Coupee Parish, Louisiana. He is buried in the Trinity Episcopal Churchyard at Rosedale in Iberville Parish, Louisiana (Find a Grave Memorial Number 7203484).

Eliza Campbell Hubbard was born in 1788; she died in 1841 at Courtland in Lawrence County, Alabama. The beloved wife of David Hubbard was buried in the Hubbard Cemetery at Courtland in Lawrence County, Alabama, Plot 1 (Find a Grave Memorial Number 127003157).

From June 15, 1844, through January 8, 1859, David Hubbard entered some 1,280 acres in the Kinlock tract which is within Township 8 South and Range 9 West (Cowart, 1991). The Kinlock Historical District now contains the remaining traces of his mill and mansion which burned in 1933 while being used as a Civilian Conservation Corp Camp and United States Forest Service Headquarters.

Kinlock Historic District

The Lawrence County Historical Commission paid for the historical marker that I, Rickey Butch Walker, originally erected a near Kinlock Spring to commemorate Hubbard's presence in Lawrence County. The following are other important historical sites included in the Kinlock District:

1) PaleoIndian occupation at the Kinlock Rock Shelter;
2) American Indian (Mobile-Nashville Trace) trail known as the Old Buffalo Trail, Cherokee Trail, or Doublehead's Trace, which later became an early white settler route known as Byler's Old Turnpike;
3) Hubbard's Grist Mill site at Kinlock Falls;
4) Hubbard Family Cemetery of the black slaves who worked the Kinlock Tract;
5) 1865 Union Army Campsite of one division of Major General James H. Wilson Cavalry; and,
6) Homesite of the famous half blood Cherokee Indian lady Elizabeth Jane (Aunt Jenny) Bates Brooks Johnston.

Today in 2019, the Kinlock Historical District is protected by the United States Forest Service as a Traditional Cultural Property. I, Rickey Butch Walker, did the paperwork to have the Kinlock Historic District recognized by the Alabama Historical Commission and added to the Alabama Register of Landmarks and Heritage. Because of its historical and cultural importance to Indian people, the Kinlock Rock Shelter is still used for traditional and ceremonial purposes.

Lamar Marshall of the Wild South organization and I wrote the grant for some $65,000.00 for some 26 historical markers including the Kinlock marker to be placed around Lawrence County, Alabama. The grant provided for 80 percent of the funding, and Lamar and I got the Lawrence County Historical Commission to match the 20 percent required to secure the markers. Hoyt Cagle and I wrote the historic marker now at Kinlock Spring. I placed the original sign at the site; however, after it was torn down, the Lawrence County Historic Commission had the sign embedded in a concrete form.

Jarman, Amos

Amos 'Squire' Jarman was born on November 12, 1789, at Trenton in Jones County, North Carolina. He was the son of John Jarman Jr. (1746-November 10,1813) and Nancy Ann Hopkins (1763-1833) of Jones County, North Carolina. John and Nancy Jarman had the following children:
1. Emanuel Jarman (1770-February 5, 1841).
2. Eleanor 'Ellen' Jarman Laney (1780-June 28, 1843).

3. Kezia Jarman (1781-1820).
4. Josiah Jarman (1784-1850).
5. Rachel Jarman (1786-1861)
6. Henry Caleb Jarman (1788-1858).
7. Amos Jarman (November 12, 1789-December 14, 1861).
8. Margaret Peggy Jarman (March 17, 1794-1874).
9. Hall Jarman (1795-1879).
10. Hardy Jarman (August 10, 1795-1827).
11. Hardy Jarman (October 10, 1796-1862).
12. John Jarman (1798-1815).
13. Nancy Anne Jarman (April 25, 1803-1847).
14. Mary Jarman (1805-).

On October 3, 1811, Amos Jarman married Mary Green, and on October 24, 1842, Amos married Mary A. E. Bilbro (1789-1873) in Wilson County, Tennessee. Amos Jarman had the following children:

1. Nathan Jarman (July 11, 1812-June 10, 1813), North Carolina.
2. Eliza Jarman (December 5, 1813-1898), North Carolina.
3. Catherine Jarman (November 15, 1815-December 22, 1850), North Carolina.
4. Henrietta Jarman (June 22, 1817-1884), North Carolina.
5. Isaac Hopkins Jarman (August 16, 1818-1864), Jones, North Carolina.
6. Mary Catherine Jarman (February 8, 1820-June 6, 1858), North Carolina.
7. Amos Green Jarman (June 29, 1822-1895), Alabama.
8. William H Jarman M.D. (August 20, 1824-1904), Alabama.
9. George Washington Lafayette Jarman (May 14, 1826-1898), Leighton, Colbert County, Alabama.
10. Durant Franklin Jarman (September 27, 1827-January 21,1853, in Texas).

Amos is called Squire because he served for many years as the squire or justice of the peace in northwest Alabama. Amos Jarman built his house when he settled in the Brick Community of Lawrence (present-day Colbert) County, Alabama. It is a historic landmark in Alabama because of its age, and because it was one of the original slave-made brick homes in the community. The Brick Community gets its name because of the early brick houses built by black slaves before the Civil War.

Amos Jarmon Plantation Home

In the 1830 Lawrence County, Alabama Census, the Amos Jarman household had three white males: 0-5, one white male 5-10, one white male 10-15, one white male 20-30, one white male 40-50, one white female: 5-10, two white females 10-15, and one white female 40-50. In 1830, Amos Jarman owned 26 black slaves.

According to the Lawrence County Archives records, Jarman Amos was appointed commissioner and overseer of Byler's Turnpike road in 1837. At that time, the Byler Road passed adjacent to the west of the plantation of Amos Jarman along the county line of Lawrence and Franklin.

According to the 1840 Lawrence County, Alabama Census, Amos Jarman household had two white males 10-15, two white males 15-20, one white male

192

50-60, one female 5-10, and one female 50-60. In 1840, Amos Jarman owned 42 black slaves.

In the 1850 Lawrence County, Alabama Slave Census, Amos Jarman owned 50 black slaves. The 1850 Lawrence County, Alabama, United States Census, House Number 217 listed: Amos Jarman, male, 60, North Carolina; Mary Jarman, female, 60, North Carolina; Jos C. Vincent, male, 32, Virginia; Wm. H. Jarman, male, 26, Alabama; and D. F. Jarman, male, 23, Alabama.

According to the Lawrence County Archives records, Amos Jarman owned the following tracts of land: Section 16, T3S, R9W; Section 17, T3S, R9W, SW¼; Section 30, T3S, R9W, NE¼, part (3 acres+); Section 17, T3S, R9W, S½, SW¼; Section 17, T3S, R9W, NW¼ and N½ of SW¼ & W½ of NE¼ NW¼ and N½ of SW¼ and W½ of NE¼; Section 30, T3S, R9W, E½; Section 29, T3S, R9W; Section 20, T3S, R9W, SE¼; Section 19, T3S, R9W, E½ of SE¼; Section 20, T3S, R9W, SE¼ Less 20 acres in NW Corner; Section 20, T3S, R9W, ½ of SW¼ Less 20 acres in NE Corner; Section 30, T3S, R9W, E½ Less 2 acres; Section 30, T3S, R9W, E½; Section 30, T3S, R9W, E½, 2 acres for Baptist Church; and, Section 20, T3S, R9W, SE¼ and E ½ of SW¼.

Amos Jarman died on December 14, 1861, at Brick in Colbert, Alabama. Today, his house is still being used as a residence.

Johnson, John-The Green Onion

Captain John H. Johnson of Virginia was married three times; his wives were Elizabeth Williams, Nancy, and an unknown wife. John Johnson was from Mecklenburg County, Virginia, and lived in Middle Tennessee before coming to North Alabama. On August 3, 1807, Captain John H. Johnson and Nancy leased 1,000 acres from Doublehead in an agreement between John D. Chisholm and the State of Georgia. Chisholm worked for Doublehead and Kattygisky who were the controlling chiefs of the Chickamauga faction of Lower Cherokees at Shoal Town on the Big Muscle Shoals, and they approved the transaction. A few days after Johnson's lease, Doublehead was assassinated on August 9, 1807, and John and Nancy's land claim was eventually revoked.

The 1807 lease of Indian lands by John Johnson was in Doublehead's Reserve near the vicinity of the present-day City of Florence; however, after Doublehead's assassination, his leases to white settlers were revoked, and the Chickasaw Indians wanted them off their land. The Chickasaw petitioned the United States Government to remove all white settlers living without permission on their tribal property. In order to comply with the Chickasaw request, the government built Fort Hampton in 1810, which was established to remove white squatters. All the land leases made by Doublehead and Kattygisky to the area of the Muscle Shoals in northwest Alabama were eventually voided by the United States government.

On September 16 and 18, 1816, both the Cherokees and Chickasaws signed the Turkey Town Treaty giving up their overlapping claims to the land on the south side of the river. The Chickasaws received $120,000.00, and the Cherokees were paid $60,000 for the land which included the present-day counties of Lauderdale, Colbert, Franklin, Limestone, Lawrence, Morgan, and southwest Madison.

After the 1816 Turkey Town Treaty and on the request of General Andrew Jackson, Major Lewis Dillahunty was sent to the North Alabama area by the fifth President of the United States James Monroe to secure the peaceful removal of the Cherokee and Chickasaw Indians on the south side of the Tennessee River. Major Dillahunty was to survey the Indian lands and secure these lands for the United States.

In 1816, Major Lewis Dillahunty and his wife, Lucinda Johnson, who was a daughter of John and Nancy Johnson, moved to North Alabama and settled at Courtland. Lewis and Lucinda Johnson Dillahaunty were the earliest white settlers and the first residents of Courtland, Alabama.

After the land cessions and removal of the Indians, the area was opened to legal white settlement in early 1818. Since their daughter and son-in-law lived in the area, the Johnsons moved to Lawrence County. The Johnsons entered land in 1818 for their farm called The Green Onion Plantation.

John Johnson House-front view
W. N. Manning, 3/8/1934

Since John Johnson was in Alabama just prior to Doublehead's death, his family was familiar with the Town Creek area; these Indian lands were sold during the federal lands sales starting in January of 1818. According to local folklore, Major Dillahunty selected the area at Kittikaska Spring for his father-in-law John H. Johnson's plantation home. Later, according to the Lauderdale County Court Records, Henry Smith purchased a large tract of land from John Johnson in 1826 near the Smithsonia Community.

On September 16, 1818, John Johnson entered 160.02 acres of land in Section 36 of Township 3 South and Range 9 West in Lawrence County, Alabama (Cowart, 1991). On September 16, 1818, he also entered an adjacent 480 acres in

Township 3 South and Range 9 West and entered an additional 280 acres in May 1831, in present-day Colbert County, Alabama (Cowart,1985).

The Green Onion Plantation included the land south of the mouth of the stream Town Creek between the north and south forks of Kittikaski Branch. The Johnson place was north of present-day Second Street and west of the River Road.

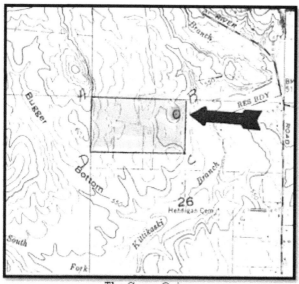

The Green Onion

Originally, all the John Johnson land was part of Lawrence County, Alabama. In 1895, the area of Lawrence County west of Town Creek, north of the Franklin County line, and east of the County Line Road that ran through White Oak, Leighton, and Ford City was annexed into Colbert County.

The Johnson plantation home was about a half mile southwest of the mouth of the Kittiakaska Creek and about 200 yards west of Kittiakaska Spring. According to local folklore, a rope and pulley system was used to pull water from the spring to the house on the hilltop. John H. Johnson built the large brick home just west of the present-day junction of the Foster's Mill Road and the River Road.

In the 1820 Lawrence County, Alabama Census, Lewis Dillahunty household had a male and female over 21, two females under 21, and three black slaves. In 1820, Thomas Dillahunty was listed as having nine black slaves, and in 1830, Harvey Dillahaunty, owned 36 black slaves.

Before 1830, John H. Johnson's daughter Maredian, who was born in Virginia in 1806, married Cordial Faircloth. In the 1820 Census of Lawrence County, Cordial Faircloth household was listed as having one male over 21, one female over 21, two males under 21, and three black slaves. According to the 1850 slave census, Cordial Faircloth had 38 black slaves; the Faircloth Family lived between the River Road and the Tennessee River north of the John H. Johnson place.

According to the 1830 Lawrence County, Alabama Census, John Johnson Sr. owned 22 black slaves. Johnson died in the early 1840s, and his son sold the house and 80 acres out of the family.

John H. Johnson had a son John T. Johnson; however, another John A. Johnson of Colbert County may be a descendant of the Johnson family of the Green Onion Plantation. The 1870 census of Colbert County shows the following: John A. Johnson, age 41, male, white, farm laborer, born in Alabama; Mary, age 30, female, white, keeping house, born in Alabama; Isaac, age 12, male, white, farm laborer, born in Alabama; Thomas, age 10, male, white, at home, born in Alabama; Newton, age 9, male, white, born in Alabama; Joshua, age 8, male, white, born in Alabama; Martha, age 4, female, white, born in Alabama; Lawrance, age 63, female, white, born in Georgia. The 1880 census listed the following John A. Johnson living in Tuscumbia, Mary E., Isaac L., Robert N., Joshua W., and Martha A.

According to the 1850 slave census, the Johnsons of northeast Colbert County had some 20 black slaves. Also in 1850, the agent for The Green Onion was listed as being Thomas Jefferson Foster who at that time had under his control some 95 black slaves.

I interviewed Huston Cobb whose family were slaves of the Johnson plantation. According to his black ancestors, Huston's great, great, grandfather Martin Johnson Sr. was a slave of the Johnson Family. Huston's great grandfather Martin Johnson Jr. was born a slave in 1820.

The Green Onion was a tidewater house built about 1825 on a hill just a hundred yards or so west of Kattygisky's Spring. Kattygisky was a Lower Cherokee who lived at Shoal Town near his spring which was about one mile southwest of the mouth of Town Creek in present-day Colbert County.

John Johnson House-rear view
W. N. Manning, 2/1/1934

On a recent visit to the home, I observed that the walls were some three or more layers of brick thick. The house is in the process of decay and disrepair with the west wall fallen and the back of the house seen in the picture is gone. The site was listed in 1850 slave survey as The Green Onion; today, it is still known by that name. During prohibition, the Green Onion was the site of a bootlegger's alcoholic establishment. The John Johnson House was placed on the National Register of Historic Places on July 9, 1986, and was assigned reference number 86001537.

According to Wikipedia, "The house has been long occupied by tenant farmers, and is now part of the Leonard Preuitt estate. The house is a one and one-half story Tidewater cottage. A single chimney sits in each gable end. The foundation rises 4 feet (1.2 m) above the ground and is laid in common bond, while above is foundation is laid in Flemish bond. The façade is three bays wide, with each door and window topped with a jack arch. Inside, a central hall separates two large rooms on each floor. A staircase in the hall connects the two floors. The house was listed on the Alabama Register of Landmarks and Heritage in 1985 and the National Register of Historic Places in 1986."

Johnson, Colonel Nicholas

Nicholas Johnson was born on August 11, 1768, in Louisa, Virginia. He was the son of Thomas Johnson (1735-1803), a Revolutionary War soldier of Virginia, and Elizabeth Ann Meriwether of Virginia. Prior to moving to Lawrence County, Alabama, he was a wealthy planter of the Broad River settlement in Wilkes County, Georgia. Nicholas Johnson served in Georgia Line during the Revolutionary War and received bounty grant of land for his services.

On January 20, 1791, Nicholas Johnson married Mary Hastings Marks of the Broad River Settlement in Georgia. Mary was the daughter of James Marks (1745-1816), a Revolutionary War soldier of Virginia and his wife Elizabeth Harvie. Nicholas and Mary had the following children:
1) Rebekah Johnson married Charles Jordan.
2) Lucy Thornton Johnson was born on February 26, 1799, and died in 1827. Lucy married John Gilmer.
3) Nancy Johnson was born on February 25, 1792, and she married Reuben Jordan. Nancy died between 1810-1826 at Monticello in Jasper County, Georgia.
4) Frank Johnson died young.
5) Edward Johnson was accidently killed during a deer hunt.
6) Betsy Johnson married Lewis B. Taliaferro.
7) Martha Johnson married George O. Gilmer.
8) Barbara Johnson married a Frazier.
9) Sarah Johnson married Jordan Smith.
10) James Johnson died young.

The Lawrence County plantation of Colonel Johnson was near the West Fork of Flint Creek and was centered along the south end of the present-day Drag Strip Road and Highway 36. The plantation joined the Alexander Plantation to the south, extending east to include the Kelly Place toward present-day Speake Community, west toward Aldridge Grove Community, and north toward the Old Moulton Road.

In the 1820 Lawrence County, Alabama Census, Nicholas Johnson's household had one white male over 21, three white males under 21, one white female over 21, and three white females under 21 with a total of eight white inhabitants. Nicholas Johnson owned 70 black slaves in 1820.

The 1830 Lawrence County, Alabama Census listed the following: males- 10-15: 1, 20-30: 1, 60-70: 1 (Nicholas), females: 40-50: 1. According to the 1830 census, Colonel Nicholas Johnson owned 135 black slaves.

The following is the story of Colonel Nicholas Johnson by James Edmonds Saunders in his book Early Settlers of Alabama (1899). "Colonel Nicholas Johnson was the son of Thomas Johnson, of Louisa County, Virginia, and Ann, daughter of Thomas Merriweather, of Albemarle County, Virginia. He had married in Georgia, Mary, daughter of James Marks, of Broad River. She died in 1815, and in 1819, he immigrated to Lawrence County, and settled on one of the branches of Flint River, some five miles Southeast of Mouton. He was an old man when he came in…Colonel Johnson was the wealthiest man who came into our county, having brought about seventy-five negroes with him….I first saw him in 1827. I was riding with a friend, to hear a debate at Oakville, between Hon. C. C. Clay, and Gabriel Moore, when he prevailed on me to call on Colonel Johnson. We passed through a very large plantation, and entered a plain but large log house. The Colonel was in his cotton field, which we had passed on the way, and observed that although it was the month of June, it had not been worked, and the hog weeds were knee high. At length he came in from the field, dressed in a straw hat, cotton shirt, and pants, and course shoes, without any socks. Nevertheless, he received us with the civility of a friend. He excused himself until he could reform his dress, and when he came in, engaged in pleasant talk, and showed remarkable conversational powers. I alluded playfully to the foul condition of his cotton field. He said, "Call it patch, sir. I plant but few acres for my force; so few that I have never built a gin house, and I never work my cotton until everything else is put in complete order. The fact is, I have a great aversion for cotton." When he heard that I had married a wife from Broad River, in Georgia, he insisted on our paying him a visit, which we did. It was midsummer when we went. We passed first, large peach orchards (always fifty acres in extent) and approached the dwelling through an avenue of 200 nectarine trees loaded with their rich, ripe, delicious fruit…His horses were of the Arabian and

Medley breeds combined. They were allowed to eat little or no corn until they were put to work. They were small, but of fine wind, and great endurance. I purchased three of them at a sale, where 100 horses were sold, and they proved to be remarkably serviceable. His hogs were raised on an excellent plan; they gleaned on his wheat fields; then consumed the oat fields, then the peaches in his enormous orchards; passed through fields of green corn, and were then fat and ready to have their flesh hardened by a short feeding on hard corn. His cows in summer were turned into the range, but brought home and penned, every night, on some poor spot. He had a very large herd….He certainly had a large estate—after his death the sale of his property lasted a week…One thing was apparent, his hogs, sheep, cattle, horses and negroes were all fat. After coming to this county he married, for his second wife, an elderly widow named Ried. Colonel Johnson died about 1832 from cancer in the stomach...Colonel Johnson live in log-cabins, for twenty years after his marriage, in the plainest style….His eldest children were daughters, and when his eldest son, Frank, was born, he was so pleased, that he planted in the fence corners of his extensive fields, a hundred thousand walnuts. According to his account, by the time the infant arrived at manhood, each of the walnuts would be grown to a tree, and worth a dollar, which would make a fortune worth talking about…Mrs. Johnson inherited her father's wit, and her mother's clear understanding…She had seven houses for chickens. A bushel of corn was usually scattered around the yard every morning. They kept forty cows, 500 sheep, and countless hogs" (Saunders, 1899).

According to the Lawrence County Archives records, Colonel Nicholas Johnson owned the tracts of land as follows: Section 17, T3S, R9W, NE¼; Section 20, T7S, R6W, E½, NW¼; Section 1, T7S, R3W, NW¼, NW¼; and Lot 69 in Mouton.

Nicholas Johnson died about 1832, and he is buried in his plantation graveyard on the present-day Dragstrip Road in Lawrence County, Alabama. Colonel Nicholas Johnson is buried on a small hill on his old plantation site within a four feet high limestone walled area. The limestone walled gravesite of Colonel Nicholas Johnson was probably built by his 135 slaves. The stones appear to be manually cut and squared. Adjacent to his burial site are several other graves, a false stone crypt that has been heavily damaged, and only one tombstone that is still readable. His grave is on the west side of the Drag Strip Road about one half mile north of Highway 36.

Colonel Nicholas Johnson
Limestone walled burial site

It is kind of ironic that the big tree in the center of his tomb site is a black walnut. My grandmother Ila Curtis Wilburn who was born of September 1, 1905, told me that when she was a little girl, that Colonel Johnson's black walnut trees with interlocking limbs covered the dirt roadway (now highway 36) for some two miles. She said that you could walk a long section of the road and never get out of the shade of those walnuts! There was a picture of some of the big walnut trees that were cut in the 1920s that were over seven feet in diameter.

Colonel Johnson's plantation had many springs and nearly all show signs of long-term aboriginal camps and villages. One site on his old plantation is still littered with an abundance of broken projectile points. The site is only one and a half miles from the Oakville Indian Mounds Park and Museum.

Jones, Colonel Benjamin B.

Colonel Benjamin B. Jones was born about 1792. In the Lauderdale County, Alabama, land records, he is listed as being from Tennessee. Other records list him as being from Nashville, Tennessee, and an army captain or colonel. His cotton plantation in Lawrence County, Alabama, was adjacent to the Seclusion Plantation that was originally owned by Llwellen Jones, father of John Nelson Spotswood Jones. John N. S. Jones' daughter Maria married James Webb Smith Donnell, who built the Seclusion Plantation Mansion.

On February 13, 1818, Benjamin B. Jones first entered 528 acres of land in Section 5 of Township 3 South and Range 6 West in Limestone County, Alabama. On March 3, 1818, he first entered land in Lauderdale County, Alabama. Then on September 14, 1818, Benjamin first entered 160 acres land in Section 10 of Township 4 South and Range 8 West in Lawrence County, Alabama. On September 16, 1818, he first entered 800 acres in Township 4 South and Range 9 West in present-day Colbert County, Alabama. In the four northwest Alabama counties, Benjamin entered hundreds of acres of land (Cowart, 1985, 1991, 1994, 1996).

In 1818, Benjamin B. Jones was a delegate from Lauderdale County, Alabama, to the Territorial Legislature for which he was paid $242.50. In 1823, he served as a State Representative from Lawrence County, Alabama.

In the 1820 Lawrence County, Alabama Census, Benjamin B. Jones household had two whites males over 21, and two white females under 21. In 1820, Benjamin Jones owned 51 black slaves.

According to the Lawrence County Marriage Records, Benjamin Jones married Martha Marie Haywood Davis on October 3, 1820. Benjamin and Martha Marie Jones had two children, Chamberlain and Flora; Flora Jones married John W. Baker.

From June 1818 through December 1824, Benjamin Jones is listed in four different pages in the Lawrence County Archives records concerning road construction in Lawrence County. He was appointed to one road from Moulton to foot of the Muscle Shoals.

By the 1830 Lawrence County, Alabama Census, there were two Benjamin Jones in the 1830 census. Benjamin Jones household had one white male under 20-30; Benjamin died in March 1830.

In 1834 some four years after the death of Benjamin B. Jones, his widow Martha Marie Davis Jones married Dr. Augustine Burkett Washington in Limestone County, Alabama. Martha Marie Davis Jones Washington died in 1847, and her husband Augustine B. Washington died in 1865 in Arkansas.

According to the Lawrence County Archives records, Colonel Benjamin B. Jones owned the following tracts of land as follows: Section 19, T4S, R8W, NE¼; Section 13, T4S, R9W, E½ of SW¼; Section 31, T4S, R8W, N½ of NE¼; Section 25, T4S, R9W, N½ of NW¼; Section 19, T4S, R8W, S½ of SW¼; Section 30, T4S, R8W, NW¼; Section 19, T4S, R8W, NW¼; Section 25, T4S, R9W, NE¼; Section 13, T4S, R9W, SE¼; Section 30, T4S, R8W, NE¼; Section 19, T4S, R8W, N½ of SW¼; Section 18, T4S, R8W, SE¼; Section 30, T4S, R9W, line between NE¼ & NW¼; Section 24, T4S, R9W, NE¼; Section 23, T4S, R9W, part of NE¼; Section 18, T4S, R8W, E½ of SW¼; Section 24, T4S, R9W, SW¼; 24, T4S, R9W, part of NW¼; Section 30, T4S, R8W, SE¼; Section 24, T4S, R9W, part of SE¼; Section 23, T4S, R9W, part of NE¼; and Section 24, T4S, R9W part of NW¼.

Jones, Littleberry Hardyman-Southdale

Littleberry Hardyman Jones was born about 1774 in Amelia County, Virginia; he was the son of Daniel Jones (1747-1795) and Susannah Stith Hardyman. On September 1, 1798, Littleberry Hardyman Jones married Elizabeth Fitzgerald at Nottoway County, Virginia; Reverend John Cameron conducted their wedding. In January 1811, Littleberry and Elizabeth were in Botetourt County, Virginia, and they conveyed land on West Creek in Nottoway County, Virginia, to his brother George William Jones. Littlebury was a half-brother to Louisa Catherine Jones Fitzgerald who married John Henry Fitzgerald, the half-brother of his wife Elizabeth Fitzgerald Jones. The children of Littlebury Hardyman Jones and Elizabeth Fitzgerald Jones were:
1. Hardyman Fitzgerald Jones was born about 1799.
2. Stith Francis Jones was born about 1801.
3. George Harrison Jones was born about 1804.
4. William Jones was born about 1807.
5. Martha Ann Jones was born about 1812.

6. Robert Fitzgerald Jones was born about March 5, 1820, in Courtland, Alabama.

Littleberry Jones owned the Southdale Plantation in Lawrence County, Alabama. According to the 1820 Lawrence County, Alabama Census, Littlebury Jones had two white males over 21, four white males under 21, one white female over 21, and one white female under 21. In 1820, Littlebury Jones owned 57 black slaves. Littlebury's cotton plantation in Lawrence County was called Southdale. In 1847, William Stuart Bankhead purchased Southdale Plantation from Littleberry H. Jones and renamed it Albemarle.

According to the Lawrence County Archives records from 1835-1840, Littleberry H. Jones, resident of Florida, held the note on the William Banks estate. Littlebury Hardyman Jones died about 1861, and he is buried in Eastern Cemetery at Quincy in Gadsden County, Florida (Find a Grave Memorial Number 179743678).

Jones, Colonel Francis Harwood-Egypt Ford

Francis Harwood Jones was the son of Vinkler Jones who died in Granville County, North Carolina, about 1818. Vinkler was originally from Mecklenburg County, Virginia. In 1774, Vinkler Jones sold to his brother, Tignal Jones Sr. his half of 600 acres in Mecklenburg County, Virginia. The land had been jointly willed to the brothers by their father Matthew Jones.

Francis Jones had a brother John and a sister Nancy Howard Jones; all three were married to the children of Thomas Booth of Mecklenburg County, Virginia. Francis married Nancy Booth, and John married her sister Judith Booth in Mecklenburg County, Virginia. Their sister Nancy Howard Jones married the Booth sister's brother, Harper Booth. The Jones and Booth families of Francis, John, and Nancy moved from Northampton County, North Carolina, to Lawrence County, Alabama, before the 1820 census.

Francis Jones settled near Egypt Ford which crossed Big Nance's Creek west of the present-day International Paper site in Lawrence County. According to the 1820 Lawrence County, Alabama Census, Francis Jones household had one white male over 21, five white males under 21, one white female over 21, two white females under 21 for a total of nine white inhabitants. According to the Lawrence County census, Francis Jones owned 72 black slaves.

According to the Lawrence County Archives records, Frances Jones owned the following tracts of land as follows: Section 5, T4S, R8W, NE¼; Section 32, T3S, R8W, SE¼; Section 4, T7S, R8W, E½ of NE¼; Section 6, T4S, R8W, SW, NW and NE¼; Section 5, T4S, R8W, NE¼; Section 32, T3S, R6W, SE¼; Section 1, T4S, R9W, E½ of NE¼; and Section 6, T4S, R8W, SW¼ and NW¼ and NE¼. Some of this land is near Egypt Ford of Big Nance's Creek or just west of the International Paper Mill site.

Jones, Colonel Richard H.-Caledonia

Colonel Richard Harrison Jones was born on June 29, 1793, in Virginia. He was the son of Harrison and Anne Jones originally of Virginia; his father was a distinguished solider of the Revolutionary War. Richard Jones graduated at the University of Georgia at Athens and served with credit as an officer in the war of 1812.

Richard married Lucy W. Early who was born on October 18, 1799. She was the daughter of the Governor of Georgia Peter Early (1773-1817) and Ann Adams Smith Sherwood (1783-1822). Lucy was the sister of Cynthia Early Swoope (1808-1886), the wife of planter John M. Swoope of Lawrence County, Alabama.

Richard and Lucy moved to Lawrence County, Alabama, from Georgia in 1822. In 1829, Colonel Richard Jones purchased a large tract of cotton land for the Caldonia Plantation which included much of the old Lower Chickamauga Cherokee village site of Melton's Bluff. Caldonia would become one of the largest antebellum cotton plantations in the Tennessee Valley. Jones built his plantation home not far from the townsite of Marathon or Melton's Bluff.

In 1841, Richard and Lucy had one daughter Daniella Ellen (Ella) Jones who was born at Caldonia. In 1859, Daniella Ellen (Ella) Jones first married Benjamin Sherrod, the son of Felix Sherrod and the grandson of Colonel Benjamin Sherrod of Halifax County, North Carolina. Felix eventually passed the Pond Spring Plantation to his son Benjamin.

After Daniella married the young Benjamin, they lived at the Pond Spring Plantation some five miles east of Courtland, Alabama, until Benjamin died. After his untimely death in 1861, Daniella inherited the Pond Spring Plantation, but she moved back to live at her Caldonia Plantation home. In the fall of 1863, she met General Joseph (Joe) Wheeler while he and his troops were camped near the Caldonia homeplace. After the Civil War ended, Daniella and General Joe Wheeler were married in 1866. They moved to New Orleans for four years before they returned to the Pond Spring Plantation where they raised their children. By marriage, Wheeler came in possession of both Caldonia and Pond Spring plantations. Richard's son Thomas Jones was accused with his brother-in-law General Joseph Wheeler of killing a man and wounding his son at the Pond Spring blacksmith shop, but both were exonerated with the influence of Richard Jones.

By 1830, Richard owned 42 black slaves, but was unable to locate the number of his slaves in 1840. According to the 1850 Lawrence County, Alabama, Slave Schedules, Richard Jones owned 82 slaves.

In the 1850 Lawrence County, Alabama Agricultural Census, Richard Jones owned 2,500 acres of land with half improved and half unimproved. His farm was valued at $25,000.00 with his equipment at $1,000.00 and livestock worth $3,500.00.

From the 1860 Lawrence County, Alabama, Slave Schedule, Richard Jones owned 107 black slaves. According to the 1860 Lawrence County,

Alabama, United States Census, Household 563, Richard Jones was a 66-year-old male from Virginia, and Lucy Jones a 40-year-old female born in Alabama. In 1860, the value of his real estate was $27,100.00, and the value of his personal property was $120,000.00.

Colonel Richard Jones died on February 3, 1883, and he was buried in the Swoope-Ussery Cemetery, Courtland, Lawrence County, Alabama (Find a Grave Memorial Number 26622385). His beloved wife Lucy Early Jones died on October 31, 1869, and he was buried by her side.

Jones, Thomas M.

Thomas Morgan Jones was born on October 6, 1820, in Georgia. On August 17, 1865, Thomas married Miley Ann Butler Jones, daughter of Georgia Ann Jones, in Elbert, Georgia. Miley was born on May 1, 1842; she was 22 years younger than Thomas. Thomas and Miley had the following children: Thomas Pierce Jones (November 14, 1866-March 10, 1925), and Georgia Ann Jones Burris (January 7, 1870-August 23, 1895).

According to the 1850 Lawrence County, Alabama Slave Census, Thomas M. Jones owned 60 black slaves. From the Lawrence County, Alabama, Slave Schedules, Northern District, June 1, 1860, by H. A. McGhee, Assistant Marshal, Thomas M. Jones owned 108 black slaves.

In the 1860 Northern Division, Lawrence County, Alabama, United States Census, Household 439, Thomas Jones was a 40-year-old male planter born in Georgia. His real estate value was listed at $26,000.00, and the value of his personal property was $104,700.00. He was the only one in his household in 1860 in Lawrence County, Alabama; he was probably in the process of moving back to his home in Georgia.

Thomas Morgan Jones died on October 20, 1894, at Elberton in Elbert County, Georgia (Find a Grave memorial Number 53444806). Miley died on June 4, 1928, at Elberton in Elbert County, Georgia; she is buried in the Bethel E. Baptist Church Cemetery (Find a Grave memorial Number 53444823).

King, Hartwell Richard

Hartwell Richard King was born on March 1, 1785, in Wake County, North Carolina. Hartwell's parents were Richard and Edith King. Hartwell's father, Richard, died on December 27, 1830. "Earlier in the year, Hartwell and his father traveled to Wake County, North Carolina, to attend to some business. While they were there Richard became ill. He implored Hartwell that if he should die to return his body to his home in his adopted state for burial. Hartwell carried out his father's wishes by preserving the body in a barrel of whiskey for the long journey back to Alabama… Though there is no written record of this event, it is recorded in family oral history handed down through four generations of family. A descendent is also in possession of the nails that were removed from the lid of the barrel" (Bowling, 2005).

Richard died during a return visit to Raleigh, North Carolina. Knowing his widow would want his remains, Hartwell had someone preserve his father Richard in a wooden barrel of whiskey and shipped the results of his corpse back to his Alabama plantation in Lawrence County for proper burial. He was buried in the King Cemetery just west of the banks of Town Creek in present-day Colbert County, Alabama.

Hartwell Richard King married Burchet Curtis on April 24, 1805. Burchet was born on February 10, 1785, Wake County, North Carolina. Burchet's father was John Curtis, Jr., and he died at age 56 in 1816. Her mother was Mary Shaw Curtis; Mary died in 1794 at age 29. Burchet's sisters were:

1) Ann Curtis married Aldridge Myatt on December 12, 1806. Ann Curtis Myatt died July 19, 1840; she was only 48 years old. Aldridge Myatt died on October 8, 1850.
2) Martha Curtis married John Rand on June 19, 1805. Martha Curtis Rand died December 25, 1845, of consumption at age 55. John Rand died in 1863.
3) Mary Curtis married Drury Vinson on December 26, 1811. On May 31, 1862, Drury Vinson died.

Hartwell Richard King and Burchet Curtis King had eleven children. Nine of their children were born in North Carolina prior to their move to Alabama in 1826. Their children were:

1) William Oswald King was born on April 27, 1806, and died in 1882. He married Martha Rebecca Delony (1811-1851) on January 14, 1830. On May 12, 1857, William Oswald married Cynthia Wright (1813-1900).
2) Robert King was born on May 7, 1809, and died on November 25, 1866, at age 57. He married Margaret Peck (1823-1900) on February 14, 1837.
3) Mary Curtis King was born on March 4, 1811, and died in 1860. She married of James Fennel on September 24, 1829. James (1803- July 9, 1848) was a cousin of the Curtis sisters. After James died, Mary moved back to Lawrence County, Alabama. In the 1850 and 1860 Lawrence County, Alabama, Slave Schedules, Mary King Fennel was listed with 38 and 54 slaves, respectifully.
4) Susan King was born on May 5, 1813, and died on April 15, 1866. She married Tignal Jones (1811-1887) on May 28, 1835.
5) Philemon King was born on July 15, 1815, and died in 1878). He married Eliza Jane Madding (1834-1906) on August 21, 1850. Eliza was the daughter of Elisha Madding and Eliza Wren Croom.
6) Martha Burchet King was born on March 31, 1818, and died in 1904. She married Thaddius William Felton (1817-1877) on September 5, 1837. After his death, she remarried her sister Susan's widower, Tignal Jones.
7) Hartwell Richard King Jr. was born on March 5, 1820, and died in 1872. He married Mary Henderson Smith (1828-1898) on March 1, 1848.
8) Paul Hartwell King was born on September 9, 1822, and died in August 29, 1871. He married Mary A. Cummings (1837-October 2, 1870) on June 12, 1856. Her father was A. J. M. Cummins, a militia Major and Baptist preacher.
9) Washington Lafayette King was born on October 1, 1824, and he died in childhood on October 25, 1827.
10) Ann Lafayette King was born on March 11, 1828, and at two months old, she died on May 18, 1828.
11) Ann Lafayette King was born on April 22, 1830, and died in 1902. On June 18, 1851, Ann married Edward Goodwin, son of Colonel John Goodwin of Aberdeen, Mississippi. On September 25, 1863, Edward Goodwin died.

On December 7, 1825, in preparation for their planned move to Alabama, Hartwell and Burchet sold 750 acres of land in Wake County, North Carolina, to John Bell for $3,500.00 (Bowling, 2005). Hartwell Richard (Dick) King was a planter, Justice of the Peace, merchant, charter member of the board of trustees of LaGrange College, and represented Lawrence County in the Alabama legislature until his death. Hartwell had property six miles east of LaGrange, in the Leighton vicinity. At one time, he was said to own some 300 black slaves.

According to the 1850 Lawrence County, Alabama, Slave Schedule, several members of the King Family were owners of black slaves. The Kings listed in this schedule are as follows: Robert, 63 slaves; Philemon, 30 slaves; Paul, 16 slaves; Hartwell Jr., 23 slaves; John A., one slave; Oswald, 50 slaves; and, Burchett, 36 slaves.

"These figures are for the preceding year ending in June 1850…the farm (Hartwell King) as having 400 acres improved and 400 acres unimproved with a value of $10,000. The value of my machinery and implements is $675. I have 6 horses, 6 mules, 8 milk cows, 4 oxen, 30 other cattle, 30 sheep, and 100 swine. The value of livestock $1,305. From June 1, 1849, until June 1, 1850, we produced 40 bushels of wheat, 50 bales of cotton, 50 lbs. of wool, 300 lbs. peas and beans, 100 lbs. Irish potatoes, 400 lbs. butter and 12 bales of hay" (Bowling, 2005).

According to the 1860 Lawrence County, Alabama, Largest Slave Holders, two members of the King family are listed: Robert owned 109 slaves; and Oswald owned 78 slaves.

"1860…agricultural census. Mr. McGee...reported the following: Acres of improved land 400, acres unimproved 230, Value of land $15,750, Value of Machinery $200, Horses 4, Mules 7, Milk Cows 6, Oxen 4, Other Cattle 6, Swine 33, Value of Livestock $1550. Crops produced during the last year ending June 1, Indian Corn 2000 bu., Rye 10 bu., Hay 25 bales, Butter 200 lbs., Cotton 53 bales" (Bowling, 2005).

Hartwell Richard King died on September 3, 1841, at the age of 56. He was buried the King Cemetery (Find a Grave Memorial Number 88379228). His wife Burchet Curtis King died 31 years later on October 23, 1872, in the Leighton area of Lawrence (present-day Colbert) County, Alabama, at the age of 87; she was buried in the King Cemetery (Find a Grave Memorial Number 88376984).

Most of the King family members were buried in the King Cemetery some six miles east of LaGrange, in what was previously Lawrence County. The cemetery is considered by some as one of the larger family cemeteries in northern Alabama.

King, Robert

Robert King was born on May 7, 1809, in Wake County, North Carolina. Robert King was the son of Hartwell Richard King and Burchet Curtis King. He married Margaret Peck King who was born May 15, 1823. Margaret was the only daughter of George Peck (1779-1826) and Celia Fennel Peck (1805-1882) of Peck's Landing at Trinity (originally called Fennel's Turnout), Alabama.

Margaret Peck King's father was George Peck who was one of the first regular merchants in Decatur, Alabama. He was also one of the founders of Decatur, and one of the five business partners of the Decatur Land Trust Company. Martha's grandfather and George's father-in-law, Wylie Fennel, was his business partner in the mercantile trade. Wylie was a wealthy North Alabama cotton planter and slave holder. The Town of Trinity was originally called Fennel's Turnout in honor of Wylie Fennel.

Margaret Peck King's mother Celia Fennel Peck was a sister to James Fennel. Mary Curtis King was the wife of James Fennel, and she was a sister to Margaret's husband Robert King. Along with other business associates, James Fennel helped establish the first railroad west of the Appalachian Mountains. The Tuscumbia to Decatur Railroad made it possible to ship cotton around the three upper Muscle Shoals of North Alabama which were extremely dangerous.

Some five miles upstream of the upper shoals, George Peck owned and operated a boat landing, called Peck's Landing, on an island near the southern bank of the Tennessee River near the Lawrence and Morgan County lines. Originally, members of the Burleson family operated a ferry from the east mouth of Fox's Creek on the Tennessee River in Morgan County to Cow Ford Landing on the north side of the river in Limestone County. It was from Peck's Landing that cotton was sent to Tuscaloosa, Alabama, via Burleson's Trace, the Byler Road, and the Black Warrior River to avoid the very dangerous and hazardous Elk River Shoals, Big Muscle Shoals and Little Muscle Shoals of the Tennessee River.

In early 1820's, Joseph Burleson was authorized by the Alabama legislature to upgrade the Indian trails to a wagon road from the ferry at the mouth of Fox's Creek and near Peck's Landing site to Moulton, then to Byler's Old Turnpike. The road became known as Burleson's Trace, but later was called the Byler Road Fork. Joseph Burleson left Lawrence County in 1834 and moved to Texas where his family became famous in the fight against Mexico and founding of the State of Texas.

Robert and Margaret Peck King had the following children:
1. Celia King McGregor (1838-1900)
2. Mary Ann King Lile (1841-1867)
3. Hartwell King (1848-1860)
4. Robert O. Walter King (1855-1867)

By 1840, Robert King owned 19 black slaves. According to the 1850 Lawrence County, Alabama, Slave Census, Robert King owned 63 slaves.

The 1850 Lawrence County, Alabama, Agricultural Census gives that Robert King owned 1,500 acres of improved land and 900 acres of unimproved land valued at $40,000.00. He also had $670.00 worth of implements and machinery with his livestock valued at $3,720.00.

The 1850 Lawrence County, Alabama Census, Household 162 listed: King Robert, 40-year-old male farmer born in North Carolina; Margarett A., 27-year-old female born in Alabama; Celia, 11-year-old female born in Alabama; Mary, nine-year-old female born in Alabama; G.P., five-year-old male born in Alabama; Bunchell, three-year-old female born in Alabama; and, Hartwell, one-year-old male born in Alabama.

The 1860 Lawrence County, Alabama Census, Household 365 has the following: Robert King 50 M Planter N.C.; Margaret A. 36 F Ala; Mary A. 17 F

Ala; George 15 M Ala; Mittie 13 F Ala; and Robert 5 M Ala." In 1860, Robert's real estate was valued at $80,000, and his personal worth valued at $100,000.00. According to the 1860 Lawrence County, Alabama, Slave Census, Page 171B, Robert King Sr. owned 109 slaves.

Robert King died on November 25, 1866, in Colbert County, Alabama. He was buried in the King Cemetery, Colbert County, Alabama (Find a Grave Memorial Number 88382176). Margaret Peck King died on September 3, 1900, at Trinity in Morgan County, Alabama. She was buried in the King Cemetery in Colbert County, Alabama (Find a Grave Memorial Number 88383688).

King, William Oswald

William Oswald King was the oldest son of Hartwell Richard King (1785-1841) and Burchet Curtis King (1785 1872). He was born on April 27, 1806, in Wake County, North Carolina, and he moved with his family to Lawrence County, Alabama, in the mid 1820's. William Oswald King first married Martha Rebecca Delony (1811-1851) on January 14, 1830, in Madison County, Alabama. Martha was the daughter of Edward Brodnax Walker Delony (1783-1858) and Margaret Bonner Fox (1793-1863). His second marriage to Cynthia Wright (June 28, 1813-September 14, 1900) was on May 12, 1857. Cynthia was the daughter of Williams Wright (1779-1835) and Sally Mitchell (1764-1825).

William Oswald King and Martha Rebecca Delony had the following children: Edward H. King (1830-1851), Robert King (1832-1905), Benjamin Rush King (1834-1918), Burchet Curtis King (1837-1918), Margaret Fox King Hubbard (1838-____), Mary T. King (1844-1848), Phileman E. King (1846-1848).

The 1850 Lawrence County, Alabama Census, household 567, lists William Oswald King as a 44-year-old farmer born in North Carolina with a farm valued at $25,000.00. Also in his house is Martha R. a 39-year-old female born in Virginia, Edward A. a 20-year-old male born in Alabama, Robert an 18-year-old male born in Alabama, B. Bush a 16-year-old male born in Alabama, B. Curtis a 14-year-old male born in Alabama, Margaret F. an 11-year-old female born in Alabama, B. a nine-year-old male born in Alabama, Oswald Jr. a seven-year-old male born in Alabama, and Martha R. a two-year-old female born in Alabama.

According to the 1850 Lawrence County, Alabama, Slave Schedule, William Oswald King owned 50 black slaves. Based on the 1850 Lawrence County, Alabama, Agricultural Census, William Oswald King owned 1,000 acres of improved land and 1,325 acres of unimproved land valued at $25,000.00. He also owned $1,100.00 worth of farm equipment and machinery including livestock valued at $2,955.00.

In the 1860 Lawrence County, Alabama, Largest Slaveholders, Page 169B, William Oswald King owned 78 black slaves.

The 1860 Northern Division, Lawrence County, Alabama, United States Census, William Oswald King was a 54-year-old male born in North Carolina. The 1860 census gives the following: Oswold King M 54 N C, Cynthia King F 48 N C, and Bruce King M 18 Ala.

The 1870 Lawrence County, Alabama, United States Census listed: Oswald King, male, 64, white, North Carolina; and, Cyntha King, female, 56, North Carolina. The 1880 Beat 4 Leighton, Lawrence County, Alabama, United States Census listed the following: Oswald King, male, 74, North Carolina; B. Rush King, son, male, 43, Alabama; Margie Hubbard, daughter, female, 40, Alabama; Billy King, other, male, 22, Alabama; Beckey King, other, female, 22, Alabama; Betsy King, other, female, 2, Alabama; Margie King, other, female, 1, Alabama; Burch King, other, female, 3, Alabama; Cynthia King, wife, female, 68, North Carolina; and George Hubbard, grandson, male, 16, Alabama.

William Oswald King died on August 18, 1882, at Leighton, Lawrence (present-day Colbert) County, Alabama, and he was buried in the King Cemetery (Find a Grave Memorial Number 94477985). His first wife Martha Rebecca Delony King died in October 31, 1851, and his second wife Cynthia Wright King died in 1900. Both of Oswald's wives were buried in the King Cemetery.

Knott, David

David Knott was born in 1762 in Granville, North Carolina; he eventually moved to Tennessee then Lawrence County, Alabama. David Knott was the son of John O. Knott Sr. (1740-1798) and Mary Forsythe (1745-1793). He was a brother of Mary Polly Knott, James Knott, Elizabeth 'Priss' Knott, John O. Knott Jr, Lucy Knott, Martha Patsy Knott, Nancy Ann Knott, Lenn William Knott, Thomas Baxter Knott, and Frances Knott Yancey.

The wife of David Knott was Isabella D. Knott. Based on Lawrence County Archives records, David and Isabella had the following children: David Alex Knott, Mary H. Knott Rutledge, James Archer Knott, Jane M. Knott Rice, John Henry Knott, and Malinda W. Knott Wood.

By 1820, David Knott moved from Tennessee to Lawrence County, Alabama. According to the 1820 Lawrence County, Alabama Census, David Knott household had one white male over 21, one white male under 21, one white female over 21, and three white females under 21. In 1820, David Knott owned 16 black slaves.

From March 16, 1830, through June 30, 1831, David Knott entered 400 acres of land in Township 7 South and Range 6 West near Oakville in Lawrence County, Alabama.

In the 1830 Lawrence County, Alabama Census, David Knott household had one white male under 5, two white males 5-10, one white male 50-60, one white female 10-15, two white females 15-20, and one white female 40-50. In 1830, David Knott was between 50-60 years old and his wife was 40-50 years old.

David Knott died in Lawrence, Alabama, before 1835. After the death of David, his wife Isabella married a Morris. It is not known exactly when David Knott died or where he was buried. For more information on David Knott, look in the records of the Lawrence County Archives.

According to the Lawrence County Archives records, David Knott owned the following tracts of land: Section 5, T7S, R6W, E½ of SE¼; Section 4, T7S, R6W, 70 acres on W side of SW¼; Section 4, T7S, R6W, E 90 acres of SW¼; Section 9, T7S, R6W NW¼; Section 5, T7S, R6W, E½ of SE¼ and 70 acres off W side of E½ of SE¼ and 70 acres off W side of SW¼.

According to the Lawrence County Archives records, John Knott owned the following tracts of land: Section 2, T7S, R6W, E½ of SE¼ & SW¼ of NW¼;

Section 2, T7S, R6W, E½ of SE¼ & SW¼ of NW¼; Section 1, T7S, R6W SW¼ of NW¼; Section 1, T7S, R6W, 40 acres on W side; and, Section 1, T7S, R6W, SW¼ of NW¼.

The Lawrence County Archives records identify members of the David Knott family. Mrs. Isabella D. Knott Morris was the widow of David Knott. The children of David Knott were David Alex Knott, James Archer Knott, Jane M. Knott Rice, John Henry Knott, Mary H. Knott Rutledge, and Matilda (Malinda) W. Knott Wood. Susan Knott was the wife of John Henry Knott.

According to the Lawrence County Archives records from June 1818 through December 1824, David Knott was appointed to find and mark closest and best route for a road from the Town of Moulton to Garner's Ferry on the Tennessee River. Garner's Ferry was originally Brown's Ferry.

Leetch/ Leitch, William

William Leetch and his brother James were born in Ireland and came to America near the end of the 1700's; both were in Mecklenberg, North Carolina by 1790's. James was born between 1778-1785, and he married Amelia Sophia Kennedy in 1810. James moved to Tennessee by 1820, and he died in 1835 in Maury County, Tennessee.

Captain William Leetch of Mecklenburg County, North Carolina, married Naomi Knox, aunt of President James K. Polk. Naomi was born in 1775 in Rowan County, North Carolina, and she died in 1854 in Moulton, Alabama. Naomi Knox Leetch's father was James Knox; he was born in 1752 in Pennsylvania and died in 1794 in Mecklenburg County, North Carolina. Naomi's mother was Lydia Gillespie; she was born in 1754 in Lancaster, Pennsylvania, and died in 1828 in Maury County, Tennessee.

William and Naomi Knox Leetch had the following children: William Leetch Jr., Sarah Leetch, James K. Leetch, Meriah Leetch Hunter, Naomi Sophia Leetch Peters, Joseph A. Leech, and Robert K. Leetch. Their daughter named Naomi Sophia Leetch was born in Lawrence County in 1820, and she died in Moulton in 1880. Naomi Sophia Leetch married Thomas Minott Peters; he was born in 1810 in Clarksville, Tennessee, and died in 1888 in Moulton, Alabama.

Thomas Minott Peters owned five black slaves in 1830, and eight slaves in 1840. Thomas Minott Peters and Naomi Sophia Leetch had the following children:

1) Sarah Naomi Peters was born in 1839 in Moulton, Alabama, and died in 1863 in Moulton, Alabama.
2) William Lemuel Peters was born in 1842 in Moulton, Alabama, and died in 1906 in Senatobia, Mississippi.
3) Martha Leigh Peters was born in 1844 in Moulton, Alabama, and died in Moulton, Alabama.
4) Anna Maria Peters was born in 1846 in Moulton, Alabama.
5) Mary Minott Peters was born in 1850 in Moulton, Alabama.
6) Lucy Alice Peters was born in 1853 in Moulton, Alabama, and died in 1918 in Moulton, Alabama.

William Leetch, an Irishman, first moved to Madison County, Alabama, prior to first entering land in Lawrence County, Alabama, in September 1818. Between 1818 and 1820, William Leetch used his slave labor to construct his home. Between September 11, 1818, and August 10, 1836, William Leetch entered some 1,000 acres in Townships 4, 6, 7 South and Ranges 7, 8, 9 West in Lawrence County, Alabama.

In 1827, when United States President James K. Polk was an ambitious young congressman, he visited his Aunt Naomi Knox Leetch of Lawrence County. William Leetch died in 1837 and willed the house to his daughter. Daniel Hodges purchased the home from the Leetch family. The Hodges family sold the house to Willie Shelton in 1907, and the William Leetch house became known as the Shelton House. The historic Leetch/Shelton House once hosted a future president and served as a temporary hospital for Confederate soldiers during the Civil War.

According to the 1820 Lawrence County, Alabama Census, William Leetch had one white male over 21, three white males under 21, one white female over 21, two white females under 21. In the 1820 Lawrence County, Alabama Census, William Leitch was listed as owning 16 slaves.

In the 1830 Lawrence County, Alabama Census, William Leetch had two white males 20-30, one white male 40-50, one white male 60-70, one white female 10-15, one white female 50-60. According to the 1830 Lawrence County,

Alabama Census, William Leetch owned 21 black slaves. William Leetch was appointed to review road building and timber used to build a causeway from Moulton to Daniel Hodges' Gate with William Brown as the road overseer. According to the 1840 Lawrence County, Alabama Census, Naomi Leetch was between 60-70 years old and had one white male 30-40 living in her house.

According to the Lawrence County Archives records, William Leetch owned the following tracts of land: Section 3, T7S, R7W; Section 4,T7S, R7W NE¼ of SE¼ of NE¼ and SE¼; Section 3, T7S, R7W part of SW¼; Section 2, T7S, R7W SW¼ of SW¼; Section 3, T7S, R7W SE¼; Section 3, T7S, R7W N½; Section 34, T6S, R7W SE¼; and Section 3, T7S, R7W 40 acres in the east part of SW¼. Most of his property was east of Moulton a few miles and south of the Old Moulton Road near his home place.

Lightfoot, Thomas M.

Dr. Thomas M. Lightfoot was born on April 26, 1764, in Virginia. By 1792, Thomas was living in Davidson County, Tennessee. In 1801, Thomas married Sarah Allen in Davidson County, Tennessee. Sarah Allen Lightfoot was born in 1780, and she was the daughter of David Allen who was born in New Jersey in 1758. Thomas migrated to North Carolina where he enlisted in the Revolutionary War from Surry County, North Carolina. On December 21, 1812, Thomas Lightfoot enlisted in the United States Army and fought in the War of 1812.

In 1819, the Thomas and Sarah Lightfoot family migrated to Lawrence County, Alabama. Shortly after arriving in Lawrence County, Thomas Lightfoot and others were appointed to mark out road from Courtland to the Big Spring in Franklin County, Alabama. Thomas and Sarah Allen Lightfoot had the following children:
1. Henry Cole Lightfoot born 1802, married Elizabeth Simmons. In 1830, the Henry Cole Lightfoot household had one male under five, one male 20-30 (Henry), one female under five, and one female 20-30 which was probably his wife. Henry Lightfoot lived next door to Thomas Lightfoot. Henry's son William Lightfoot owned 24 slaves.
2. John Frazier Lightfoot born 1805, married Maleana McKissack.
3. Narcissa W. Lightfoot born 1810, married John Miller.

4. Nancy Ann T. Lightfoot born 1812, married Asa Messenger.
5. Robert W. Lightfoot born 1815, married Adelia Reid.

In the 1820 Lawrence County, Alabama Census, Thomas Lightfoot owned 17 black slaves. Living in his house was one white male over 21, four white males under 21, one white female over 21, and three white females under 21 for a total of nine white inhabitants.

In the 1830 Lawrence County, Alabama Census, Thomas Lightfoot owned 22 slaves. Living in his house was two males 15-20 years old, one male 60-70 years old (Thomas), one female 5-10 years old, one female, 10-15 years old, one female 15-20 years old, and one female 40-50 years old.

According to the Lawrence County Archives records, Thomas Lightfoot owned the following tracts of land: Section 17, T3S, R8W, E½; and Section 17, T3S, R8W, W½. Thomas M. Lightfoot died on February 11, 1831. He was buried in Lightfoot-Porter Cemetery or Westmoreland Cemetery located on the property of W. J. (Bill) Lee near Wheeler Dam Village in Lawrence County, Alabama (Find a Grave Memorial Number 111832673).

John Frazier Lightfoot

John Frazier Lightfoot was the son of Thomas and Sarah Lightfoot. He came to Alabama with his parents in 1819. John served in the Alabama Militia. In 1830, John F. Lightfoot was the only one in his house, and he was listed as having one male 20-30 years. According to the Lawrence County Archives records, John F. Lightfoot owned a tract of land in Section 29, T3S, R8W, N½ of E½ of NW¼.

John married Melanie J. McKissach, daughter of Archibald McKissach of Tennessee. John Frazier Lightfoot and Melanie McKissach Lightfoot had the following children:
1) Captain Thomas Lightfoot, the eldest, was born July 20, 1834, in Pulaski, Tennessee. His first marriage in 1856 was to Mattie Tweedy of Lawrence County, Alabama. His second marriage in 1879 was to Mary Maxey of Savoy, Texas, and they had four children. Thomas served as a captain in the Confederate army under General Sterling

Price, and when the war ended, he settled in Fannin County, Texas. Thomas died on February 15, 1895, and Mary Maxey Lightfoot died in 1910. Thomas and Mary were buried at Paris in Lamar County, Texas.

2) Henry William Lightfoot (1846-1901) of Paris in Lamar County, Texas, was a power of attorney.

3) Lucy Lightfoot, born in 1851 at Myrtle Grove, came to live in Mulberry at the residence in 1897. In Nashville, Tennessee, on March 28, 1872, she had married Thomas Jefferson Moore.

In the 1840 Lawrence County, Alabama Census, John F. Lightfoot had five white males with the oldest 30-40 and four white females with the oldest 20-30. According to the 1850 Lawrence County, Alabama, United States Census, House Number 274, John H. Lightfoot is listed as a 44-year-old white male, born in Tennessee. Others in the household are as follows: Malene J. Wright, female, 37, Tennessee; Thomas Lightfoot, male, 15, Tennessee; Sarah A. Lightfoot, female, 14, Alabama; A. M. Lightfoot, male, 12, Alabama; John F. Lightfoot, male, 9, Alabama; James M. Lightfoot, male, 7, Alabama; W. H. Lightfoot, male, 3, Alabama; Oval M. Lightfoot, male, 1, Alabama; Richard Miller, male, 19, Alabama; Manuel Miller, male, 17, Alabama; Philip Miller, male, 14, Alabama; Martha Miller, female, 12, Alabama; and, Jonathan Gelson, male, 22, Alabama.

According to the 1850 Lawrence County, Alabama, Slave Schedules, John F. Lightfoot owned 58 slaves, and Robert M. Lightfoot owned 14 slaves. Melanie, the wife John Frazier Lightfoot, was the executor of his estate. After he died, Melanie married James A. Patterson sometime after 1853. By December 1857, James and Melanie settled in Fannin County, Texas, where she died in 1862.

Madding, Captain Elisha

Captain Elisha Madding was born on May 31, 1783, in Pittsylvania County, Virginia. Elisha was the son of Thomas Madding and Rachel Dodson. His siblings were Allis Madding, Thomas Madding, Raleigh Madding, Albert Madding, Robert Madding, Wilmont Madding, Mary "Polly" Madding, Elizabeth Madding, and Rawley Madding.

Elisha Madding married Elizabeth Marie Wren Croom, daughter of Dr. Richard Croom, on November 11, 1827, in Lawrence County, Alabama. They had the following children:

1. Richard Thomas Madding (1829-1862).
2. Mary Ann Madding was born on July 10, 1828, and she married Charles Augustine Toney Jr. She died on November 17, 1907 (Find a Grave Memorial Number 94765453).
3. James Allen Madding (1832-1880)
4. Eliza Jane Madding married Philemon King in Lawrence County, Alabama on August 21, 1850;
5. Isaac Croom Madding (1838-1863);
6. Edwin Price Madding (1841-1852);
7. Camilla Wilmont Madding married Alexander Donelson Coffee.

According to the 1850 Lawrence County, Alabama, Slave Schedule, Elisha Madding owned 62 black slaves. In the 1850 Lawrence County, Alabama, Agricultural Census, Elisha had 800 acres of improved land and 300 acres of unimproved land. The cash value of his farm was $10,000.00 with $400.00 worth of machinery and implements plus $1,620.00 of livestock.

In the 1850 Lawrence County, Alabama Census, Household 187, Elisha Madding was a 66-year-old farmer born in Virginia. Also in his house was Eliza M. a 42-year-old female born in North Carolina, Rich a 21year old male born in Alabama, James A. an 18-year-old male student born in Alabama, Franklin a 16-year-old male born in Alabama, J.H. a 12-year-old male born in Alabama, E.P. a nine-year-old male born in Alabama, and Carmella a seven-year-old female born in Alabama.

According to the 1860 Northern Division, Lawrence County, Alabama, Slave Schedule done on June 1, 1860, by H. A. McGhee Asst. Marshall, Eliza Madding, the wife of Elisha, owned 30 black slaves.

Elisha served in the War of 1812, and he was in the 5th Regiment of the Tennessee Militia; Elisha became a Captain in the 7th Regiment. Elisha Madding died on December 4, 1852. He was buried in the Madding Cemetery at Leighton in Colbert County, Alabama.

Martin, Joseph

Joseph Martin was from Georgia, and he married a sister of his neighbor George Walton. Joseph Martin and his neighbor George Walton left Georgia together, and they settled in Lawrence County some seven miles northwest of Courtland, Alabama. Some of the children of Joseph Martin and the sister of George Walton are:

1) Neaty or Nealy Martin Gallagher who was identified in the Lawrence County Archives as the daughter of Joseph Martin.
2) Walton Martin, son of Joseph Martin died in the epidemic of 1824; Walton Martin was probably named in honor of his Uncle George Walton.
3) Rachel Martin, sister to Walton, married Abraham Battle. Abraham and Rachel lived on the place occupied by their son-in-law John H. Houston. Rachel died in 1873, and her husband preceded her in death.

In the 1820 Lawrence County, Alabama Census, Joseph Martin household had two white males over 21, three white males under 21, one white female over 21, four white females under 21. In 1820, Joseph Martin owned 23 black slaves. Also, in 1820, Joseph Martin's brother-in-law George Walton owned 20 black slaves.

The 1830 Lawrence County, Alabama Census listed the household of Joseph Martin: one white male 15-20, one white male 20-30, one white male 60-70 (Joseph Martin), and one white female 40-50. In 1830, Joseph Martin owned 27 black slaves. Also, in 1830, George Walton owned 44 black slaves. In the census, Joseph was listed on microfilm page 295, and George was listed on microfilm page 293.

On September 14, 1818, both Joseph Martin and George Walton first entered land in Lawrence County, Alabama; they were brothers-in-law and slave holders. On the same date, Joseph Martin and George Walton each entered 320 acres of land in Township 4 South and Range 8 West. Joseph entered another 480 acres from November 27, 1830, through August 29, 1837. George entered another 395 acres from March 20, 1830, through January 19, 1835 (Cowart, 1991). These entries are verified by the Lawrence County Archives records.

Another person by the name of Joseph E. Martin came into Lawrence County prior to the 1830 Census, and evidence showed that many people confused Joseph E. Martin with the slave holding Joseph Martin who died before 1838. Census records did not show Joseph E. Martin as owning any slaves; he moved to Arkansas and died in 1863. The 1830 Lawrence County, Alabama Census listed Joseph Martin as being between 60 and 70 years old, and the Joseph E. Martin was between 30 and 40 years old.

According to the Lawrence County Archives records, Joseph Martin owned the following tracts of land as follows: Section 24, T6S, R6W, SE¼ of NE¼; Section Section 2, T4S, R8W, part of NE¼; Section 2, T4S, R8W, NW¼; Section 29, T3S, R8W, W½ of E½ of NW¼; Section 33, T3S, R8W, E½ of NE¼; Section 34, T3S, R8W, W½ of SE¼; Section 34, T3S, R8W, NW¼; Section 34, T3S, R8W, SW¼; Section 34, T3S, R8W, E½ of SE¼; Section 29, T3S, R8W, N½ of E½ of NW¼; Section 33, T3S, R8W, E½ of NE¼; Section 34, T3S, R8W, E½ of SE¼; Section 34, T3S, R8W, W½ of SE¼; Section 34, T3S, R8W, SW¼; and Section 34, T3S, R8W, NW¼. Some of this land is south of Red Bank near Egypt Ford of Big Nance's Creek and a few miles west of the International Paper Mill site.

McDonald, Colonel William A.

On July 6, 1851, William McDonald married Laura Matilda Bynum in Lawrence County, Alabama. Laura Matilda Bynum was the daughter of Junius Bynum and Margaret Josephine Saunders Taylor of Courtland. Laura Matilda Bynum was born on December 17, 1833, which matches the 1860 census record.

According to the 1850 Lawrence County, Alabama, United States Census, Household 559, William A. McDonald was a 23-year-old male farmer who was born in Alabama; therefore, he was born about 1827. On December 2, 1850, the 1850 Lawrence County, Alabama, Slave Schedule listed William A. McDonald as owning 52 black slaves. In 1850, William A. McDonald had $410.00 worth of farming equipment and $1,280.00 worth of livestock.

The 1860 Lawrence County, Alabama, United States Census, Northern District, Household 92 gives William McDonald as a 32-year-old male born in Alabama, Matilda McDonald a 26-year-old female born in Louisiana, William

McDonald a seven-year-old male born in Alabama, Wade McDonald a one-year-old male born in Alabama, and James Hughes a 49-year-old male born in Virginia is listed as his overseer. William A. McDonald was located between the wealthy planters Samuel Shackelford in household number 86 and John Swoope in household number 102; both had a personal property value over $100,000.00.

In 1860, William McDonald had a real estate value of $6,920.00 and a personal property value of $55,000.00. According to the 1860 Lawrence County, Alabama, Slave Schedule, William and Matilda McDonald owned 58 black slaves.

Laura Matilda Bynum Tabb McDonald first married Thomas Bolling Tabb, and then she married Colonel William A. McDonald; she died July 29, 1879, at age 45. Her mother Josephine died on June 25, 1879. The following is found in Footprints in Time (1993) by Myra Borden: "Thursday, July 7, 1879, Mrs. Josephine Bynum died at the residence of Colonel William McDonald of Courtland, on the 25th instant." The Bynum family and McDonald family were connected through marriage. Oakley H. Bynum married Effie L. McDonald (12/9/1822-5/23/1894) and Colonel William A. McDonald (born about 1827) married the niece of Oakley H. Bynum.

McMahon, John Jordan

Even though John Jordan McMahon was not a slave owner, he and his family benefitted greatly by the cotton produced by slave labor. In 1860, his father-in-law Jack Shackelford and his brother-in-law Samuel Shackelford owned 43 and 86 black slaves, respectively.

In 1828, John Jordan McMahon settled at Courtland in Lawrence County, Alabama, and entered a business partnership with Andrew Bierne, a fellow Virginian gentleman. John managed the Courtland branch of the Huntsville cotton mercantile firm of Bierne and McMahon. John quickly made a fortune dealing in the slave produced cotton of the Tennessee Valley planters. John McMahon spent many years in New Orleans as a cotton broker, leaving his family in Courtland.

John Jordan McMahon was born on October 22, 1805, in Harrisonburg, Virginia. John's parents were Colonel William McMahon, born in Augusta County, Virginia, and Rebecca Bibb Patton (b. 1783); they were married in 1802. After their son John got settled in Courtland, his parents came to Lawrence County, Alabama, to be near him. About 1838, they settled on a plantation not far from Courtland. All of William and Rebecca's children were born in Rockingham County, Virginia:

1. John Jordan McMahon,
2. William P. McMahon,
3. Charles J. McMahon,
4. Mary E. McMahon,
5. Robert Grattan McMahon,
6. Asher Waterman McMahon,
7. Maria Rebecca McMahon, and
8. Ethelbert S. McMahon.

According to land records, John Jordan McMahon migrated from Virginia to the Tennessee Valley of Alabama in the 1818. On July 6, 1818, John entered 165.87 acres of land in Section 30 of Township 5 South and Range 1 West in Morgan County, Alabama (Cowart, 1981). On September 28, 1818, he first entered 160 acres of land in Section 12 of Township 7 South and Range 8 West in Lawrence County, Alabama. From September 28, 1818, through November 26, 1852, John J. McMahon entered an additional 400 acres in Townships 5, 6 South and Ranges 6, 7, 8 West in Lawrence County, Alabama (Cowart, 1991).

On August 20, 1835, John J. McMahon married Harriet Catherine Shackelford, the daughter a local physician Dr. Jack Shackelford. Harriet Shackelford was born on November 16, 1812. John and Harriet had the following children:

1. Fortunatus Shackelford (Nate) McMahon was born in 1836.
2. William Jackson McMahon was born in 1839.
3. Robert B. McMahon was born in 1845.
4. Lillie McMahon was born in 1850.

John J. McMahon's home in Lawrence County was placed on the National Register of Historic Places on October 27, 1987. According to the register, "The McMahon House is a two-story...house is constructed in brick...Built circa 1828...John Jordan McMahon is the earliest documented owner...After the war, Dr. Fortunatus McMahon returned to Courtland and set up practice. A nameplate inscribed "Doctor McMahon" is still on the north door of the McMahon House...The house was...donated to the Alabama Historical Commission in 1987 and listed on the National Register of Historic Places in the same year.

The McMahon house is one of the oldest brick dwellings still surviving in

McMahon House

North Alabama, and it is one of only six two-story brick dwellings south of the Tennessee River believed to pre-date 1830. It is estimated that less than 50 Federal-style brick dwellings survive throughout the state. The significance of the McMahon House is seen in the sophisticated Federal-style interior woodwork which is virtually unchanged since its construction. This includes the staircase, six mantelpieces and built-in cupboards."

John Jordan McMahon died on June 2, 1857, in New Orleans, Louisiana. Harriet Catherine Shackelford McMahon, the wife of John Jordan McMahon, died in 1902.

Moseley, William Finnell Sr.

In September 1818, members of the Moseley family came to North Alabama, with family and friends. Based on land records of Madison and Lawrence Counties, the Moseleys came to Alabama with the families of Matthew Clay and Arthur F. Hopkins, and they settled on adjoining land.

From February 2, 1818, through February 4, 1818, Clement C. Clay, Arthur F. Hopkins, John Moseley, Thomas and William Moseley entered land in Madison County, Alabama (Cowart, 1979). From September 8, 1818, through September 14, 1818, Matthew Clay of Madison County, Arthur F. Hopkins of Madison County, Pamelia Moseley of Madison County, John F. Moseley of Madison County, William F. Moseley, and Thomas B. Moseley of Bedford County, Tennessee, entered land in Lawrence County, Alabama (Cowart, 1991). Most of the land they entered was adjacent to each other.

The Moseleys were probably brothers and sister or cousins. In the 1820 Lawrence County, Alabama Census, William F. Moseley owned 11 black slaves, John Moseley owned 18 black slaves, John F. Mosely owned 14 slaves, Permelia Moseley Hopkins owned 9 slaves, and Robert Moseley owned 10 slaves. In the 1830 Lawrence County, Alabama Census, William F. Moseley owned 29 slaves, John F. Moseley owned 28 slaves, and Robert G. Moseley owned seven slaves.

William Finnell Moseley was born about 1785 in Amelia County, Virginia; he died about 1832 at Wheeler in Lawrence County, Alabama. William married Jane Merrico about 1812, and Unity Hughes Pamplin about 1815. William's parents were John Moseley and Anna Finney. William F. Moseley Sr. had the following children:
1. William F. Moseley Jr. was born about 1813.
2. John Merrico Moseley
3. George Moseley
4. Dr. Robert Goode Moseley was born about 1820 in Lawrence County, Alabama; he married Mary Macon.
5. Thomas A. Moseley was born about 1823 in Lawrence County, Alabama.
6. Elizabeth Williamson Moseley was born on April 8, 1824, in Lawrence County, Alabama; she died on October 14, 1867, at Huntsville in Walker

County, Texas. On September 16, 1840, Elizabeth married John McCaw Smith at Macon in Noxubee County, Mississippi. They had the following children: Robert McCaw Smith, Edward Baker Smith, Virginia Smith, Mary Kate Smith, and Unity Smith.

7. Virginia Moseley was born about 1825 in Lawrence County, Alabama; she married James M. Maxey.
8. Malinda Moseley was born about 1826 in Lawrence County, Alabama.
9. Catherine Moseley was born in 1831 in Lawrence County, Alabama.

William F. Moseley Jr.

In the 1850 Lawrence County, Alabama, Slave Schedules, William F. Moseley owned 11 slaves. In 1860, William F. Moseley owned 33 slaves.

According to the 1860 Northern Division, Lawrence County, Alabama, United States Census: William F. Moseley was a 46-year-old white male born in Virginia; Sarah E. Moseley was a 12-year-old female born in Alabama; and, L. B. McCrary was a 22-year-old male born in Alabama.

John Moseley

According to the Lawrence County Archives records, the following tracts of land were owned by the Mosely family: John Moseley owned Section 19, T5S, R6W, SE¼; John F. Moseley owned Section 23, T3S, R8W, NW; Robert G. Moseley owned Courtland Lots 221, 222, 223, 224, 268, 271, 272, 273, and 274; the former residence of the deceased William F. Moseley was Section 17, T4S, R7W, SE¼, and he also owned Section 17, T4S, R7W, SW¼.

According to the Lawrence County Archives records, Circuit Court records of 1831, John Moseley was listed as an heir of Matthew Clay. Elizabeth Moseley was listed as a wife of John Moseley. Mary E. F. Moseley was also listed as the wife of John F. Moseley. Elizabeth and Mary E. F. may be the same person, and John and John F. may be the same person. In the 1838-1841 records, John F. Moseley had a bill due to the Hamlin Eppes estate.

In the Lawrence County Archives records from June 3, 1818, through December 1824, John Moseley was one of the men the court appointed to mark out and build road to Cox's Ferry (Brown's Ferry) from the north boundary line of the Widow Moseley's land. In 1827, another road was authorized from Hickman's Spring (Pond Spring) to Moulton. Another road from Hickman's Spring (Pond Spring) north to Cox's Ferry (Brown's Ferry) was assigned to Pleasant Mosely, Thomas Hart, Thomas Ashford, John J. Ormond, executive, and W. Lynn, administrator.

Napier, Dr. John Smith

Dr. John Smith Napier was born on December 23, 1807, in Pittsylvania County, Virginia. His father was John Meredith Napier who was born about 1773 in Virginia, and his mother was Sarah "Sally" Smith of Maury County, Tennessee. John Napier married Mary Ann Curtis Matt, daughter of Ann Curtis and Aldridge Matt, on October 20, 1833, at LaGrange, Alabama. Mary Ann was born on August 17, 1817, in North Carolina. John and Mary had the following children born in Alabama:
1. Mary Ann Curtis Napier Stephenson (1835-1903).
2. James Myatt Napier (1837-1893).
3. John Smith Napier (1841-1914).
4. Sarah Araminta "Sallie" Napier Kinnard (1844-1911).
5. William Samuel Napier (1849-1914).
6. Ernest Vinson Napier (1854-1937).
7. M. Ella Napier (1858-   ).

In 1840 Lawrence County, Alabama Census, the John Smith Napier household had one male under 5 years old, one male 20-30 years old, one male 30-40 years old, one female under 5 years old, and one female 20-30 years old. In 1840, John S. Napier owned 32 black slaves. In 1847, Dr. John S. Napier built his home near Leighton on land originally owned by his father-in-law Aldridge Matt.

According to the 1848 Tax Assessment, John Smith Napier of Lawrence County, Alabama, had five black slaves less than 10 years old: Johnson, Nathan, Susan, Francis, and Henry; six slaves between 10-20 years old-Tennessee, Andrew, Emily, Cynthia, Judia, and Clark; three slaves between 20-30 years old-Henry, Moses, and Charles; and, three slaves between

30-40 years old-Chaney, Becky, York; two slaves between 40-50 years old-Aaron and Isaac; and two slaves 50-60 years old-Peggy and Simon.

In the 1850 Lawrence County, Alabama, United States Census, Household 166, listed the following: Dr. John S. Napier, a 42-year old-planter, born in Virginia; Mary C., a 32-year-old born in North Carolina; Mary M.E., a 15-year-old; James M., a 12-year-old; John S. Jr., a nine-year-old; Sarah A., a six-year-old; and, William, a one-year-old. According to the 1850 Lawrence County, Alabama, Slave Schedules of the Seventh District, enumerated by A. N. Faris, Assistant Marshal, John Smith Napier owned 25 black slaves.

In 1851, John S. Napier sold his home and land W. Richard Preuit, who developed the property into a large cotton plantation known as Preuit Oaks. Napier then moved to Franklin (Colbert) County as evidenced by the following 1856 Lawrence County Commissioners Court document. "An election was held for the purpose of electing a member of this court to fill the vacancy occasioned by John S. Napier removed to Franklin County where as Edward R. Stanley was duly elected a Commissioner of Roads and Revenue for Lawrence County, Alabama, to fill said vacancy." By 1860, he was again enumerated in census records as living in Lawrence County.

In the 1860 Courtland, Lawrence County, Alabama, United States Census, John Smith Napier was a 52-year-old planter born in Virginia. Also in his household was Mary C. a 41-year-old female born in North Carolina, J.M. a 22-year-old male planter, J.S. a 19 year ols male, S.A. a 16-year-old female, Wm. S. a ten-year-old male, E.V. a six-year-old male, M.E. a two-year-old female, and Mariah Hunter a 21-year-old female born in Tennessee.

The 1860 Lawrence County census listed John Smith Napier's real estate valued at $60,000.00 and personal estate valued at $80,000.00. The 1860 Lawrence County, Alabama, Slave Schedules stated that John Smith Napier owned 64 black slaves.

According to the 1870 Waco, McLennan County, Texas, United States Census, Household 302, John Napier was a 62-year-old retired farmer born in Tennessee. Also in his household was Mary a 52-year-old born in North

Carolina, Ernest a 15-year-old born in Alabama, Ella a 12-year-old born in Alabama, and Louisa a 14-year-old domestic servant born in Texas.

Find A Grave records for Dr. John Smith Napier stated, "During his childhood his family moved to Tennessee and finally to Alabama. Napier attended Princeton College in Kentucky with a concentration in the field of medicine. Afterwards he settled in Colbert County, Alabama, and became a member of the Resident Board of Directors of La Grange Military Academy in La Grange, Alabama. A well know and extensive planter, Napier owned a 30,000-acre plantation in Colbert County near the present day town of Mussel Shoals. Because of the deterioration of his plantation after the Civil War, Napier moved to Waco in May of 1868 and bought a small brick house on South 4th Street from H.S. Morgan. Now known as the Earle Napier Kinard House, the building is essentially as the Napiers constructed it."

According to the Waco Graver, "The Day, 1889, Saturday, December 14; Dr. John S. Napier died yesterday at the residence of his son-in-law, Amos DuBois; aged 81. He was born in Southern Virginia, December 21, 1807. Studied medicine at Princeton College, Kentucky. Settled in Waco Jan. 27, 1870. His children: Mrs. J. C. Stephenson, J. M. Napier, John S. Napier Jr., Mrs. D. C. Kinnard, W. S. Napier, E. G. Napier, Mrs. Amos DuBose. The widow was in Alabama on a visit. Funeral tomorrow from the DuBose residence on South 9th, J. A. McKamy officiating. Tueday, Dececember 17: The funeral for Dr. J. S. Napier was Sunday, with burial at Oakwood; Masonic rites." According to the Waco Graver article, it was obvious that Dr. Napier married a second time, since his wife Mary Curtis Matt Napier died in 1872; therefore, she could not be in Alabama on a visit.

232

Dr. Napier's wife Mary Curtis Matt Napier died on April 28, 1872, at Waco in McLennan County, Texas (Find a Grave Memorial Number 116986329. Dr. John Smith Napier died on December 13, 1889, at Waco in McLennan County, Texas. He was buried in Oakwood Cemetery at Waco in McLennan County, Texas, Plot: Block 11, Lot 62 (Find a Grave Memorial Number 9925490).

Norment, Nathaniel Ellis

Nathaniel Ellis Norment was born on March 14, 1783, in Virginia; he was the son of Samuel Norment of Caroline County, Virginia, and Elizabeth Crenshaw. Nathaniel E. Norment was married three time. His first marriage was to Amelia Bridges on October 27, 1803, in Caroline County, Virginia. The children of Nathaniel and Amelia were Richard Norment and Nathaniel Ellis Norment, Jr.

The second marriage of Nathaniel E. Norment was to Susannah Anderson Burrus, daughter of Charles and Mary Burrus. On March 24, 1822, Susannah Burrus Norment died. She was listed as being buried in Rocky Hill Cemetery in Lawrence County, Alabama. The children of Nathaniel and Susannah Burrus Norment were as follows:
1. Nancy Ellis Norment was born on May 14, 1808; she married John Elgin and died on August 26, 1831(Find a Grave Memorial Number 28421620).
2. Mary Ann Norment
3. Thomas Butler Norment
4. Sarah Burrus Norment was born in Virginia on May 31, 1818. Sarah first married Robert Lewis Wood on March 2, 1835. Her second marriage was to George W. Wilkerson on October 20, 1843. Her third marriage was to C. W. Henry on December 10, 1851. Sarah died on December 12, 1857, and she was buried in Norment Cemetery in Hardeman County, Tennessee (Find a Grave Memorial Number 29321966).

The third marriage of Nathaniel E. Norment was to Sarah Menefee. The children of Nathaniel and Sarah Menefee Norment were the following:
1. John Samuel Norment was born on January 31, 1828, and he died in 1911 (Find a Grave Memorial Number 23263834).

2. William Menefee Norment was born on September 21, 1829, and he died March 20, 1924 (Find a Grave Memorial Number 22333291).
3. Frances E. Norment was born on November 23, 1831, and she died on May 5, 1838 (Find a Grave Memorial Number 23507848).
4. Ellis R. Norment

In the 1820 Lawrence County, Alabama Census the Nathaniel Norment household had one white male over 21, two white males under 21, one white female over 21, and three white females under 21. In 1820, Nathaniel Norment owned 19 black slaves. The 1830 census of Hardeman County, Tennessee, had Nathaniel E. Norment, Sr. as a resident.

Nathaniel Ellis Norment died on July 1, 1839, and he was buried in Norment Cemetery at Whiteville in Hardeman County, Tennessee. His tombstone inscription said, "Sacred To the Memory of N. E. Norment, Born 14 Mar 1783, Died 1 July 1839. An honest man, a Patriot and a Christian" (Find a Grave Memorial Number 22333225). Most of his children are buried in the Norment Cemetery in Hardeman County, Tennessee.

Petway, Hinchey

Hinchey Petway Sr. was born in Virginia on September 23, 1776. He left Sussex County, Virginia, and arrived at Nashville in Davidson County, Tennessee, about 1803. On October 23, 1807, Hinchey Petway married Susannah Caroline Parrish (1789-1858) in Williamson County, Tennessee; they had nine children.

Hinchey Petway was listed in Davidson County, Tennessee, in 1812 and 1830 through 1850 censuses. On September 16, 1818, Petway Hinchey entered 320 acres of land in the NW¼ and SW¼ of Section 23 of Township 4 South and Range 9 West in Lawrence County, Alabama. The land was later assigned to William Dearing. In 1820, Hinchey was in Lawrence County, Alabama, with 27 slaves and no family members. Based on court records, he left Lawrence County in 1828.

Hinchey Petway Sr. died on September 12, 1856, in Tennessee. He was buried in Mount Olivet Cemetery at Nashville in Davidson County, Tennessee, Plot: Section 1, (Find A Grave Memorial Number 129045002).

Preuit/Pruett/Prewitt, Captain Jacob

According to Life and Legend of Lawrence County by Dorothy Gentry (1962), "Two brothers, William and Henry Preuit, who came from Scotland and settled in Virginia, have descendants in Lawrence County who lived in the old Preuit house…"

According to Early Settlers of Alabama (1899), "The Prewitt…family were among the earliest settlers of our county. The eldest of the Prewitts…came from Clinch River in East Tennessee. He settled his family in Madison County, Alabama…His sons, James and Jacob, came to Lawrence County…James…removed to another State. Jacob purchased a place (farther south) from John McKinney…"

Jacob Preuit was born about 1765 in Rowan County, North Carolina; he was the son of William Preuit (1714-1817) and Mary Elizabeth Martin (1722-1812). Jacob Preuit was a private in the American Revolutionary War and a captain with the Tennessee Mounted Volunteers during the War of 1812.

On March 12, 1786, Jacob Preuit married Nancy Agnes Richey in Greene County, Tennessee. Nancy Agnes Richey, daughter of Thomas Richey and Elizabeth Davis, was born about 1766 in Virginia. Jacob and Nancy had the following children:
1) William Madison Preuit was born on December 22, 1786, in Greene County, Tennessee, and died on July 5, 1841, at Moulton in Lawrence County, Alabama. He first married Sally Cavitt, and then married Martha Patsy Looney (1797-6/1/1869).
2) Margaret Peggy Preuit was born on October 16, 1788, and died October 15, 1855. She married John Hellums (1782-1852).
3) Mary Ann Preuit was born about 1788, and she died August 15, 1855, at Jeddo in Bastrop County, Texas. She married R. H. Hallmark (1785-January 30, 1854) on September 14, 1807.
4) Elizabeth Preuit was born about 1791; she married Isaac Lee.

5) Nancy W. Preuit (1798-1837) married John Welch Preuit, a first cousin.
6) James M. Preuit (1798) married Mariah Carter.
7) Rebecca Preuit (1799) married Levy Roden.
8) John Preuit was born on March 10, 1803, and died on August 4, 1894, in Texas. He married Martha 'Mattie' H. Hart (6/6/1808-5/20/1842) on November 22, 1827.
9) Lavina Preuit (1805) married A. J. Underwood.
10) Tabitha Preuit (1811) married Levy Warren

Original Preuit House built before 1815

Captain Jacob Preuit had owned land in at least two states and three north Alabama counties. About 1807, he moved with his family to Madison County, Mississippi Territory, which is now Alabama. He lived there before the land sales of 1809. From September 18, 1809, through November 14, 1810, Jacob Preuit entered land in Townships 1, 3 South and Range 1 East in Madison County, Alabama (Cowart, 1979).

In 1818, Jacob Preuit moved to Lawrence County where he became quite prosperous. From September 15, 1818, through October 12, 1818, Jacob Preuit entered 403 acres in Township 7 South and Ranges 7, 8 West in Lawrence County, Alabama (Cowart, 1991).

The Lawrence County home that Jacob lived in was described by Dorothy Gentry (1962) as follows: "The house was built in 1815 and torn down the first part of February 1959 for a new residence. The original house was a log structure and consisted of two rooms, separated by a "dog-trot" and was built by Robert Price (In 1820, Robert owned 44 black slaves.), who came to Moulton from Virginia and obtained the original land grant from the government."

In the 1820 Lawrence County, Alabama Census, the Jacob Preuit household had one white male over 21, two white males under 21, one white female over 21, and three white females under 21. In 1820, Jacob Preuit owned 28 black slaves.

In 1824, Captain Jacob Preuit bought a tract of land from John McKinney on the Byler Road northeast of what is now Haleyville and near New Prospect Church. He and his slaves constructed a two-story poplar log dwelling for himself and wife Nancy, and nearby built a log two story tavern on the Byler Road. On December 16, 1819, Captain John Byler was authorized by the Alabama legislature at Huntsville to make the old the Indian trail wider and free of stumps. The old route was originally known as the Old Buffalo Trail, Cherokee Trail, or Doublehead's Trace. John Byler was buried at Rock Springs Cemetery at Mt. Hope in Lawrence County, Alabama.

The Preuit tavern was a rest stop for people traveling the Byler Road, which was a land route connecting the Tennessee River with the Warrior River at Tuscaloosa. According to Early Settlers of Alabama (1899), "The old gentleman, hale and hardy, still active and past 80, when chasing a bear, his horse fell in a pine hole and threw him on the pomel of his saddle which caused his death three days later."

Captain Jacob Preuit died May 14, 1845 (Find a Grave Memorial Number 55727304), and Nancy Agnes Richey Preuit died May 14, 1850, in Marion County, Alabama (Find a Grave Memorial Number 81589130). They are buried at New Prospect Baptist Church Cemetery at Haleyville in Winston County, Alabama. Captain Preuit died after falling from his horse while chasing a bear.

William Madison Preuit

According to Dorothy Gentry (1962), "The history of the Preuit family as far as records can be found, dates back to 1687, Henrico County, Virginia…William Madison Preuit, who married Sallie Cavitt…came to Lawrence County from Madison County and bought the Preuit farm in 1825 from the Price family."

William Madison Preuit was born on December 22, 1786, in Greene County, Tennessee. He was the oldest son of Captain Jacob Preuit and Nancy Agnes Richey. William Madison Preuit and Sally Cavitt (April 3, 1782-August 30, 1830) were married 25 years and had 11 children: William C. Preuit, Ruthy Preuit, William Richard Preuit, Nancy Ann Preuit, Polly Ann Preuit, Jacob Madison Preuit, James Alexander Preuit, Betsy Ann Preuit, Orleans Preuit, Moses Preuit, and John T. Preuit.

After the death of Sally, William M. Preuit married Martha Patsie Looney (1796-June 1, 1869). William and Martha had the following children: Richard H. Preuit, John William Preuit, Thomas G. Blewit Preuit, and Sarah Jane Preuit.

According to Early Settlers of Alabama (1899), "William came from Madison County at the same time with his father, and improved a place Southeast of Moulton about five miles. He, too, was born in Tennessee. He was a prosperous planter, and purchased the plantation belonging to the Price estate, which was one of the finest in the Southern end of the county. His first wife was Nancy (Sally) Cavit of Madison County. By this marriage he had two sons, Jacob and Richard. Jacob moved to Texas…William Prewit married for his second wife

238

the widow of Fleming Hodges, Sr., and died at the age of 56 years....The eldest (son), Robert,... one son named Talbot....The remaining son is John W. Prewit, who lives on the Price place, where his father died. He is a first rate planter, and is now the largest taxpayer in Lawrence County."

According to the Lawrence County, Alabama, census records, William Madison Preuit owned six black slaves in 1820. The census showed that he owned 25 in 1830. By 1840, William Madison Preuit owned 63 black slaves.

According to Life and Legend of Lawrence County by Dorothy Gentry (1962), "In 1825, the house was acquired by William Preuit, who had moved from Madison County. Mr. Preuit remodeled the house with wood siding, ceilings and four room addition which included two upstairs rooms and two behind the original log structure. The house was unharmed by soldiers during the Civil War, and evidence that Yankee troops did pass nearby can be seen by the fact that three Union soldiers were buried on the farm by slaves who found the bodies shortly after the troops passed through on a retreat through the area.

One story handed down in the family related that all the meat in the smokehouse was hauled to the family graveyard about one and a half miles behind the house. A small brick house had been built around the grave of the body of William Preuit and this became the hiding place for the family meat until military troops left the area.

The chimney brick, made by slave labor, is believed to have been made in 1815 at the same time brick was made for the old Bass place on Penitentiary Gap. The mantle in the house was whittled with a pocketknife by Finis and Walter Bass' grandfather."

William Madison Preuit died on July 5, 1841, and he was buried in Preuit Cemetery Number 1 in Lawrence County, Alabama (Find a Grave Memorial Number 73767488).

Ward and John Preuit at Preuit Home 1959

239

William Richard Preuit-Preuit Oaks

William Richard Preuit was born on September 19, 1808; he was the son of William Madison Pruitt (1786-1841) and Sally Jane Cavett Pruitt (1782-1830). William Richard Preuitt married Mariah Hodges (1812-1875). The tombstone of Mariah Hodges Preuit has not been found, and she was not mentioned in the 1870 census as living in the house of Richard Preuit.

According to Early Settlers of Alabama (1899), "Richard lives near Leighton….When I first knew him he lived on a plantation five miles Northeast of Moulton, well stocked with slaves and mules…he was seized with the ambition of being the largest planter in the county, and I think he became so, for he had some 1500 acres in cotton when, unluckily, the war broke out, and he was crippled in his estate." After the Civil War, the holdings of Richard Preuit declined to only 400 acres upon his death in 1882.

In 1851, William Richard Preuit bought the home of Dr. John Smith Napier who built the house in 1847. Richard called his plantation Preuit Oaks, and he accumulated some 2,500 acres of land with over 200 black slaves. His Preuit Oaks Plantation was east of Leighton on Cottontown Road and was originally in Lawrence County, Alabama. In 1892, the area was annexed from Lawrence County into present-day Colbert County.

According to the 1850 Lawrence County, Alabama, United States Census, Richard Preuit was a 41-year-old male planter born in Alabama, and worth $15,000.00. Also in his household was Mariah a 38-year-old female born in Alabama, Valentine a 20-year-old male planter born in Alabama, William an 18-year-old male born in Alabama, and Sarah a 15-year-old female born in Alabama.

According to the 1850 Lawrence County, Alabama, Agricultural Census, Richard Preuit owned 1,050 acres of improved land and 370 acres of unimproved land valued at $15,000.00. His farm equipment was valued at $1,500.00, and his livestock was worth $3,350.00. In the 1850 District 7, Lawrence County, Alabama, Slave Schedules, Richard Preuit owned 91 black slaves.

According to the 1860 Lawrence County, Alabama, United States, Census, Household 167, Richard Preuit was a 50-year-old male planter born in Alabama. Others listed included Mariah a 48-year-old female born in Alabama, William V. a five-year-old male born in Alabama, Frank Bates a 30-year-old male born in Tennessee, Eliza Bates a 26-year-old female born in Alabama, and Fannie Bates a six month old female born in Alabama.

According to the 1860 United States Census, Richard Preuit had real estate valued at $106,000.00 and his personal property valued at $120,000.00. On June 1, 1860, Northern District, Lawrence County, Alabama, Slave Schedules, Assistant Marshall H. A. McGhee surveyed the Preuit Oaks Plantation. At that time, W. Richard Preuit owned 207 black slaves.

According to the 1870 Lawrence County, Alabama, United States Census, several Preuit households were mentioned which included mulatto and black families which were probably former slaves of Richard Prewit. In household 179, Richard Prewit was a 60-year-old white male farmer born in Alabama. Also, in the household was Josevine a 22-year-old female born in Alabama, Sallie a three-year-old female born in Alabama, Rich Bates an 11-year-old white male born in Alabama. Richard's real estate value was $12,350.00, and his personal property value was $1,750.00.

The following are the 1870 Mulatto or Black families listed in the census: Household 180-Prewit, Jourdan, 50, male, black, farmer, Alabama; Mina, 42, female, black, South Carolina: Riley, 19, male, black, Alabama; and Lizzia, 13, female, black, Alabama. Household 182-Prewit, Ab, 18, male, mulatto, Alabama; and Mullins, Martha, 38, female, mulatto, Alabama. Household 183-Prewit, Frank, 23, male, black, farmer, Alabama; Laura, 19, female, mulatto, Alabama, and Matilda, two, female, mulatto, Alabama. Household 184-Prewit, Sydney, 27, male, black, farmer, Alabama; Milia, 22, female, black, Alabama; Mothen, four, male, black, Alabama; and George, two, male, black, Alabama. Household 185-Bates, Andrew, 30, male, black, farmer, Alabama; Anna, 26, female, black, Alabama; and Julia, three, female, black, Alabama. Household 186-Prewit, Mart, 25, male, black, Alabama; Cindarilla, 23, female, black, Alabama; and John, six, male, black, Alabama. Household 187-Prewit, Samuel, 37, male, black, farmer, Alabama; and Cindrilla, 34, female, black.

The Preuit Oaks plantation house on Cotton Town Road near Leighton, Alabama, was added to the National Register of Historic Places on May 8, 1986,

and the Alabama Register of Landmarks and Heritage on November 26, 1978. The home has a Greek Revival architectural style and was built in 1847. The plantation house was a one and a half story structure with a gable roof and two dormer windows on the front. The house has a center hall plan with two rooms on either side. A one-story addition projects from the rear of the house. In addition to the house, Preuit Oaks has 14 buildings constructed between 1850 and 1890, including an office, kitchen, cook's house, corn cribs, barn, gin house, tenant house, smokehouse, and blacksmith shop. A family cemetery is also located on the property.

Richard Preuit died on November 23, 1882. He was buried in the Preuit Cemetery near Leighton in present-day Colbert County, Alabama (Find a Grave Memorial Number 66021108).

John William Preuit

John William Preuit was born on August 8, 1834; he was the son of William Madison Preuit and Martha Patsie Looney. He married Martha 'Mattie' E. McDaniel who was born on August 13, 1839. John William and Martha McDaniel Preuit had the following children: Cora Anne W. Preuit Cartwright (1859-1939), Travis L. Preuit (1860-1892), Vastia A. Preuit (1862-1867), Clebe P. Preuit (1871-1932), and Minnie M. Preuit Simms (1878-1902).

John William Preuit was the grandson of Jacob. John William Preuit lived in the original home of Robert Price. Price built the first log dwelling in 1815 which was three years before the first white settlers were allowed to legally own land in Cherokee territory; therefore, he was probably related to the Cherokee people through marriage.

The home that John William Preuit and Martha McDaniel lived in was located at the intersection of two Indian trails-Coosa Path and Old Chickasaw Trail. The Coosa Path continued through Moulton and on to Tuscumbia Landing while the Chickasaw Trail led to Russell's Settlement (Russellville) in Franklin County and then to Cotton Gin Port on the Tombigbee River.

In 1830, John William Preuit owned 20 black slaves. In 1840, John and Martha McDaniel Preuit owned 65 slaves. In 1850, John and Martha owned 54 black slaves.

John William Preuit died on August 19, 1923, and he was buried in the Preuit Cemetery Number 1 in Lawrence County, Alabama, behind his family's original home (Find a Grave Memorial Number 135447919). Martha 'Mattie' E. McDaniel Preuit died on September 20, 1907, and she was buried next to her husband John William Preuit (Find a Grave Memorial Number 135447978).

Old Preuit Homeplace

Today in 2019, I, Rickey Butch Walker, own and live on the old Preuit home site in Lawrence County, Alabama; one of the Preuit Cemeteries is in my back yard. My home is probably the fourth house that has stood on the site of the homes of the original Preuits who came to Lawrence County, Alabama. My home is about 150 yards east of a huge spring that flows out of a limestone outcropping. Based on the aboriginal artifacts that I have found in my garden and yard, the habitation of the site dates to the early archaic period. I found a beautiful Decatur projectile point about 50 feet from my house, and several archaic points have been found in the surrounding area. In my garden, I found a piece of galena about three inches long and two inches square. Although most of the surrounding area of the Preuit farm is now in cattle pastures with row crops including cotton to the east and west. The remains of the old Preuit cotton gin was destroyed by the same tornado that destroyed my original home on February 6, 2008.

Price, Robert

Robert Price was born on April 25, 1779, in Henrico County, Virginia; his father was Charles Price. In 1806, Robert married Frances Smith Chappell in Charlotte County, Virginia; Frances was born on December 24, 1792, in Virginia. Robert Price was a Revolutionary War patriot in Virginia.

On September 6, 1818, Charles Price entered 160 acres in Section 2 of Township 3 South and Range 2 West in Madison County, Alabama. On September 18, 1809, both Charles and William Price each entered 160 acres in Township 3 South and Range 2 West in Madison County, Alabama. On October 4, 1809, William Price entered 160 acres in Section 2 of Township 3 South and Range 2 West in Madison County, Alabama (Cowart, 1979). Therefore, based on land records, the Price family was in Madison County, Alabama, by 1809.

After he moved with his family from Buckingham County, Virginia, to Lawrence County, Alabama, Robert Price died in 1821 at the home he constructed some three miles southeast of Moulton. After his death, Frances married Reverend Thomas Strain and moved to Morgan County, Alabama.

The following excerpt is from Early Settlers of Alabama by James E. Saunders (1899). "Charles Price…lived near Richmond, Virginia. He had only two sons. The eldest, Robert, came to Alabama, and William, went to Missouri…Robert Price was married in 1806, in Charlotte County, Virginia, to Frances S., daughter of Reverend John Campbell, a local preacher of the Methodist Church. The ceremony was performed by Reverend Alexander Sale…Robert Price sent out some of his hands to Lawrence County in 1819, and he followed with his family in 1820. He brought with him from Virginia six children; another was born in Alabama, but lived only a few years.
1. Edwin S. Price…married Mildred, daughter of Robert Wood, of West Tennessee….Edwin S…was married a second time to Mrs. Jane Redd, of Brownsville, Tennessee, in 1845, and died in 1853.
2. William H. Price…was married to Elizabeth, daughter of William Dixon, near Florence Alabama in 1831, and moved to Franklin County, and died in 1866…William H…was married a second time to Mrs. Catharine Peters (of Texas).

3. Robert J. Price…first married to Martha A., daughter of Major James Moore, near Aberdeen, Mississippi. He moved to Fayette and thence to Lawrence County, Alabama, where he died in 1841…Robert, was married a second time to Mrs. Elizabeth Douglas.
4. John C. Price…married Margaret, daughter of Colonel William Hodges…was married a second time to Miss McCarty of Columbus, Mississippi, and died two months afterward.
5. Dr. Charles Wesley Price (1817-1883)…in Morgan County, Alabama. He married Mary F. Moore, a sister of his brother Robert's wife.
6. Mary Ann E. Price Neville (1819-1851).
7. Joseph Price (1821-1822)" (Saunders, 1899)."

According to the 1820 Lawrence County, Alabama Census, the Robert Price household had one white male over 21 (Robert), five white males under 21 (William, Robert, John, Charles, and Joseph), one white female over 21 (Frances), and one white female under 21 (Mary Ann). In 1820, Robert Price owned 44 black slaves.

According to the Lawrence County Commissioner's Court Minutes, June 1818 through December 1824, Robert Price was one of the men appointed by the court to help establish a road in Lawrence County from Lamb's Ferry to intersect the road running from Courtland to Big Spring.

Robert Price died on August 17, 1821, and he was buried in Preuit Cemetery Number 1 in Lawrence County, Alabama, (Find a Grave Memorial Number 123679407). Frances Smith Chappell Price Strain died on December 21, 1848; she was buried in the Price Cemetery at Priceville in Morgan County, Alabama (Find a Grave Memorial Number 29612354).

Reynolds John

John Reynolds was the son of Pryor Reynolds Sr. Pryor was born on September 30, 1783, in Henry County, Virginia; he was the son of George Reynolds (1750-1813) and Susannah Lansford. On May 11, 1809, Pryor married Prudence Morehead (1792-1860) in Virginia; she was the daughter of John Morehead and Obedience Motley. Pryor and Prudence had 10 children.
1. George Reynolds

2. John Morehead Reynolds (1810-1860)
3. Susan Morehead Reynolds Winston (1813-1898)
4. James Turner Reynolds (1816-1904)
5. Thomas Edwin Reynolds (1819-1872)
6. Martha Edwin Reynolds (1821-1824)
7. Pryor Reynolds (1824-1896)
8. Annie Gray Reynolds (1828-1906)
9. Samuel Morehead Reynolds (1830-1862)
10. Mary Scales Reynolds (1833-1905) married Madison M. Millner.

Pryor Reynolds and his family moved to Tennessee in 1809, living in Williamson County until 1819. John Reynolds, the son of Pryor, owned some land in Tennessee. The family then moved to Lawrence County, Alabama, where Pryor lived until 1827.

Pryor Reynolds moved to Rockingham County, North Carolina, in the neighborhood of where he was reared. Pryor Reynolds died on October 5, 1858, and he was buried in the Reynolds Family Cemetery at Eden in Rockingham County, North Carolina (Find A Grave Memorial Number 26184214).

The 1820 Lawrence County, Alabama Census listed the following Reynolds slave owners: John Reynolds owned four black slaves; Mason Reynolds owned 21 black slaves; Pryor Reynolds owned three black slaves; and William Reynolds owned one black slave. In the 1830 census, John Reynolds owned 17 black slaves.

According to the Lawrence County Archives records, John Reynolds owned the following tracts of land: Section 17, T6S, R8W, W½ of SE¼; Section 17, T6S, R8W, N½ of E½ of SE¼; Section 17, T6S, R8W, W½ of SE¼; Section 17, T6S, R8W, N½ of E½ of SE¼; Section 17, T6S, R8W, N½ of E½ of SE¼; and, Section 17, T6S, R8W, W½ of SE¼.

Other Reynolds were listed as follows: James Reynolds owned Section 31, T6S, R8W, N½ of W½ of SE¼; Leland Reynolds owned Section 26, T7S, R9W, SW¼; and Mearcellus L. Reynolds owned Section 22, T7S, R9W, E½ of NE¼.

The Lawrence County Archives records identified some of the children of John Reynolds as follows: Elizabeth Reynolds Tubb; John Reynolds Jr.; Peter Reynolds; Bennett Reynolds; Rebecca Reynolds Driver; and Susan Reynolds Coopwood.

Saunders, Turner

According to Dorothy Gentry in <u>Life and Legends of Lawrence County, Alabama</u> (1961), "Turner Saunders was born January 3, 1782, in Brunswick County, Virginia, son of Thomas and Ann (Harper) Saunders…On July 24, 1799, before he reached the age of 18, he was married to Frances Dunn, of the same county, and in 1808, he removed from Virginia and settled upon a tract of land six miles from Franklin, Tennessee…Saunders and his wife moved to the Town of Franklin where he went in to mercantile business. He practically monopolized the trade in furs and peltries of the Cherokee and Chickasaw Indians who lived along the Tennessee River. Also a preacher of the Methodist church, he afterward removed to Courtland in 1821 and became a planter on a large scale."

Frances Dunn Saunders, the first wife of Turner Saunders and two of her sons Thomas and Franklin died of malaria in less than a month apart. After Frances died in 1824, Turner Saunders married Henrietta M. Weeden Millwater, a widow who was born and reared in the City of Baltimore. Henrietta had two young daughters, Sarah and Mary Eliza Millwater when she married Turner on July 1, 1826. Turner and Henrietta had four sons, Turner, Thomas, Franklin and Hubbard, born after their marriage.

Some of the children of Turner Saunders were as follows:

1. Sophia Dunn Saunders Parish, 1802-1829
2. Louisa Turner Saunders Foster, 1803-1879
3. Narcissa Hubbard Saunders Foster 1805-1845
4. James Edmonds Saunders, 1806-1896
5. Frances Ann Saunders Billups, 1808-1890
6. Martha Maria Saunders Bradford, 1812-1856
7. William H. Saunders, 1819-1895
8. Amanda S. Saunders, 1823-?
9. Eliza Jane Saunders
10. Turner Saunders
11. Thomas P. Saunders, 1827-1882
12. Franklin Saunders, 1833-1909
13. Hubbard Saunders.

REV. TURNER SAUNDERS.

In 1830, Turner Saunders was elected the first president of LaGrange College. That same year, Turner built a historic cotton plantation home about five miles north Town Creek, Alabama. After living in the plantation home for some 14 years, Saunders sold the house to Freeman Goode on February 12, 1844.

The house was later acquired by the Hall family. In the 1940s, the Mauldin family purchased the 1,000-acre farm that included the house. On October 1, 1974, the Saunders-Goode-Hall House was added to the National Register of Historic Places, due to its architectural significance. Today, the

Mauldin family still owns the place, but they have never lived there; however, they have tenants that live in the house.

Saunders Hall
Alex Bush, Library of Congress, 1935
Rear-north and east elevation

The house was built on a Palladian plan and was thought to be designed by Thomas Jefferson who was born in Saunders' native Virginia. The entire house including the columns was constructed with brick above a raised basement. The outside of the basement portion has windows spaced around the house at ground level. On the inside of the basement portion, shackles were attached to some of the walls for securing black slaves of the plantation.

According to the 1830 Lawrence County, Alabama Census, Turner Saunders owned 50 black slaves. In 1844, Turner Saunders moved to Aberdeen, Mississippi. On March 5, 1853, Turner Saunders died at age 71. He was buried in Odd Fellows Rest Cemetery at Aberdeen in Monroe County, Mississippi (Find a Grave Memorial Number 114573122).

Saunders, James E.-Rocky Hill

Colonel James Edmonds Saunders was the son of Turner Saunders and Frances Dunn. He was born on May 7, 1806, in Brunswick County, Virginia. James and his wife Mary Frances Watkins Saunders had the following children:

1. Robert Turner Saunders (1827-1888)
2. Elizabeth D. Saunders Poellnitz (1829-1852)
3. Mary Louise Saunders Blair (1832-1859)
4. Dudley Dunn Saunders (1835-1908)
5. Sarah Jane Saunders Hayes (1836-1896)
6. Prudie Saunders (1842-1864)
7. Lawrence Watkins Saunders (1846-1867).

COL. JAMES EDMONDS SAUNDERS
When a young man.
Born in Virginia 1806, died 1896.

According to Dorothy Gentry in <u>Life and Legends of Lawrence County, Alabama</u> (1961), "On July 14, 1824, James Edmonds Saunders, married Mary Frances Watkins, oldest daughter of his neighbor, Major Robert H. Watkins....In 1825, the young husband-student, was installed in the law office of Foster and Fogg in Nashville....The first year of practice began in Moulton and his earliest clients were by chance, widows, rich and poor and among the former was Mrs. Naomi Leetch, honored aunt of the President James K. Polk, who visited her in 1827 and formed a friendship with Saunders. In 1828, he formed a law partnership in Courtland with Judge John J. Ormond, who later became a member of the Alabama Supreme Court. The old historic road, cut by General Andrew Jackson as a highway through Lawrence County by his troops, runs parallel with the former Memphis and Charleston Railroad (now Southern). Here, three miles west of Courtland is Rocky Hill, the family home, to which James Edmonds Saunders came in 1832."

According to the 1830, Lawrence County, Alabama Census, James Edmonds Saunders owned nine black slaves. By the 1840 census, he owned 32 black slaves.

Main staircase in Rocky Hill Castle

According to the 1850 Lawrence County, Alabama, Agricultural Census, James E. Saunders owned 600 acres of improved land and 800 acres of unimproved land worth $14,000.00. He had $1,000.00 worth of farming equipment and $2,100.00 worth of livestock. In the 1850 Lawrence County, Alabama, Slave Schedules, James Saunders owned 41 black slaves.

In 1858, Rocky Hill Castle construction was started by a Frenchman. In 1861, construction slowed because of the Civil War, but the house was just about completely built. However, James Edmonds Saunders refuse to pay the architect for his work. The builder died before getting paid for completing the home, but according to folklore, his spirit returned to haunt the house.

The Rocky Hill Castle of James Edmonds Saunders was described by Mrs. Elizabeth G. Irwin in her pamphlet Famous Homes in Alabama. "Rocky Hill Castle is largely Greek in character. Its almost identical one-story porticoes both in the front and rear have an exquisite cornice of the triglyph motif adorning the four fluted columns. Wings added to either side also have small porticoes with two columns each. A profusion of cornice brackets buttresses the over-hanging eaves of the roof, and a cupola with arched windows."

The house and tower were built of brick which was plastered over with stucco. The tower was a replica of Winsor Castle tower in England and was attached to the main house by a supporting wall. The top of the observation tower provided a view of the plantation cotton fields where the overseer could keep watch over Saunders' black slaves. The watch tower had six floors which were used to house and/or to imprison slaves. The interior of Rocky Hill Castle had beautiful walnut spiral staircases and a large arched entrance leading to the parlor. The fireplace mantles were made of Italian marble.

The 1860 Lawrence County, Alabama Census, Household 242 listed the following: James Saunders, 54, male, Virginia, planter; Mary, 52, female, Georgia; Sally, 21, female, Alabama; Prudence, 18, female, Alabama; Laurence, 15, male, Alabama; Ella, 12, female, Alabama; and Lizzie, seven, female, Alabama. In 1860, James Edmonds Saunders had real estate valued at $250,000.00 and personal property valued at $115,000.00.

During the Civil War, Rocky Hill Castle served as a Confederate hospital for wounded soldiers. William Forrest, the brother of General Nathan Bedford Forrest, was brought to Rocky Hill to mend from the wound that he received at Battle Ground near the edge of Morgan and Cullman Counties. Later, Confederate General Nathan Bedford Forrest stopped at Rocky Hill to thank Saunders for taking care of his brother. In addition, Confederate General P. G. T. Beauregard was dined and entertained at the mansion. On one occasion, a meeting of the Military Court of the Army of Tennessee was held at Rocky Hill.

Colonel James Edmonds Saunders died on August 23, 1896, at the age of 90. He was buried on his cotton plantation at Rocky Hill Cemetery between Town Creek and Courtland in Lawrence County, Alabama (Find a Grave memorial Number 21629362).

After the death of his grandfather, Dudley Saunders and his family were the last of the Saunders family to live in the Rocky Hill Castle. The family of Dudley moved from the home in the 1920s because of ghosts that haunted the old castle. Shortly after the last Saunders that occupied the house left, the plantation was sold to H. D. Bynum and R. E. Tweedy. They used the land for growing cotton and never lived in Rocky Hill Castle. After the house was sold in the 1920's, the abandoned Rocky Hill Castle fell to destructive vandalism, disrepair, and decay. In 1961, the once magnificent plantation mansion was bulldozed and destroyed.

Shackelford, Jack

Dr. Jack Shackelford was born in Richmond, Virginia, on March 20, 1790, the son of Richard Shackelford and his third wife Joanna Lawson. The mother of Jack Shackelford died when he was an infant. Catharine Allgood, a sister of one of the first wives of Richard, reared Jack with all the love of a devoted mother. Jack was educated as a physician and surgeon. In 1811, he moved to Winnsboro, South Carolina, where he began his practice and married Maria Young, the daughter of a prominent Presbyterian minister (Saunders, 1899).

Dr. Jack Shackelford and his wife Maria Young Shackelford had four children.
1. Fortunatus S. Shackelford was killed at Goliad, Texas.
2. Samuel W. Shackelford first married Margaret McMahon, who lived but a short time. Samuel then married Susan Addie, daughter of Colonel Benjamin Sherrod; they had two children-Jack and May.
3. Harriett C. Shackelford married John J. McMahon and, they had four children:1) Dr. Fortunatus S. S. McMahon, a physician in Courtland, served in the Confederate Army. 2) Dr. W. Jack McMahon, Confederate Army surgeon, married Miss Cutter of New Orleans. 3) Robert McMahon was a soldier in the Civil War. 4) Lillie McMahon.

4. Edward P. Shackelford married Caroline Watkins. Their children were Frank W., Harriet C., and Elizabeth.

Most of the following information was derived from <u>Early Settlers of Alabama</u> (1899). Dr. Jack Shackelford served on the staff of General Andrew Jackson in the British War of 1812. In 1818, Jack moved his family to Shelby County, Alabama, where he bought a cotton plantation. Jack was elected to the Alabama state Senate in 1822, 1823, and 1824. As security for a cousin whose business failed, Shackelford was forced to sell his plantation in Shelby County.

About 1829, Jack Shackelford was appointed to head the United States Land Office in Courtland, Alabama. In 1828, the United States Congress approved the sale of 400,000 acres of government land for the construction of a canal around the Big Muscle Shoals. Jack succeeded in selling the land in four years; however, the canal proved unusable during most of the year and fell into disuse. By the Civil War, the canal was full of debris and abandoned.

Jack Shackelford

After the land for the canal was sold, Dr. Jack Shackelford served as one of the twelve members of the board of directors for the Tuscumbia, Courtland and Decatur Railroad. Jack was elected treasurer of the first railroad west of the Appalachian Mountains. At a cost of slightly more than $4,000/mile, the railroad was 43 miles long when completed from Tuscumbia to Decatur in 1834. Since most of the board were slave holding cotton planters, the primary use of the railroad was to transport cotton around the Muscle Shoals.

The railroad tracks consisted of wooden strings five inches square which were laid on ties of red cedar. To the stringers, iron bars three inches wide were placed and spiked down. A graveled horse path was in the middle of the track for mules or horses to pull the railcars. In December 1834, a steam locomotive engine which had arrived from England made the initial trip from Tuscumbia to Decatur and back in one day.

Dr. Jack Shackelford, officers, and members of the board of directors were among those who rode the train on its initial run with the steam engines.

With the start of the Texas Revolution against Mexico, Dr. Jack Shackelford recruited, mustered, and organized a company of military volunteers in the fall of 1835. The company included his son Fortunatus, two nephews, and local young men from the Courtland area. The soldiers were uniformed in red jeans, hence they became known as the Red Rovers. Dr. Shackelford drilled his company as its captain before joining the struggle against Mexico for Texas independence. The command of Shackelford was placed under James W. Fannin and fought in the battles at Coleto and Goliad. The company of Dr. Jack Shackelford was captured near Goliad and executed. In the Goliad massacre that followed Fannin's surrender, Dr. Shackelford was spared in order to aid the Mexican wounded.

Dr. Jack Shackelford remained in San Antonio until the retreat of the Mexican army following the Battle of San Jacinto allowed his escape. He traveled to Goliad where he lost his company of men and joined General Thomas J. Rusk. Shackelford asked Rusk to bury the massacred victims. Dr. Shackelford continued to Velasco where he met with President David G. Burnet and confronted the captured Antonio López de Santa Anna. Upset over the honorable treatment given the Mexican general, Shackelford obtained his discharge and returned to Courtland, Alabama, where he received military honors.

On February 4, 1839, Dr. Jack Shackelford visited Houston, Texas, and attended a dinner sponsored in his honor. During the Mexican invasions of 1842, Shackelford again tried to secure volunteers for the Texas cause. In 1846, he traveled to Houston and Austin, Texas. In 1858, Shackelford County, Texas, was established and named in honor of Dr. Jack Shackelford. In addition, Jack County, Texas, was also named in honor of his services. More than to any other man, Texas was indebted for the vivid account of Captain Jack Shackelford of the battle and massacre at Goliad.

After his return from Texas, Dr. Jack Shackelford resumed his medical practice in Courtland. His wife died in 1842, and he married Mrs. Martha Chardavoyne, the widow of William V. Chardavoyne. On January 22, 1857, Dr. Jack Shackelford died at Courtland in Lawrence County, Alabama, and he was buried in the Courtland Cemetery.

Shackelford House

The following was a letter to the editor by William Crawford Sherrod, the son of Colonel Benjamin Sherrod. The letter appeared in the Courtland Enterprise on Thursday, June 28, 1900. "Wichita Falls, Texas, June 18, 1900, Editor Enterprise. I am satisfied that the old gun found at the creek…belonged to a lot of guns furnished to the Militia of Alabama about the year 1833. At the beginning of the War with Mexico, Dr. Jack Shackelford raised a company of men in and around Courtland to assist the Texans…He and his Company…were forced to surrender at Goliad, Texas. With the exception of Dr. Shackelford, Smith Whitefield, Brooks, and Joseph Fenner, the entire Company was massacred by the Mexicans. Dr. Shackelford was taken as a captive and carried to the City of Mexico…held prisoner for two years. He soon learned to speak the Spanish language fluently and being small in stature, with a very swarthy complection and straight black hair, he easily passed for a pure Castillian. After two years of imprisonment and suffering, and with the aid of a Mexican woman, he succeeded in making his escape, and made his way back to Courtland, reaching there the night that Dr. McMahon was born. His return was a great surprise as friends and kindred, had mourned him dead for two years, as he was thought to have been murdered with his Company at Goliad. His Company, The Red Rovers, belonged to Fannin's Command….There was a distribution of arms to the citizens soldiers known as the Militia and a lot of the guns like the old musket described in the Enterprise were sent to Courtland and placed in charge of Dr. Shackelford, I am not sure they were ever called in. As a boy, I remember shooting one of them that was loaned to my older brother, Charles, by Dr. Shackelford. It was an old flint

256

lock musket, with a walnut stock running the entire length of the barrel and with an iron ram rod…Smith and Whitfield Brooks were nephews of my mother, being the children of her sister, Francis Burt. Another of his nephews was murdered along with Fortunatus Shackelford, a son of Dr. Shackelford. There were representatives murdered by the Mexicans of almost every prominent family living around Courtland at the time…So small a community never before or since has made so bloody a sacrifice to aid a struggling republic in throwing off the yoke of oppression. Quite different from the verdict of the civilized world in standing quietly by with folded arms while the Boers are being murdered and plundered of their country and government. W. C. Sherrod"

Samuel W. Shackelford

Samuel W. Shackelford was born on December 23, 1816; he was the son of Dr. Jack Shackelford. Samuel married Susan Adelaide 'Addie' Sherrod, daughter of Colonel Benjamin Sherrod (1777-1847) and Tabitha Watkins Goode Sherrod (1792-1873). Susan was born on September 14, 1825; she and Samuel W. Shackelford had a son that they
named Jack Shackelford (November 3, 1859-November 21, 1937). Susan had the following siblings: Charles Fox Sherrod (1827-1885), William Crawford Sherrod (1835-1918). She had the half siblings: Felix Alonso McKinzie Sherrod (1809-1845); Samuel W. Sherrod (1809-1845), Maria Antoinette Sherrod Swoope (1810-1829); Frederick O. A. Sherrod (1812-1848).

It is very possible that Samuel and his wife Susan lived and oversaw the Hard Bargain Plantation. Colonel Benjamin Sherrod provided most of his children with a cotton plantation and slaves. Hard Bargin was close to the Cotton Garden, the personal plantation of Colonel Sherrod. Since census records show that the Colonel and his daughter lived next to each other, it is highly probable that Susan and Samuel Shackelford lived at Hard Bargin.

In the 1850 Lawrence County, Alabama, Slave Schedule and 1850 Lawrence County, Alabama, Agricultural Census, Samuel W. Shackelford does not appear in either of these records, but in 1860, he was shown as owning 86 black slaves. He and his wife, Susan Sherrod Shackelford are in house # 2 next to Ben Sherrod's Cotton Garden Plantation.

William C. Sherrod says that he was born at Cotton Garden Plantation, and he was still in the household #1 on the 1850 census mentioned below. Since Susan is the daughter of Ben Sherrod, she and her husband Samuel must have been living and working on her father's Hard Bargain Plantation which was adjacent to the Cotton Garden Plantation.

According to 1850 Lawrence County, Alabama United States Census, Household 2 was next door to House 1 of Tabitha Sherrod, wife of Colonel Ben Sherrod, Charles F. Sherrod and William C. Sherrod. House 2 was where Ben Sherrod's daughter Susan who married to Samuel W. Shackelford was living. The census record of house number 2 is as follows: S. W. Shackelford, male, 32, white, South Carolina; W. Watkins, male, 40 Tennessee; John C. Watkins, male, 11, Alabama; Caroline E. Watkins, female, 7, Alabama; Susan A. Watkins, female, 10, Alabama; W. W. Watkins, male, 6, Alabama; Frank B. Watkins, male, 3, Alabama; A. E. M. Lemore, female, 18, Alabama; S. W. Shackelford, male, 32, South Carolina; S. A. Shackelford, female, 25, Alabama; Ella Shackelford, female, 1, Alabama; A. Alexander, male, 39, Tennessee; Mary Alexander, female, 42, Georgia; Sarah Alexander, female, 14, Alabama; Cena Alexander, female, 12, Alabama; Wm. H. Alexander, male, 10, Alabama; G. W. Alexander, male, 8, Alabama; James Alexander, male, 3, Alabama. Obviously, with ten people living in the house number 2, the dwelling had to be quite large.

In the 1860 Northern Division, Lawrence County, Alabama, United States Census is the following: Samuel Shackelford, male, 41, white, South Carolina; Susan A. Shackelford, female, 34, Alabama; Mariah Shackelford, female, 2, Alabama, Jack Shackelford, male, 0, Alabama; Talitha Sherrod, female, 67, South Carolina. In the 1860 Lawrence County, Alabama, Slave Schedule, Samuel W. Shackelford owned 86 slaves.

The 1870 Lawrence County, Alabama United States Census had the following: S. W. Shackelford, male, 53, South Carolina; Susan A. Shackelford, female, 44, Alabama; Mariah A. Shackelford, female, 12, Alabama; and, Jackson Shackelford, male, 10, Alabama.

The 1880 Leighton, Lawrence County, Alabama United States Census has the following: S. W. Shackelford, male, 63, married, white, farmer, South Carolina, father's birthplace Virginia, mother's birthplace South Carolina; M. A. Shakelford, daughter, female, 22, Alabama; Jack Shakelford, son, male, 20, Alabama; Peleg Burt, other, male, 23, Mississippi; Charlott Thomes, other, female, 38, Alabama; Selena Goode, other, female, 50, Alabama; S. A. Shackelford, wife, female, 56, Alabama; and, Emma Goode, other, female, 25, Alabama.

Samuel W. Shackelford died on April 6, 1893. He was buried in the Courtland Cemetery at Courtland in Lawrence County, Alabama (Find a Grave Memorial Number 44210407). Susan Adelaide Sherrod Shackelford died on February 7, 1890 (Find a Grave Memorial Number 44242036). According to the Moulton Advertiser on Thursday, February 27, 1890, "Susan Adelaide Sherrod Shackelford died, at her residence, near Courtland, Alabama on February 7th, 1890. Mrs. S. Adelaide Shackelford, wife of Colonel Samuel W. Shackelford. Sister Shackelford was the daughter of Colonel Ben Sherrod, one of the early settlers of the Tennessee Valley."

Sherrod, Colonel Benjamin

Colonel Benjamin Sherrod was born January 16, 1777, in Halifax County, North Carolina. His father was also named Benjamin Sherrod, who was born in Halifax County, North Carolina, on October 29, 1751. His mother was Mary Ricks who was born in Halifax County, North Carolina, in 1758. She was the sister of Isaac Ricks, the father of Abraham Ricks of The Oaks Plantation; Abraham first entered land in Franklin County, Alabama, on April 3, 1818. After losing both parents as a young boy, Benjamin Sherrod grew up in tidewater North Carolina in the care of his mother's only brother, Issac Ricks.

On January 1, 1808, Colonel Benjamin Sherrod first married Eliza H. Watkins in Elbert County, Georgia. Eliza was born on May 2, 1789, and she died on January 27, 1818. She was the daughter of Samuel Watkins and Eleanor Thompson. Benjamin and Eliza had six children:

1. Felix Alonso McKinzie Sherrod, born March 29, 1809; he married Sarah Ann Parrish. Felix died June 21, 1845, and he was buried in Wheeler Cemetery at Wheeler in Lawrence County, Alabama (Find a Grave Memorial Number 32782001).
2. Mariah Antonette Sherrod was born on September 19, 1810, and she died on February 25, 1829. On May 15, 1828, Mariah married Jacob Swoope, and they had one son William (Find a Grave Memorial Number 47671249). After Maria died, Jacob married Frances Saunders, daughter of Turner and Frances Dunn Saunders.
3. Frederick Oscar Alexander Sherrod was born on December 3, 1812, at Washington in Wilkes County, Georgia. He married Anne Bolton, daughter of Colonel John Bolton of Baltimore. His children were (1) John Bolton Sherrod of Montgomery, Alabama, married Judith Winston, daughter of Colonel Isaac Winston of Tuscumbia, Alabama. (2) Frederick O. Sherrod of Birmingham, Alabama, married Mittie, youngest daughter of Orrin Davis of Lawrence County, Alabama. (3) Felix O. A. Sherrod. (4) Frances. (5) Benjamin Watkins Sherrod married an Alexander. Frederick Oscar Alexander Sherrod died November 24, 1848, at Tuscumbia in present-day Colbert County, Alabama. He was buried in the Sherrod Cemetery near Bear Creek west of Tuscumbia (Find a Grave Memorial Number 86464266). After Frederick died, his wife Anne married Dr. Farrar of Jackson, Mississippi.
4. Samuel Watkins Sherrod was born on November 16, 1814; he married Frances Parrish, sister of his brother Felix 's wife. His children were: (1) Henry Sherrod died leaving a considerable fortune. (2) Walter Sherrod of Town Creek in Lawrence County, Alabama, married Laura, daughter of Orrin Davis of Lawrence County. (3) Henry Sherrod was born in 1864, and married Ella, daughter of Mr. James Irvine of Florence, Alabama. (4) Virginia Irvine Sherrod. Samuel Watkins Sherrod died on November 28, 1848; he was buried in Wheeler Cemetery at Wheeler in Lawrence County, Alabama (Find a Grave Memorial Number 32781882).
5. George Sherrod.
6. Eliza Sherrod.

The second marriage of Colonel Benjamin Sherrod was to Talitha Goode Watkins on July 12, 1821, in Madison County, Alabama. Talitha Goode first married Coleman Watkins and they had two sons: Willis Watkins and Goode

Watkins. Talitha was born on April 22, 1792, and she was the daughter of John Goode and Ann Freeman. Benjamin and Talitha had four children:

1. Susan Adelaide Sherrod, who married Samuel W. Shackelford, was born September 14, 1825, in Alabama, and she died on February 7, 1890, at Courtland in Lawrence County, Alabama (Find a Grave Memorial Number 44242036).
2. Charles Fox Sherrod, who married Susan Billups of Columbus, Mississippi, was born on November 3, 1827, at the Cotton Garden Plantation in Courtland, Alabama. He died on May 7, 1886, at Columbus, Mississippi (Find a Grave Memorial Number 12914968).
3. William Crawford Sherrod, who married Amanda Morgan, daughter of Samuel Morgan of Nashville, was born on August 17, 1832, at the Cotton Garden Plantation in Courtland, Alabama. William died on March 26, 1918, and he was buried in Riverside Cemetery at Wichita Falls, Texas (Find a Grave Memorial Number 8649022).
4. A. Eliza Sherrod died as a young child.

Sherrod Plantations

About 1818, Colonel Benjamin Sherrod settled in North Alabama where he established several cotton plantations in Lawrence and Franklin Counties of the Tennessee River Valley. At one time, it is believed that he owned over 700 black slaves. Some of the Sherrod plantations include Alamance, Chantilly, Cotton Garden, Hard Bargin, Bear Creek, Locust Grove, Patton Island, and Pond Spring.

Alamance Plantation

According to the 1850 Lawrence County, Alabama, Agricultural Census, the Alamance Plantation had 1,100 acres of improved land and 1,150 acres of unimproved land with $3,600.00 worth of livestock. According to the 1850 Lawrence County, Alabama, Slave Schedules, the Alamance Plantation had 90 black slaves.

There was an Alamance County in north central North Carolina, and a Great Alamance Creek where the Battle of Alamance was fought, an important early battle in the Revolutionary War. This may be where the plantation name Alamance came from.

The author does not know the exact location of Alamance Plantation except that it was in the Tennessee River Valley in Lawrence County, Alabama. If Alamance is like other plantations of Benjamin Sherrod, it is highly probable that one of his children resided there.

MARION,

The thorough Bred and Distinguished Stallion

THE stockholders of marion, influenced by the repeated requests of many Gentlemen, have at length, yielded to their urgent solicitations, and the favorite son of a peerless sire (Old Archie) arrived a few days since from North Carolina, in high health and spirits.— He will stand the ensuing season, at Chantilly (my plantation) two miles from Tuscumbia, on the road leading to Courtland, at the reduced price of *sixty dollars*, if paid within the season, or *seventy* within four weeks after it's close, one dollar to the groom in every instance.

The rare and exquisite beauty—the faultless symmetry—the great developement of muscular power and the pure unblemished pedigree of this noble animal, combined with his brilliant performance as a racer, and his surity as a foal getter, richly entitle him to the patronage of the community.

FRED'K. O. A. SHERROD.

P.S. His description, performances and pedigree will be shortly issued in bills.

Tuscumbia Dec. 22 1837. 23-tf

☞The Florence Gazette, Advocate and Democrat, Huntsville, and the papers at Tuscaloosa, will each insert the foregoing 6 weeks and forward their accounts to this office for collection.

Speculation is that Charles Fox Sherrod might have lived at the Alamance Plantation. Since he is the only other son of Colonel Benjamin Sherrod who lived to adulthood that is not listed as living on a cotton plantation in Lawrence County or a surrounding county, Charles would be the most likely child living at Alamance.

Chantilly Plantation

Chantilly was a Sherrod cotton plantation in Franklin (present-day Colbert) County, Alabama. Frederick Oscar Alexander Sherrod lived on the Chantilly Plantation about two miles southeast of Tuscumbia on the old Tuscumbia Road that passed from Decatur to Courtland to Tuscumbia (present-day highway 20, alternate highway 72). In addition to growing cotton, Fredrick obviously loved racing horses and posted several advertisements in local papers about his stallions at Chantilly Plantation.

In the 1840 Franklin County, Alabama Census, Frederick O. A. Sherrod owned 66 black slaves. Since Fredrick died in 1848, by the 1850 Franklin

County, Alabama, Slave Schedules, his wife Anne Sherrod owned 84 black slaves.

Fredrick Sherrod died on November 24, 1848, and he is buried in the Sherrod Cemetery just east of Bear Creek some five miles west of Tuscumbia. Today, the cemetery is in a wooded area and is not easily accessible.

Cotton Garden Plantation

Colonel Benjamin Sherrod and his second wife Talitha Goode Watkins Sherrod lived at their home on the Cotton Garden Plantation which was located north of the nearby Town of Courtland. Most of the children of Benjamin and Talitha were born at the Cotton Garden Plantation Mansion.

In the 1850 Lawrence County, Alabama, Agricultural Census, the Cotton Garden Plantation had 1,400 acres of improved land and 850 unimproved land with $6,000.00 worth of livestock. According to the 1850 Lawrence County, Alabama, Slave Schedules, the Cotton Garden Plantation had 125 black slaves.

Hard Bargin Plantation

Susan Adelaide Sherrod Shackelford, daughter of Colonel Benjamin Sherrod, and her husband Samuel W. Shackelford were thought to have lived at the Hard Bargain Plantation. Part of Hard Bargin eventually became the old Courtland Air Base. In 1850, the plantation had 1,100 acres of improved land and 900 acres of unimproved land with $4,000.00 worth of livestock. According to the 1850 Lawrence County, Alabama, Slave Schedules, the Hard Bargin

Plantation had 85 black slaves, but there were no slaves listed for Samuel W. Shackelford.

In 1860 Lawrence County, Alabama, United States Census, Household 86 listed the following: Samuel W. Shackelford was a 41-year-old male planter born in South Carolina; Susan A. was a 34-year-old female born in Alabama; Mariah was a two-year-old female born in Alabama; Jack was a six month old male born in Alabama; and Talitha Sherrod was a 67-year-old female born in South Carolina.

Samuel W. Shackelford had real estate valued at $42,000.00 and personal property valued at $105,664.00. According to the 1860 Lawrence County, Alabama, Slave Schedules, Samuel W. Shackelford owned 86 black slaves.

Bear Creek Plantation

The Sherrod Plantation on Bear Creek in present-day Colbert County, Alabama, was five miles west of Tuscumbia; there is another Bear Creek in Franklin County. The plantation was the location of the Sherrod Cemetery, the burial site of Frederick Oscar Alexander Sherrod, who lived on a Chantilly Plantation two miles southeast of Tuscumbia. The plantation was on Bear Creek just south of the old Tuscumbia Road (present-day Highway 72) which was also an Indian trail known as the Upper South River Road; the farm was east of the creek and Hawk Pride Mountain Road.

Probably Samuel Watkins Sherrod, the third son of Colonel Benjamin Sherrod, lived for a short while at the Bear Creek Plantation. In the 1840 Franklin County, Alabama Census, Samuel W. Sherrod is listed as owning 57 black slaves. Prior to the Civil War, the Bear Creek land was located in Franklin County (now present-day Colbert County). However, Samuel died on November 28, 1848, and he was buried at Wheeler in Lawrence County, Alabama.

Locust Grove Plantation

William Crawford Sherrod, the youngest son of Colonel Benjamin Sherrod, lived at the Locust Grove Plantation in Franklin (Colbert) County,

Alabama. William C. Sherrod was born at the Cotton Garden which he also managed for his father.

According to the 1850 Franklin County, Alabama, Agricultural Census, William Sherrod owned 1,100 acres of improved land and 1,600 acres of unimproved land worth $40,000.00. His farm equipment was worth $1,200.00, and his livestock was valued at $7,500.00.

Patton Island

In 1821, Colonel Benjamin Sherrod bought from the State of Alabama an entire island of over 600 acres in the Tennessee River. The earliest settlers called it Cane Island because of the dense growth of river cane. On an 1844 map, the island is called Tinnin's Island. Today, the island is known as Patton's Island. It got that name when Robert Miller Patton, the twentieth Governor of Alabama, who lived at the Sweetwater Plantation in Florence, Alabama, bought the island. By 1860, Patton owned 113 slaves and 3,800 acres of land.

The island was located at the place where Singing River Bridge (Patton Island Bridge) now crosses the Tennessee River from the City of Muscle Shoals in Colbert County to Florence in Lauderdale County. O'Neal Bridge crosses the river between Sheffield and Florence and is near the lower or western end of Patton Island. The island extends from near Wilson Dam on the upstream end to near O'Neal Bridge on the downstream end. Colonel Benjamin Sherrod originally sold the island to Waddy Tate in 1830. The island is located in part of Sections 12, 13, and 14 of Township 3 South and Range 11 West in Lauderdale County, Alabama.

Pond Spring Plantation

Pond Spring Plantation was east of Courtland in the Tennessee Valley of Lawrence County, Alabama. The first land in the plantation was entered in 1818 by John Pryor Hickman. Hickman was in partnership with Colonel Sherrod in purchasing some of the property. According to the 1820 census of Lawrence County, John Hickman's family had 11 members, and he owned 56 slaves. He and his slaves built the first log cabins at Pond Spring. There was an early county proposal to build a road from Sherrods Spring to Meltons Bluff.

In 1827, Colonel Sherrod bought the property at Pond Spring from Hickman which included 1,760 acres. After Colonel Benjamin Sherrod purchased the interest of Pond Spring from Hickman, his oldest son Felix Alonso McKinzie Sherrod moved to the plantation and eventually became the owner of Pond Spring Plantation. In the 1830's, Felix Sherrod greatly expanded the larger of the two log dogtrot cabins on the property. The larger Sherrod House was used by Felix and his family, and the smaller dogtrot home was used for housing slaves.

Upon the death of Felix, the Pond Spring Plantation passed to his son, Benjamin Sherrod, a grandson of Colonel Benjamin Sherrod. In 1859, the young Benjamin married Daniella 'Ella' Jones, daughter of Richard Harrison Jones and his wife Lucy Early of the nearby Caledonia Plantation.

According to the 1850 Lawrence County, Alabama Agricultural Census, Pond Spring had 900 acres of improved land and 700 acres of unimproved land with $4,000.00 worth of livestock. According to the 1850 Lawrence County, Alabama Slave Schedules, the Pond Spring Plantation had 94 black slaves.

In the 1860 Lawrence County, Alabama United States Census, Household 112, Benjamin J. Sherrod was a 24-year-old male planter born in Alabama, Ella an 18-year-old female born in Alabama, Richard J. a six month old male born in Alabama, and Alice C. a 15-year-old female born in Alabama. In the 1860 census, Benjamin J. Sherrod had a real estate value of $40,000.00 and a personal property value of $25,000.00. According to the 1860 Lawrence County, Alabama, Slave Schedule, the Pond Spring Plantation of the young Benjamin Sherrod owned 80 black slaves.

In 1861, the young Benjamin died, and Pond Spring Plantation passed to his widow Daniella 'Ella' Jones Sherrod. Ella married the famed Confederate Calvary General Joseph 'Joe' Wheeler in 1866.

In the early 1870s, Joseph Wheeler and Daniella Jones Sherrod Wheeler returned from New Orleans after four years to Lawrence County, and they built a new home that became known as the General Joe Wheeler Home, adjacent to the older Sherrod House at Pond Spring.

On April 13, 1977, the General Joe Wheeler home was placed on the National Register of Historic Places. In 1993, the General Joe Wheeler homesite of the Pond Spring Plantation was given by the Wheeler Family to the Alabama Historical Commission. The property included 50 acres and 13 historic buildings. The General Joe Wheeler home became the main museum housings the Wheeler family's original furnishings.

According to the Lawrence County Archive records, Colonel Benjamin Sherrod owned the following land: Section 35, T4S, R8W, NW¼; Section 10, T3S, R7W, SW¼; Section 15, T4S, R7W, N½; Section 21, T3S, R8W, SW¼; Section 34, T4S, R7W, WSE; Section 2, T5S, R7W, WSW; Section 28, T4S, R7W, SW; Section 33, T3S, R6W; Section 32, T3S, R6W; Section 10, T4S, R6W; Section 34, T3S, R6W; Section 2, T4S, R6W, Island, TN River; Section 3, T4S, R6W, all of; Section 4, T4S, R6W; Section 11, T4S, R6W; Section 2, T5S, R7W, ENW; Section 19, T6S, R7W, ESE; Section 26, T4S, R7W, E½ of NW¼; Section 33, T4S, R7W, W½ of SW¼; Section 18, T3S, R8W, E½; T4S, R8W, Cow Island; T4S, R8W, 159 acres; 4 Courtland Lots; Courtland Lot # 92 & House; T3S, R7W, Cow Island; Section 34, T4S, R7W, WSE; Section 2, T4S, R6W, Island in TN river; Section 2, T5S, R7W; and, Section 33, T4S, R7W.

Benjamin Sherrod History

Benjamin Sherrod was educated at the University of North Carolina; in 1800, he moved to Wilkes County, Georgia. He served in the War of 1812 as an Army contractor with the commissary department, and acquired the title of colonel.

In 1808, Benjamin Sherrod married Eliza Watkins of Elbert County, Georgia, and she died in 1818. After Eliza's death, he moved from Wilkes County, Georgia, to Courtland in Lawrence County, Alabama. On July 12, 1821, Colonel Sherrod married a second time to Talitha Goode Watkins; they lived at the Cotton Garden Plantation near Courtland.

Colonel Benjamin Sherrod

At Courtland, Alabama, on February 11, 1832, under the leadership of Benjamin Sherrod, the Board of Directors accepted the charter of the Tuscumbia and Courtland Railroad. Colonel Sherrod was selected the first president, David Deshler was selected as chief engineer, and Dr. Jack Shackelford was elected treasurer. The Tuscumbia and Courtland Railroad was the first railway in the south and west of the Appalachians. The object of the promoters of this road was to get around the Mussel Shoals of the Tennessee River which was practically impassible most of the year. After the railroad ran into financial trouble, Benjamin Sherrod had to pay the entire indebtedness of $300,000.00 to the State of Alabama. This obligation was met promptly and was the largest debt ever paid by any individual to the State.

The railroad consisted of cross ties that were laid about every four feet. On top of the ties, wooden stringers with flat strips of iron were nailed in place which created the rails. The passenger cars were short and flat, and they were about the size of the old mule pulled wagons. The power was provided by a pair of horses or mules which made the trip of 23 miles from Tuscumbia to Courtland in one day. When the iron rails on top of the stringers would bend up at the end, they were called snake heads and would cause a car to derail. The passengers would be called out by the conductor to nail down the snake head and put the car back on the track. The work fixing the rails and replacing the cars on the track would sometimes take a half a day.

1830's Fulton Train Engine

About the year 1837, the railroad extension was approved to Decatur some twenty miles; the corporation became the Tuscumbia, Courtland and Decatur railroad. In 1838, the Tuscumbia, Courtland and Decatur Railway Company purchased the first locomotive engine brought to America. The engine was delivered from Baltimore by ocean steamer to New Orleans up the Mississippi River to Paducah, Kentucky, then transferred to a river steamer to Tuscumbia Landing where it was placed on the railroad tracks.

The locomotive was operated by Captain Lawson who was its engineer on the Baltimore Road until 1838 when it was purchased by the Tuscumbia, Courtland and Decatur Railway Company. Captain Lawson was paid to bring the locomotive to Tuscumbia. Captain Lawson ran the locomotive from Tuscumbia to Decatur until the start of the Civil War. The old Tuscumbia, Courtland and Decatur Railroad was eventually extended to Stevenson on the east and Memphis on the west. This was the third railroad in the United States and became a part of the Memphis and Charleston Railroad.

Colonel Benjamin Sherrod owned the steamboat Benjamin Sherrod which caught fire and sank in the Mississippi River on May 8, 1837. The Tennessee River was then navigable from Paducah to Tuscumbia Landing and from Decatur to Chattanooga, leaving about 35 miles of dangerous shoals, which no steamboat could pass. The extremely treacherous rapids included Little Muscle Shoals, Big Muscle Shoals, and Elk River Shoals. The Tuscumbia, Courtland and Decatur Railroad allowed commerce to be transported around these unforgiving Muscle Shoals of the Tennessee River.

Death of Benjamin and Talitha

"Talitha Goode Watkins Sherrod died on May 14, 1873, at Courtland in Lawrence County, Alabama. Died at the residence of her son-in-law, Colonel Samuel W. Shackelford, near Courtland, Alabama, on the 14th instant, Mrs. Tabitha Goode Sherrod, relict of the late Colonel Benj Sherrod, aged 81 years and 1 month. Mrs. Sherrod was born in Edgefield District, South Carolina, April 22nd, 1792," Moulton Advertiser, Friday, May 23, 1873.

Benjamin Sherrod died on February 25, 1847, in Courtland at the age of 70. The epitaph on his tomb at Cotton Garden Plantation near Courtland, Alabama, reads as follows: "They who loved thee living and lament thee dead pay this last tribute to thy noble shade. Sacred to the memory of Colonel Benjamin Sherrod; Born 16th January 1777; Died 25th February 1847; aged 70 years 1 month 9 days. An honest man's the noblest work of God. He died in the hope of a blessed immortality."

Alabama Historical Commission

Today in 2019, the Alabama Historical Commission owns Pond Spring, and the commission stated the following: "The property of Pond Spring, the General Joe Wheeler Home was first purchased by the Hickman family in 1818. The log cabin on the site was originally, a 'one-pen,' or one room cabin, likely built by the Hickman family, although there is evidence that the structure may have been erected by early squatters on the site before John Hickman and his family arrived. The pre-1818 structure was the original west cabin room, where the Hickmans lived with their nine children until 1820. Needing more space, they added a second room, creating a double pen 'dogtrot' cabin. This cabin was referred to as the kitchen from 1820-1850.

The second property owner, Colonel Benjamin Sherrod, renamed the site Pond Spring, circa 1827. Pond Spring was passed down to the Colonel's grandson, Benjamin who was married to Daniella Jones from 1859 until his death in 1861; the property remained in the Sherrod family until Daniella married General Joe Wheeler in 1866.

In 1994, General Joe Wheeler's granddaughter donated 50 acres of land, the building, and collections to the Alabama Historical Commission, the state historic preservation agency charged with protecting and interpreting the history of generations who called Pond Spring home. The Wheeler House Museum is open to the public on Wednesday through Sunday. Admission is charged. Special tours are available by appointment. For more information about Pond Spring, please call 256 637-8513 or visit www.ahc.alabama.gov ."

Swoope, Jacob-Dixie Plantation

Jacob Swoope was born on July 9, 1766, in Philadelphia, Pennsylvania, and he died on March 26, 1832. Jacob was buried in the Trinity Episcopal Cemetery in Staunton, Virginia (Find a Grave Memorial Number 7685410). In

Dixie

1790, he married Mary Elizabeth McDowell (1772-1816). His father was Colonel Micheal Swoope who came from Germany to America in 1727 at the age of one year old on a ship called the William and Sarah.

According to <u>Early Settlers of Alabama</u> (Saunders, 1899), "Jacob had been well educated and was an accomplished merchant…had learned to read and speak the English language fluently….Mr. Swoope was a merchant, a handsome man, and usually well dressed. He resided in Staunton, Augusta County. He came to Rockingham dressed in German fashion….Mr. Swoope served in Congress from 1809 to 1811, and then very wisely returned to his merchandising, in which he was very successful.

Jacob was the father of three of the best merchants Courtland ever had- John M., Jacob K., and Edgar M. Swoope. They brought to the place a substantial cash capital, and did business under, the style of "J. & J. Swoope," and in a few years reaped large profits. The planters then cultivated fresh, productive lands, made large cotton crops, and sold for high prices. No wonder then that the merchants of that day grew rich. We shall now notice each of the merchants in detail…John M., Jacob K., and Edgar M. Swoope were three brothers of German descent who came to Courtland, Alabama, from Staunton, Virginia. Together, they owned some 380 black slaves; some of the slaves were listed by first name only in the wills of the brothers. Probably many of the Swoope Afican American descendants might be from the plantations of the Swoope brothers and took the last name of Swoope as their last name."

Jacob Swoope
7/9/1766-3/26/1832

According to the 1840 Lawrence County, Alabama Census, Jacob K. Swoope owned 111 black slaves. In the 1850 Lawrence County, Alabama, Slave Schedule, the Swoope's of Courtland owned many black slaves; John McDowell Swoope owned 129 black slaves; Edgar M. Swoope owned 142 black slaves; and I. R. Swoope owned 107 black slaves. In the 1860 Lawrence County, Alabama Slave Schedule, E. M. Swoope owned 164 black slaves and John M. Swoope owned 117 black slaves.

John M. Swoope, Jacob K. Swoope, and Reverend Edgar M. Swoope were brothers and merchants in Courtland. They printed their own money at Courtland in Lawrence County, Alabama.

Jacob K. Swoope

Jacob K. Swoope was born on September 21, 1800, in Pennsylvania and he died on March 2, 1841 (Find a Grave Memorial Number 84952098). Jacob was buried in Swoope Cemetery Number 4 at Wheeler in Lawrence County, Alabama; he was married two times. His first marriage was to Marie Antoinette Sherrod who was born on September 19, 1810. Jacob and Marie were married on May 15, 1828, in Lawrence County, Alabama. They had one child William who died prior to adulthood; Marie died in 1829.

According to <u>Early Settlers of</u> <u>Alabama</u> by James E. Saunders (1899), Jacob's second marriage was to Frances Anne Saunders (1808-1890) who was the daughter of Reverend Turner Saunders. Frances was born in Franklin, Tennessee, on April 12, 1808. They were married on November 16, 1830, in Columbus, Lowndes, Mississippi. Jacob and Frances had five children:

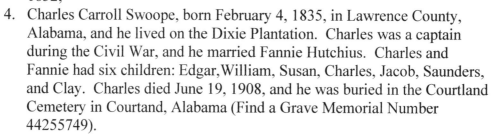

1. Lou Swoope;
2. James Saunders Swoope, born in Columbus, Mississippi;
3. Jacob K. Swoope Jr., born July 26, 1832;
4. Charles Carroll Swoope, born February 4, 1835, in Lawrence County, Alabama, and he lived on the Dixie Plantation. Charles was a captain during the Civil War, and he married Fannie Hutchius. Charles and Fannie had six children: Edgar, William, Susan, Charles, Jacob, Saunders, and Clay. Charles died June 19, 1908, and he was buried in the Courtland Cemetery in Courtand, Alabama (Find a Grave Memorial Number 44255749).
5. Frances Swoope, born 1838.

John McDowell Swoope

John McDowell Swoope (1804-11/22/1861) married Cynthia Early who was the daughter of Peter Early and Anne Smith. Cynthia's older sister Lucy Early married Colonel Richard Jones, a wealthy planter of Caldonia Plantation.

"John M. Swoope…was one of the best judges of goods in the place, and for several years spent a large part of his time in New York and Philadelphia in making purchases for the firm. Everything he did was well done. He was always neatly and richly dressed; never appeared on the street without having his clothes well brushed and his hat as slick as when it came from the block of the hatter.

Indeed, he was fastidiously neat in everything. His house and garden were kept in complete order…he became a cotton planter" (Saunders, 1899).

John M. Swoope

According to the 1850 Lawrence County, Alabama, United States Census, John M. Swoope was a white male born in Virginia of 52 years of age with an estimated year of birth being 1798. In addition to John M. Swoope in house number 545, the census lists Cyntha A. (Early) Swoope as a female of 38 years born in Georgia; Mary A. Swoope, female of 18 years and born in Alabama; Emma C. Swoope, female of 16 years born in Alabama; Virginia A. Swoope, female of 14 years born in Alabama, Jacob R. Swoope, male of 18 years born in Alabama; and, Charles C. Swoope, male of 16 years born in Alabama.

In the 1860 census, John M. Swoope is listed as a 62-year-old male born in Virginia. The value of his real estate was $53,000.00, and his personal property was worth $110,000.00. Also listed was Cynthia Swoope a 48-year-old female born in Georgia.

John McDowell Swoope was buried in the Swoope-Ussery Cemetery at Courtland in Lawrence County, Alabama (Find a Grave Memorial Number 26620428).

Edgar M. Swoope

Edgar M. Swoope was born in 1805; he was the son of Jacob and Mary Elizabeth McDowell Swoope. On June 7, 1831, Edgar married Elmira C. Watkins (1812-1886) in Lawrence County; she was the daughter of Samuel Watkins (1765-1835) and Eleanor Thompson (1771-1831). They had five children: Samuel Watkins Swoope (1832-1857); Maria E. Swoope (1834-1837); Orrin D. Swoope (1835-1840); infant Swoope (1838-1838); and, Mary Eleanor Swoope, who was born in 1848, and she married James Ballentine of Pulaski, Tennessee, on September 4, 1866.

According to the 1860 Lawrence County, Alabama, United States Census, Household 364, Edgar Swoope was a 55-year-old male Methodist Clergy born in Virginia. The value of his real estate was $62,000.00, and his personal property value was $170,500.00. Also in his household was E. C. Swoope a 49-year-old female born in Georgia, M. E. Swoope a ten-year-old female born in Alabama, and M. Taylor a 20-year-old male born in New York.

According to the <u>Moulton Advertiser</u> of Saturday March 23, 1867, "Edgar M. Swoope was born in 1805 and died on Wednesday evening, March 20, 1867, after a long and painful illness." Edgar is buried in Swoope Cemetery # 1 at Courtland in Lawrence County, Alabama (Find a Grave Memorial Number 47670427).

Sykes, James Turner

James Turner Sykes was the son of Dr. William Sykes and Birchett L. Turner. James Turner Sykes (1799-June 25, 1849) married Sarah 'Sallie' Winfield Dancy (July 26, 1794-January 29, 1835). James was elected to the state legislature in 1828, and he served as president of the Branch Bank at Decatur. James and Sallie had the following children:
1. Dr. Francis 'Frank' Winfield Sykes (1819-1883)
2. James Turner Sykes (1823-1852)
3. Winfield Sykes Malone (1827-1854)
4. Dr. Andrew Jackson 'Jack' Sykes (1830-1887).

According to the 1840 Lawrence County Census, James Turner Sykes was between 30 and 40 years old, and he owned 33 black slaves. James Turner Sykes died on June 25, 1849; he was buried Odd Fellows Rest Cemetery at Aberdeen in Monroe County, Mississippi (Find a Grave Memorial Number 1394225).

Dr. Francis 'Frank' W. Sykes

Francis 'Frank' Winfield Sykes was born on April 19, 1819, in Chatham County, North Carolina; he was the son of James Turner Sykes and Sarah Dancy Sykes. Frank W. Sykes attended Nashville and Transylvania University where he earned a diploma as a medical physician. Dr. Frank W. Sykes married Susan Elizabeth Garth (August 13, 1823-November 16, 1875). Susan was the daughter of General Jesse W. Garth (1788-1867), who lived near Decatur, and Unity S. Dandridge (1799-1833).

Dr. Frank Sykes purchased the plantation owned by Mr. George W. Foster, and retired from his medical practice. He was elected to the State House of Representatives several times, and in 1865 as State senator. During the reconstruction period, he was fairly elected United States senator, but he was unjustly excluded from his seat.

Frank and Elizabeth had one son John that died early and two daughters: Eunice Dandridge Sykes Michie (1844-1888) married Captain Michie of Charlottesville, Virginia; and Molly Sykes Groesbeck.

The 1850 Lawrence County, Alabama, United States Census, House Number 319, listed the following: Francis W. Sykes was a 31-year-old male born in North Carolina; S. E. Sykes was a 26-year-old female born in Alabama; Eunice Sykes was a five-year-old female born in Alabama; F. T. Sykes was a two-year-old male born in Alabama; and A. J. Sykes was a 20-year-old male born in Alabama.

The 1850 Lawrence County, Alabama, Slave Schedules state that Frank W. Sykes owned 36 black slaves. According to the 1850 Lawrence County, Alabama, Agricultural Census, Frank W. Sykes owned 700 acres of improved land and 700 acres of unimproved land valued at $14,000.00. His farm equipment was valued at $1,017.00, and he owned $2,300.00 worth of livestock.

The 1860 Northern Division, Lawrence County, Alabama, United States Census, listed the following: F. W. Sykes was a 40-year-old male planter born in North Carolina; Susan E. Sykes was a 38-year-old female born in Alabama; Emma Sykes was a 16-year-old female born in Alabama; Frances D. Sykes was a 11-year-old male born in Alabama; and Mary W. Sykes was a four-year-old female born in Alabama.

In the 1860 census, Frank W. Sykes had a real estate value of $23,800.00, and his personal property was worth $99,500.00. According to the 1860 Lawrence County, Alabama Slave Schedule, Frank W. Sykes owned 58 black slaves.

In the 1870 Lawrence County, Alabama, United States Census, Household 324, F. W. Sykes is a 53-year-old male farmer born in Alabama with a real estate value of $7,000.00 and his personal property was worth $1,800.00. Also in his household was Elizabeth S. a 46-year-old female born in Alabama, F. D. a 22-year-old male born in Alabama, and Mollie a 13-year-old female born in Alabama.

According to the <u>Moulton Democrat</u> on January 10, 1883, "Dr. Francis W. Sykes of Lawrence County, Alabama, died at Decatur, Alabama, January 6, 1883. Dr. Sykes was a native of North Carolina and at an early age came to Morgan County, afterwards settling near Courtland in Lawrence County. He represented Lawrence County repeatedly in the Legislature and in the Constitutional Convention of 1875. A Democratic Legislature elected him to the U. S. Senate since the War, but a radical Senate refused him his seat."

Frank W. Sykes died on January 6, 1883. He was buried in the Garth Cemetery at Decatur in Morgan County, Alabama (Find a Grave Memorial Number 21561527).

Dr. Andrew Jackson 'Jack' Sykes

Andrew Jackson Sykes was the son of James Turner Sykes and Sarah Dancy Sykes. Andrew married Emma Swoope who was born about 1833; she was the daughter of John M. Swoope and Cynthia Early. In the 1850 Lawrence County, Alabama, United States Census, Andrew is listed in household 319 with his brother Frank W. Sykes as a 20-year-old male born in Alabama.

According to the 1860 Lawrence County, Alabama, United States Census, Household 234, Andrew Jackson Sykes was a 30 year male old physician born in Alabama with a real estate value of $5,000.00 and a personal property value of $20,000.00. Also, listed in his house is E. C. Sykes a 27-year-old female born in Alabama, and Lucy a one-year-old female born in Alabama. In 1860, Andrew J. Sykes owned 15 black slaves.

Dr. Andrew Jackson 'Jack' Sykes, who served as a surgeon during the Civil War, died at the age of 56 on April 8, 1887, and he was buried in the Swoope-Ussery Cemetery at Courtland in Lawrence County, Alabama (Find a Grave Memorial Number 26622080). His wife Emma Swoope Sykes died in February 1922 at the age of 92.

Tinker, Dr. Harris

Around March 18, 1818, Dr. Harris Tinker married Susan King Croom who was born in 1793 in Lenoir County, North Carolina. Susan died before July 23, 1825, in Lawrence County, Alabama.

According to the 1820 Lawrence County, Alabama Census, the Harris Tinker household had one white male over 21, and two white females under 21. In the 1820 census, Harris Tinker owned 33 black slaves.

According to the 1830 Lawrence County, Alabama Census, the Harris Tinker household was listed without any occupants. In 1830, Harris Tinker owned 43 black slaves.

By 1840, Harris Tinker was listed in the Greene County, Alabama, United States Census. His household had three white males under 20, two white males 30-40, one white male 40-50, three white females under ten years old, and one white female 20-30.

According to the Lawrence County Archives records, Harris Tinker of Franklin County, Alabama, owned the NE¼ of Section 4, T4S, R9W; NE¼ of Section 5, T5S, R9W; NW¼ of Section 5, T5S, R9W; and, SE¼ of Section 32, T4S, R9W. His wife Susan R. Croom Tinker owned the NE¼ of the NW¼ of Section 10, T4S, R9W.

Tweedy, Joseph M.

Joseph M. Tweedy was born in Campbell County, Virginia, on April 6, 1806, and he died on July 2, 1875. He was buried in the Old Tweedy Cemetery at Courtland in Lawrence County, Alabama (Find a Grave Memorial Number 48174338). The Old Tweedy Cemetery is three miles northeast of Courtland, Alabama. Joseph married Mary Martin; they had two sons:

1. Robert Tweedy was born on February 28, 1831; he married Harriett Ophelia Featherston (Find a Grave Memorial Number 44602809). Robert and Harriett had the following children: Robert Howell Tweedy (1860-1936); Charles Eldrige Tweedy (1880-1955); and Alice Tweedy Durbin (1889-1977).
2. Joseph M. M. "Brother Mack" Tweedy was born on July 21, 1833, and he died on May 5, 1858, at age 24 (Find a Grave Memorial Number 48174392).

The Tweedy plantation home in Courtland was one of the oldest dwellings in Lawrence County being built between 1818 and 1819. The house was one of the earliest brick homes in North Alabama.

According to the 1850 Lawrence County, Alabama, Agricultural Census, Joseph M. Tweedy owned 430 acres of improved land and 162 acres of unimproved land worth $7,344.00. He had $590.00 worth of farming equipment and $1,320.00 worth of livestock. According to the 1850 Lawrence County, Alabama, Slave Schedules, Joseph M. Tweedy owned 29 black slaves.

Tweedy Home

Wade, Daniel

According to Early Settlers of Alabama, "Daniel Wade…came with the Booths, Fitzgeralds and Benjamin Ward from Virginia. He was a house builder, who employed many carpenters, and was doing a good business….He had married Martha Booth, a lovely daughter of William Booth, Sr., a planter living south of Courtland, and being anxious to own a home, contracted for a small plantation, and borrowed from a Shylock in Huntsville, four thousand dollars, at twenty per cent per month. His friend, Littleberry Jones, kindly became responsible for the debt, and succeeded in lowering the interest, but it eventually broke Wade and bent Jones, and Wade went to Florida with the small colony…It may seem strange that any sane man should have borrowed, as Wade did, a large sum of money at such a bloody rate of interest; but he was very sanguine, and having several houses going up, felt certain that he could meet the payment. The debt was sued upon; the case went up to the Supreme Court, and the decision made there was afterward one of the grounds of impeaching three of the Supreme Court judges" (Saunders, 1899).

In the Lawrence County Archive Minutes from June 1818 through December 1824, Daniel Wade was listed on reference page numbers 15, 16, 36, 49, 63, and 68. Most of these minute records concern court appointments on marking roads or other early items as the county began. Each one of these pages are available in their handwritten forms online at this site if copies are desired.

According to the Lawrence County Archives marriage records, Daniel Wade married Charlotte Booth on July 6, 1820. In the 1820 Lawrence County, Alabama Census, the Daniel Wade household had one white male over 21, and two white males under 21. In 1820, Daniel Wade owned 20 black slaves.

According the Lawrence County Archives records, Charlotte Booth Wade owned the SW¼ of Section 5 of T7S, R7W, and the W½ of the NE¼ of Section 36 of T5S, R8W. Daniel Wade owned Lot 116 in Courtland. Daniel also owned the SW¼ of Section 5 of T7S, R7W and the W½ of the NE¼ of Section 36, T5S, R8W.

Walker, David H.-Pleasant Ridge

According to Lawrence County Archives records, David H. Walker was born on June 23, 1797, in Virginia. He married Elizabeth Walker of Virginia who was born on July 12, 1800. David's wife Elizabeth died on October 16, 1847. On March 9, 1849, David H. Walker married the second time to Sarah A. Lester who was born on June 22, 1796. Based on census records, David H. and Elizabeth Walker had the following children:

1. John N. Walker was born about 1826. On September 30, 1846, John married Elizabeth Nance Walker who was born about 1827.
2. Benjamin F. Walker was born about 1828. Benjamin married Margaret Walker who was born in Alabama about 1834. In the 1860 census, his stepmother Sarah Walker was living in his household, and she was listed at age 66 born in Virginia. Benjamin owned 36 black slaves in 1860 with a real estate value of $3,000.00 and personal property value of $30,000.00.
3. David H. Walker Jr. was born about 1830. David married Virginia who was born about 1838. David H. Walker Jr. owned 24 black slaves in 1860 with a real estate value was $3,500.00 and personal property value of $22,985.00.

David H. Walker Sr. was not found in Lawrence County, Alabama, until 1830, but in 1830, David owned 21 black slaves. By the 1840, Lawrence County, Alabama Census, David H. Walker owned 51 black slaves, and he was living at his Pleasant Ridge home. According to the 1850 District 8, Lawrence County, Alabama, Slave Schedules, David H. Walker owned 58 black slaves.

In the 1840 Lawrence County, Alabama, United States Census, the David H. Walker household had four males under 20 years old, one male 40-50 years old, two females under 20 years old, and two females 40-50 years old.

In the 1850 Lawrence County, Alabama United States Census, House Number 395, David H. Walker was a 51-year-old male born in Virginia, Sarah Walker was a 53-year-old female born in Virginia, Benjamin Walker was a 22-year-old male overseer born in Alabama, David Walker was a 20-year-old male born in Alabama. In 1850, the value of the David H. Walker farm was $4,000.00.

David H. Walker Sr. died on November 28, 1855. According to Lawrence County Archives records, David H. Walker's estate was handled by his son John N. Walker, administrator in 1858. In 1860, Sarah Walker, the second wife of David, had 15 black slaves.

The Walker Family Cemetery is located west of Moulton about five miles in Lawrence County, Alabama. The following burials are found in the Walker Family Cemetery:
1. Walker, David H., born June 23, 1797, died November 28, 1855 (Find a Grave Memorial Number 130842757);
2. Walker, Elizabeth, born July 12, 1800, died October 16, 1847 (Find a Grave Memorial Number 130842815);
3. Walker, Elizabeth Nance, born May 9, 1827, died July 30, 1852 (Find a Grave Memorial Number 130842936);
4. Walker, Franklin Pope, born June 22, 1854, died July 20, 1855, son of B. F. and Margaret Walker (Find a Grave Memorial Number 130842998);
5. Walker, Infant c/o John N. and Elizabeth Walker (Find a Grave Memorial Number 130843034);
6. Walker, John D., born 1855, died January 2, 1857, son of B. F. and Margaret Walker Walker (Find a Grave Memorial Number 130843092). According to the Moulton Democrat, Friday, January 9, 1857, "Departed

this life on Friday the 2nd inst., at the residence of B.F. Walker, John D., infant son of B.F. and Margaret Walker-aged 1 year, 9 months, and 2 days;"

7. Walker, Kate, born July 12, 1859, died September 5, 1860, daughter of B. F. and Margaret Walker Walker (Find a Grave Memorial Number 1308423169);
8. Walker, Sarah H., born June 22, 1796, died June 24, 1860, in Dreing County, Arkansas; she was the second wife of David H. Walker Sr. (Find a Grave Memorial Number 130843221);
9. Walker, William J., born July 1, 1838, died June 14, 1841 (Find a Grave Memorial Number 130843281);
10. Walker, William J., born April 15, 1832, died March 28, 1836 (Find a Grave Memorial Number 130843255).

John N. Walker

John N. Walker was the son of David H. Walker. On September 30, 1846, John N. Walker married Elizabeth Nance Walker in Lawrence County, Alabama; she was the daughter of Samuel and Catherine Young Walker. Elizabeth was born on May 9, 1827, and she died on July 30, 1852.

The 1850 Lawrence County, Alabama United States Census, House Number 313, listed the following: John N. Walker was a 24-year-old male born in Alabama; Elizabeth Walker was a 23-year-old female born in Alabama; and Sarah Walker was a two-year-old female born in Alabama. In 1850, the farm of John N. Walker was worth $2,500.00. In the 1850 Lawrence County, Alabama, Slave Schedules, John N. Walker owned 10 black slaves.

According to the 1850 Lawrence County, Alabama Agricultural Census, John N. Walker had 150 acres of improved land and 164 acres of unimproved land valued at $2,500.00. He owned $100.00 worth of farm equipment and $392.00 worth of livestock.

In 1858, John N. Walker was the administrator of the estate of his father David H. Walker Sr. John N. Walker's first wife and infant child were buried in the Walker Family Cemetery. Elizabeth Nance Walker, wife of John N. Walker and daughter of Samuel and Catherine Young, died on July 3, 1852. She was buried in the Walker Family Cemetery in Lawrence County, Alabama. On April 11, 1855, John N. Walker married the second time to S. A. McKelvey.

LouAllen Farms

Today in 2019, the old David H. Walker homeplace and some 80 acres of the original plantation belongs to the Larry LouAllen family who still farms the area; however, instead of cotton, Larry specializes in strawberries, peaches, tomatoes, and green house plants, flowers, and shrubs. His fruit farm is known as LouAllen Farms and consists of six green houses, a huge peach orchard, strawberry beds, as well as various types of vegetables.

Larry's parents were Jerry Freeman LouAllen and Helen Cameron who were childhood sweethearts. Jerry and Helen attended Bera (Berryman) School together when they were in elementary grades. The school was located at Muck City some five miles west of Moulton on old Highway 24. On February 3, 1938, Jerry and Helen went to the Lawrence County Courthouse in Moulton where they were married by Probate Judge Charles Bragg. Mrs. LouAllen stated that she and her husband got electricity in their home after being married a few years.

In 1946, Jerry and Helen LouAllen bought a portion of the old David H. Walker plantation including the original home which was built in 1830. They purchased the property from Arthur Young who had bought the land from Cliff

David H. Walker Home

Long. Not long after buying the place, Jerry and Helen LouAllen moved into the plantation house of David H. Walker. They lived in the old Walker plantation log house for 19 years before building their own home. Mrs. Helen LouAllen said, "The Walker log house was over 100 years old when we moved there, and we were told that it was built by black slaves. This old man who was a relative of the Walker family came from Birmingham, and he told us that his family's ancestors stood in the yard and watched a battle during the Civil War." The Walker family could see the fight which was probably during Streight's Raid around April 28, 1863, as he moved his some 1,500 Union troops from Mt. Hope to Moulton, Alabama, and passed by the plantation.

Mrs. LouAllen stated, "The field near the old house was full of arrowheads." This indicates prehistoric long-term human habitation and an Indian village site in the area that became the David H. Walker Plantation. It also suggests that Indian trails and roads connected the Indian settlement to other villages and passed through the plantation site. The Chickasaw Trail which passed through Moulton to Russellville crossed through or in close proximity to the Walker plantation.

When the Jerry and Helen Louallen first bought the place, they farmed small tracts of cotton for their living with a pair of mules named Ider and Ader. Jerry eventually sold the mules to Jess Barrett, and later bought the same pair of mules back from Jess. Mrs. LouAllen said, "I think we farmed ten to fifteen acres of cotton with those mules. The first year after we were married, we got our crops gathered and paid our bills. We did not have but thirty dollars left, and could not pay his daddy what we owed him."

Jerry and Helen LouAllen had the following children: Shirley Glenn LouAllen, Hershel LouAllen, Mary LouAllen Borden, Margaret LouAllen Dixon, Larry LouAllen, Janice LouAllen Welch, Harold LouAllen, Randall LouAllen, and Ronnie LouAllen. Ms. Helen LouAllen said that before school started each year that they would go to Ed King's department store in Moulton and buy all the kids school clothes.

Jerry and Helen LouAllen also grew some sugar cane that they had made in molasses at the syrup mill owned by Jerry's father. Jerry also cut stave bolts and cedar fence posts for a little extra money. Helen plucked geese to make feather beds; when I interviewed her in 2017, she said that she still had three feather beds in her home. Jerry and Helen finally found the Lord at the old schoolhouse at Muck City where they first met. After that meeting, they attended church on a regular basis.

The old David H. Walker plantation house stood on its original site for many years before it burned to the ground in the late 1990s. The LouAllen's had rented the house to some folks who built a big fire in the fireplace which caught the house on fire. Today, the old Walker plantation homeplace is still known as Pleasant Ridge.

Walker, John A.

According to the marriage records of Lawrence County, Alabama, John A. Walker married Mary Goggans. According to the 1820 Lawrence County, Alabama Census, John A. Walker owned 101 black slaves. In the 1830 census, John owned only 24 slaves.

In the 1830 Lawrence County, Alabama Census, the John A. Walker household had one male five and under, one male 20-30, one male 40-50, one female 5-10, two females 20-30, and one female 50-60. In the state census of October 8, 1835, John A. Walker was listed two names under Colonel Ben Sherrod.

According to Lawrence County Archives records, John A. Walker owned the following land: Section 17, T4S, R7W, NE¼; Section 23, T3S, R8W, WSE; Section 18, T3S, R8W, E½; Section 21, T3S, R8W, E½ of NE¼; Section 22, T3S, R8W, W½ of NW¼; Section 16, T3S, R8W, SE¼ and NE¼; Section 18, T3S, R8W, Part of E½; Section 18, T3S, R8W, E½; Section 17, T4S, R7W; and Section 17, T4S, R7W, SW¼.

Walton, George Sr.

Joseph Martin was from Georgia and married a sister of George Walton. Joseph Martin and his neighbor George Walton left Georgia together and settled in Lawrence County, Alabama, seven miles northwest of Courtland.

George Walton, son of Jesse, was born 1774 in Goochland County, Virginia. He died on August 5, 1850, in Panola County, Texas. Around 1800, George married Rebecca Isaacs, daughter of Colonel Elijah Isaacs. Rebecca was born about 1778. She died before 1850 in Panola County, Texas. George and Rebecca had the following children:

1. Samuel W. Walton married Mary Wilkinson Loe.
2. Martin Walton was born 1801 in Georgia. On August 5, 1824, he married Abigail Jones of Lawrence County, Alabama.
3. Jesse Walton of Mississippi was born 1803 in Georgia; he married Ellen Steen.
4. George J. Walton was born 1805 in Georgia. On January 7, 1835, he married Frances B. Linthicum of Lawrence County, Alabama.
5. Robert Walton was born 1808 in Tennessee. He first married Betsy Loe and later Sarah Woodley of Texas.
6. Killis Walton was born 1810 in Tennessee; he married Margaret Ross of Mississippi.
7. Sarah Walton married a Young of Alabama.
8. Mary Walton was born 1813 in Tennessee; she married Champion Smith of Alabama.
9. Andrew J. "Jack" Walton was born 1817 in Alabama. On November 21, 1837, Jack married Permelia M. Bowling of Lawrence County, Alabama. Jack and Permelia became heirs of her father James M. Bowling.
10. Elizabeth Walton was born 1819 in Alabama; she married George Bowling of Alabama.
11. Verlinda Walton married Jabez Booker of Alabama.
12. William W. Walton was born 1824 in Alabama, and was buried in Oakwood Cemetery at Austin, Texas. William married Caroline Standefer of Texas.

Samuel W. Walton and Mary Wilkinson Loe Walton had the following children:

1. Major William 'Buck' Martin Walton, Confederate States of America, was born January 17, 1832, in Canton, Mississippi. He died on July 1, 1915, in Austin, Texas. On February 9, 1854, William married Letitia 'Lettie' Ann Watkins. She was the daughter of Dr. Thomas Alexander Watkins and Sarah Epes Fitzgerald, at Forest Place in Carrollton, Mississippi. Lettie was

born March 21, 1835, in Courtland, Alabama, and she died June 23, 1914, in Austin, Texas.

2. George Lowe (Loe) Walton was born January 27, 1830, near Courtland in Lawrence County, Alabama. On April 5, 1855, George married Amanda Moore, daughter of Dr. Charles Hamilton Moore and Matilda C. Graham. Amanda was born 1833 in Concordia Parish, Louisiana. She died on January 10, 1922, in Concordia Parish, Louisiana, and was buried in Natchez City Cemetery. George died February 21, 1909, in Concordia Parish, Louisiana; he was buried in Natchez City Cemetery.

According to the 1820 Lawrence County, Alabama Census, the George Walton household had one white male over 21, seven white males under 21, one white female over 21, and three white females under 21. In 1820, George owned 12 black slaves. In the 1830 census, George Walton owned 44 black slaves.

According to the Lawrence County Archive records, George Walton owned the SE¼ of Section 7 of T6S and R8W and the SW¼ of Section 6 of T6S and R8W. Martin Walton owned the SW¼ of Section 11 of T5S and R9W and the SW¼ of the NW¼ of Section 11 of T6S and R9W. The Lawrence County Archives from June 1818 through December 1824 stated that George Walton and other men were appointed by court to mark out a road from Courtland to Tennessee River.

Warren, Levi Ford

Levi Ford Warren was the son of Thomas Warren (1759-1819) and Mary McWilliams Warren (1764-1850). Levi was a brother of Robert B. Warren who owned 20 slaves in 1860. According to Lawrence County Archives marriage records, on February 4, 1845, Levi F. Warren married Tabitha Jane Preuit in Lawrence County, Alabama.

The 1850 Lawrence County, Alabama, United States Census, House Number 849, listed the following: Levi F. Warren was a 49-year-old male born in South Carolina; Tabatha J. Warren was a 40-year-old female born in Alabama; Jacob Warren was a 20-year-old male born in Alabama; Andrew Warren was a 15-year-old male born in Alabama; Eliza Warren was a 12-year-old female born in Alabama; Martha Warren was a ten-year-old female born in Alabama; Susan Warren a six-year-old female born in Alabama; Julia Warren a four-year-old female born in Alabama; and Levi Warren a one-year-old male born in Alabama. In the 1850 Lawrence County, Alabama, Slave Schedules, Levi F. Warren owned 50 black slaves. On June 26, 1853, Levi F. Warren married Nancy Ann Ferguson Rose of Lawrence County, Alabama; she was born in Tennessee in 1811.

The 1860 Southern Division, Lawrence County, Alabama, United States Census, listed the following: Levi F. Warren was a 58-year-old male farmer born in South Carolina; Nancy A. Warren was a 51-year-old female born in Tennessee; Andrew J. Warren was a 25-year-old male born in Alabama; Susan Warren was a 16-year-old female born in Alabama; Julia Warren was a 13-year-old female born in Alabama; Levi Warren was an 11-year-old male born in Alabama; and Rebecca Warren was a nine-year-old female born in Alabama. According to the 1860 census, Levi Ford Warren had real estate value of $16,800.00 and a personal property value of $61,000.00. In the 1860 Lawrence County, Alabama Largest Slave Holders, Levi F. Warren owned 67 black slaves.

Levi F. Warren was a deputy with Andrew Kaiser for Hugh M. Warren, the third sheriff of Lawrence County. Hugh M. Warren's deputy, Andrew Kaiser, studied medicine, found some mineral springs in Winston County that he called Kaiser's Springs and settled there. His other deputy, Levi F. Warren, lived near Moulton and amassed a very large fortune as a cotton planter. Levi F. Warren died before 1880.

Levi Ford Warren's second wife Nancy Ann Ferguson Rose Warren died on November 11, 1891, at Hillsboro in Lawrence County, Alabama. Nancy was the daughter of William Ferguson and wife of James A. Rose (1797-1850). She was buried in Rose Cemetery in Lawrence County, Alabama (Find a Grave Memorial Number 76639395). According to information on record in the Lawrence County Archives, the Rose Cemetery in a family cemetery located in a pasture in a small stand of trees, approximately 400 yards off County Road 222 just to the right of a home at 7888 County Road 222, near County Road 431, between Trinity and Hillsboro in Lawrence County, Alabama.

According to the Lawrence County Archives, Levi Ford Warren owned the following land: Section 18, T7S, R7W, SW¼; Section 3, T8S, R6W, NW¼ of

NW¼; Section 27, T7S, R6W, W½ of NW¼; Section 28, T7S, R6W, E½ of S½ of SW¼; Section 28, T7S, R6W, S½ of W½ of SE¼; Section 28, T7S, R6W, W½ of NE¼; Section 34, T7S, R6W, S½ of SE¼; Section 34, T7S, R6W, N½ of SE¼; Section 36, T7S, R6W, NW¼ of SW¼; Section 29, T4S, R8W, SW¼; and, Section 29, T4S, R8W, SW¼.

Watkins, Robert H.-Oak Grove

Robert H. Watkins Sr. was born on October 1, 1782, in Prince Edward County, Virginia. On April 25, 1805, Robert married Prudence Thompson Oliver in Petersburg, Georgia. Prudence was born on October 22, 1788; she was the daughter of John and Frances Thompson Oliver of Petersburg, Georgia. Robert Watkins Sr. and Prudence Thompson Oliver Watkins had the following children:

1) Mary Frances Watkins was born November 13, 1809, and she died on February 6, 1889. She married James E. Saunders, of Lawrence County, Alabama.

2) Sarah Independence Watkins was born July 4, 1811, and she died on January 30, 1887. She married George W. Foster of Florence, Alabama.

3) James Lawrence Watkins was born on May 10, 1814, and he died in 1891. James married Eliza Patton of Huntsville, Alabama.

4) Virginia Prudence Watkins was born on October 22, 1816, and she died on May 12, 1837. Virginia married Thomas Jefferson Foster of Florence, Alabama.

5) Louisa Matilda Watkins was born on December 29, 1819, and she died in 1892. Louisa married Stephen W. Harris of Huntsville, Alabama.

6) Robert H. Watkins was born on May 10, 1824, and he married Margaret Lindsay Carter of Pulaski, Tenn.

According to James E. Saunders (1899), "Robert H. Watkins moved to Lawrence County, Alabama, in 1821, bringing with him his wife's brother, John Oliver....He settled in Lawrence County, Alabama, four miles north of Courtland, and built a large red brick mansion called Oak Grove. In old age, he partitioned out his lands and slaves to his children. In 1849, Robert and his wife moved to Pulaski, Tennessee, and made their home near their youngest child, Robert H. Watkins Jr. Here they lived in great content until his death. His widow, with an ample income, thenceforth resided alternately with each of her children, driving to their homes with her own carriage, maid, and coachman.

Major Robert H. Watkins was over six foot in height, and had a finely proportioned person….Major Watkins was the neighbor and intimate friend of Colonel Sherrod, but they were rivals in cotton planting. In their rapid accumulation of wealth (which was only equaled by one planter in Madison County)….Major Watkins owned all the land from the first hill north of Courtland to the

Oak Grove

Tennessee River; and when Colonel Sherrod, for want of room, took his flight to the Chickasaw cession, Major Watkins passed the Tennessee River and made large purchases on Elk River….Major Watkins, a man of wonderful physical strength and endurance, superintended his overseers as closely as they did the hands and he moved business on with great energy. While Colonel Sherrod, whose health would not bear exposure, accomplished about as much by systematic management; but to do this he had to employ overseers of a higher grade and at greater costs. But there was a principle of action which was common to both of those great managers, and that was never to expend labor on poor land….On the plantations I cultivate, it requires double the number of laborers it did before the emancipation, to work the same land; and it is therefore very costly. No matter on what contract you work, labor must be paid in some form labor must have food and clothing, and houses and fuel, in winter; therefore you should work (as the eminent planters did) none

Robert H. Watkins Sr.

292

but rich lands…In their old age Major Watkins and his excellent wife moved to Pulaski, and after some years they died (Saunders, 1899).

Robert H. Watkins Sr. and Jr. owned the Oak Grove Plantation. In 1849, Robert H. Watkins Sr. and his wife moved to Pulaski, Tennessee. Their son Robert H. Watkins Jr. ran the plantation for his parents.

According to the 1850 Lawrence County, Alabama, Slave Schedules, Robert H. Watkins owned 140 black slaves. In 1850, Lawrence County, Alabama, Agricultural Census, Robert H. Watkins owned 2,033 acres of improved land and 3,000 acres of unimproved land worth $30,000.00. He also had $1,112.00 worth of farm equipment and $4,887.00 worth of livestock.

According to the 1850 Lauderdale County, Alabama, Slave Schedules, Robert H. Watkins owned 85 black slaves. In 1850, Lauderdale County, Alabama, Agricultural Census, Robert H. Watkins owned 800 acres of improved land and 700 acres of unimproved land valued at $18,000.00.

Major Robert H. Watkins died on September 10, 1855, in Pulaski, Tennessee. He was buried Maplewood Cemetery at Pulaski in Giles County, Tennessee (Find a Grave Memorial Number 46356342). Prudence Thompson Oliver Watkins died in Huntsville, Alabama, in October 20, 1867. Prudence was buried in the Maple Hill Cemetery at Huntsville in Madison County, Alabama (Find a Grave Memorial Number 53674726).

Watkins, Samuel

Samuel Watkins was born in Prince Edward County, Virginia, on May 17, 1765; he was the son of James B. Watkins and Martha Watkins. His siblings were: 1) William Watkins; 2) James Watkins, Jr.; 3) Sarah Herndon Thompson; 4) Robert H. Watkins; 5) John Watkins; 6) Garland Thompson Watkins; 7) Joseph Watkins; 8) Isham Watkins; 9) Lucy Johns; and 10) Thompson Watkins.

Samuel Watkins married Eleanor Thompson Watkins, and they had the following children:
1. Eliza H. Watkins Sherrod
2. Paul J. 'Don' Watkins (1795-1861)

3. Eleanor Watkins Thompson (1801-1826)
4. Edgar Watkins (1805-1887)
5. Elmira Watkins Swoope (1812-1886).

According to Early Settlers of Alabama by James E. Saunders (1899), "Samuel Watkins…removed to Elbert County, Georgia, about 1783, and there married Eleanor Thompson, daughter of Robert Thompson….She had been born also in Virginia….Mr. Samuel Watkins was not only a large cotton planter on Broad River, but a merchant doing a large business in the town of Petersburg, Georgia….Mr. Samuel Watkins purchased a large tract of land in Lawrence County, extending from the head of Spring Creek southward to the Brown's Ferry Road, and his eldest son, Paul J. Watkins, moved out, and prepared the lands for cultivation, and built the houses, so that

Samuel Watkins

his father, when he came to his new home, had to hang up his hat….Mr. Samuel Watkins and his wife were members of the Methodist Church. They had a family of five children. Eliza, the first wife of Colonel Sherrod, who died in Georgia, Paul J., Edgar, and Elmira, who married Rev. Edgar M. Swoope….Eleanor, daughter of Mr. Samuel Watkins, married Jessie Thompson, and died in a short time after her marriage, without issue" (Saunders, 1899).

Samuel Watkins was the only Watkins listed in the 1820 Lawrence County, Alabama Census. He was over 21 years old, and he owned 31 black slaves. In 1830, he owned 96 black slaves. Samuel Watkins died on October 8, 1835, in Lawrence County, Alabama.

According to the Lawrence County Archives, Samuel Watkins owned the land in the SW¼ of Section 22 of T4S and R6W, the SE¼ of Section 13 of T4S and R7W; the S½ of Section 15 of T4S and R7W, and the E½ of the NW¼ of Section 26 of T4S and R7W.

Paul James "Don" Watkins-Flower Hill

Paul James 'Don' Watkins was born on November 1, 1795, at Petersburg in Gordon County, Georgia. His parents were Samuel Watkins (1765-1835) and Eleanor Thompson Watkins (1771-1831). In 1820, Paul preceded his parents to Alabama, for whom he purchased a plantation. After clearing up the Spring Creek place for his father, he purchased a large tract of land on the Tennessee River below Brown's Ferry that he called 'Flower Hill Plantation.' His place was used primarily for the growing and cultivation of cotton, but he also planted many varieties of flowering plants, thus the name 'Flower Hill' became the name of his plantation. "Like his mother, Eleanor Thompson, he made his home a floral kingdom, and his exquisite collection was noted throughout North Alabama. He preserved much of his family history of which he wrote an abstract in 1853" (Saunders, 1899).

In 1822, Paul J. Watkins married Elizabeth Watt in Madison County, Tennessee. Elizabeth who was born on July 21, 1804, in Lawrence County, Alabama; she was the daughter of John Watt and Nancy Scales. Elizabeth Watt Watkins (1804-1856) was a sister to Alfred Watt (1806-1840) and Amelia Ann Watt Sykes (1816-1847). Paul J. and Elizabeth Watt Watkins had the following children:

1. Eliza Sherrod Watkins (1824-1879) married John T Phinizy.
2. Susan Watkins married Ephraim H. Foster of Nashville, Tennessee.
3. Amelia A. Watkins (1829-1855) married Colonel Edward Munford of Virginia.
4. Martha Jane Watkins (1832-1852) married William S. Bankhead of Courtland, but they did not have children.
5. Mary E. Watkins was born in 1833. On October 16, 1855, she married James Branch of Virginia. Mary died on March 7, 1888, at Courtland in Lawrence County, Alabama. She was buried at the Watkins-Watt Cemetery at Flower Hill Plantation.

According to the 1830 Lawrence County, Alabama Census, Paul James 'Don' Watkins owned 42 black slaves. In 1840, his number of slaves is missing, but in the 1850 slave schedules, he owned 161 slaves. In the 1860 records, Paul Watkins is listed with 148 slaves.

Paul J. Watkins married the second time in 1857 to Mary Morrison of Huntsville, Alabama. Paul James "Don" Watkins died on November 6, 1861, at Flower Hill Plantation in Lawrence County, Alabama. From <u>Footprints in Time</u> by Myra Borden (1993), "Huntsville Democrat Newspaper Nov 6, 1861 Died at his residence in Lawrence County on Tuesday the 20th of October, Paul J. Watkins, aged 66 years less 5 days." Paul James "Don" Watkins is buried in the Watkins-Watt Cemetery at Flower Hill Plantation in Lawrence County, Alabama (Find a Grave Memorial Number 47649058).

From <u>The Southern Advocate</u> on July 31, 1856, "Died in Lawrence County, Alabama on 18th, Mrs. Elizabeth Watkins consort of Paul J. Watkins aged 52 years." Her parents were John Watt (?-1821) and Nancy Scales Watt (1787-1841). Elizabeth was buried in the Watkins-Watt Cemetery at Flower Hill Plantation in Lawrence County, Alabama (Find A Grave Memorial Number 47634068). The Watkins-Watt Cemetery was on the Flower Hill Plantation in Lawrence County, Alabama. The cemetery is on a small hill in a field on the east side of the Mallard Creek Road.

Winston, Isaac, Jr.

Isaac Winston was born on February 1, 1829, in Alabama; he was the son of Isaac Winston (January 22, 1795-August 13, 1863) and Catherine Baker Jones Winston (December 15, 1798-July 25, 1884) of Belle Mont Plantation in Franklin County, Alabama. The siblings of Issac Winston Jr. were Mary Susan Winston Armistead (1822-1879), Infant Winston son (1830), Catherine Baker Winston Burt (1832-1876), Elizabeth Jane Winston Bowling (1834-1892), and Infant Winston daughter (1836), Madora V. Winston (1839-1852), and Ella Walker Winston Thornton (1840?-1904).

Isaac Winston Jr.

On October 11, 1852, Issac married Olive Bland Michie in Fayette County, Tennessee. Olive Bland Michie Winston was born on November 6, 1834, in Tennessee. Issac and Olive had the following children:

1. Isaac 'Ike' Winston (1853-1923)
2. Charles 'Charlie' Winston (1855-1888)
3. Walker Winston (1858-1913)
4. Sarah 'Sallie' Mann Winston MacArthur (1861-1950)

Olive Winston

The following were enumerated in the 1850 Lawrence County, Alabama, United States Census, House Number 184: John J. Ray, agent for Isaac Winston, male, 36, white, Virginia, $36,600.00; Julia Ray, female, 36, Virginia. The 1850 Lawrence County, Alabama Slave Census lists John J. Ray as an agent for Isaac Winston who owned 77 black slaves.

In the 1850 Lawrence County, Alabama, Agricultural Census, Isaac Winston owned 1,500 acres of improved land 500 acres of unimproved land with a cash value of his farm being $30,000.00. The value of his farming equipment was $1,000.00 and his livestock was valued at $4,454.00.

According to the 1860 Lawrence County, Alabama Slave Schedules, Isaac Winston owned 80 black slaves. The 1860 Lawrence County, Alabama, United States Census, Household 255 gives Isaac Winston real estate value at $30,000.00 and the value of his personal property at $68,000.00. Issac was listed as a 30-year-old male planter born in Alabama with Olivia a 25-year-old female born in Tennessee, Isaac, Jr. a six-year-old male born in Alabama, Charlie a four-year-old male born in Alabama, and Walker a one-year-old male born in Alabama.

By 1870, Olivia Winston and her children were back in Fayette County, Tennessee. Her husband Issac Winston died in 1863 during the Civil War.

Olive Bland Michie Winston died on March 29, 1913, at Manhattan in New York County, New York. Her death notice was in the <u>Washington Post</u> on

April 01, 1913; she was listed as a daughter of Charles Michie and wife of Isaac Winston.

Isaac Winston Jr. died during the Civil War on May 1, 1863. He was buried in Congressional Cemetery in Washington, District of Columbia, on October 18, 1894 (Find a Grave Memorial Number 10170937).

During the first years of the Civil War, the plantation Issac Winston Jr. was under the control of Union forces. The following transcribed letter from Isaac Winston Jr. is a desperate plea to General Buel concerning his plantation and family in Town Creek, Alabama.

"Maj Gen Buel, Commanding U. S. Forces at Tuscumbia: General Buel, I am a Southerncr, but hope neverless that common justice will induce you to listen to my protest against being made the victim of the petty spite of Col Straight of the 51st Indiana Regiment commanding U. S. Forces at this Point, Because I dared to avow my principles and remonstrate with the men who intruded upon my Family at all hours robbed my Garden and Shops and refused to sell them articles I could not spare I was threatened with arrest and forced to fly from home leaving my Wife and Children unprotected, Col. Straight has had hauled from my cribs nineteen wagon loads of corn under protest from me that he was depriving my Family of Bread and knowing I will never accept one cent by way of compensation. What is money worth when we want Bread? I had no corn to spare will now be compelled to buy. And Secondly was not willing to trade with the Enemies of my Country. The Quarter Master of the Mechanics Engineers concurred in all Col. Straights exactions and took three Beeves from me knowing I received no compensation, because when he avowed his readiness to sweep the Southern Country even Women and Children I unable to control my feelings expressed my horror of the man who could acknowledge such Sentiments. Col Straight has written me a note now in my position, saying, "I ought to be tried for treason and hung. I write because I have been informed that you are disposed to deal honorably toward all Southerners and think it but common justice to myself that you should be made aware of the manner in which Col Straight has acted towards me. I desire no pay for what has been taken from me, but merely call your attention to Col. Straight's proceedings. Col Shumaker of the 31st Michigan Regiment is cognisant of the whole affair, and although I have no authority from him for doing so I refer you to him for his version as I believe him to be truly honorable and willing to see justice awarded even an Enemy. Col. Shumaker has protected my Family since I left, so far as lay in his power, for which kindness I am indeed grateful. When Gen Mitchells Division were here they took from me forty ham's of Bacon besides constantly intruding upon my Family threatening me with violence, forcing locks and robbing constantly. When I heard of the advance of your Army, I hoped for at least Justice knowing you to be a Western man and having heard praises of your moderation and leniency from even your political Enemies. I am a true Southerner can submit to a military necessity, at the same time as a freeman have rights and privileges upon which no one can trample You can obtain other evidence that this was a particular case. On no other plantation was such a large quantity of corn taken (leaving so little), thus proving it was done through malice and spite. Respectfully, Isaac Winston Jr.

P.S. The first morning on which corn was sent for I addressed a note to Col. Shumaker informing him I had no corn to sell not having more than my Family would consume, he merely replied that he was not commanding here and of course he was not the proper person to whome to apply but to Col Straight the latter sent a verbal message through the Officer that if I preferred to burn my property to letting them have it, a few hours would be allowed me I wrote to enquire if my Family would be molested in consequence and requesting him to specify the time he could allow. When I received the note to which I have referred threatening me with hanging and informing me it was his duty to enforce the laws. Respectfully, I.W. Jr.

The following is the reply to Issac Winston Jr. letter from a Union Army Captain: Town Creek Bridge, July 28, 1862, Hon. Isaac Winston
Dear Sir: Some difficulties which have occurred at Courtland today many of the cavalry of that place are destitute of rations without any means of supplying the same at this time. You know the difficulty of producing supplies with consent of _____. Therefore, any damage done your property shall be promptly accepted for our being p_____ the disturbed condition? of the country around? --------f-ming at a distance from camp-------- and labor----. Yours Respectfully, Captain W.Mc????? --

Woolridge, Thomas F.

Thomas Wooldridge was born about 1752 in Chesterfield, Virgina, and he died before 1830 in Alabama. His parents were William Wooldridge and Sarah Flournoy. William and Sarah had the following children: Absolum Wooldridge, William Wooldridge, Sarah Wooldridge, Penina Wooldridge, Cinthy Wooldridge, Pamelia Emily Wooldridge, Thomas Wooldridge, Augustus B. Wooldridge, Teressa Wooldridge.

Thomas first married Cheriah (Chreia) Davis, and his second marriage was to Martha Easter Aycock. Chirial Davis Woolridge was born about 1760, and she died in 1836 in Lawrence County, Alabama or Texas. Thomas F. Woolridge and Chirial Davis Woolridge had the following children:

1. Frances J. Woolridge was born on October 11, 1800, in Abbeville, South Carolina. She died on December 25, 1835, in Matagorda, Texas. Frances married James Harris on February 19, 1818, in Abbeville, South Carolina. He was born on August 5, 1797, in Abbeville, South Carolina, and died June 30, 1838, in Goliad, Texas.

2. Permelia Emily Woolridge was born on March 7, 1801, in Elbert County, Georgia. She died on August 31, 1881, near Center Creek at Heber City in Wasatch County, Utah. Permelia first married Jordan Yarbrough Hundly on October 27, 1817, at Huntsville in Madison County, Alabama. He was born about 1784 in Bedford County, Virginia, and died before July 27, 1835, in Mississippi. Permelia married the second time to Samuel McRae Rooker on July 27, 1835, at Macon in Noxubee County, Mississippi. He was born on October 5, 1813, in York County, South Carolina, and he died on November 16, 1894, near Center Creek at Heber City in Wasatch County, Utah.

3. Thomas Davis Woolridge was born on July 22, 1802, in Elbert County, Georgia, and he died on January 7, 1860, in Texas. Thomas married

Nancy Banks on February 13, 1821, in Elbert County, Georgia. Nancy was born in 1803 in Elbert County, Georgia.

4. Absolom Davis Woolridge was born in 1804 in Elbert, County, Georgia, and died in 1822 at Chattahoochee, Georgia.

The 1820 Lawrence County, Alabama Census listed the following: Thomas Woolridge, white males over 21: 1, white males under 21: 4, white females over 21: 1, white females under 21: 1, total whites: 7. According to the 1820 census, Thomas F. Woolridge owns 17 black slaves.

According to the Commissioner's Court of Lawrence County, Alabama, June 1818 through December 1824, the document stated that the court wanted a road from the place of Melton's Bluff at Marathon to the house of Thomas Woolridge in the Town of Courtland.

References

1820 Lawrence County, Alabama, United States Census

1830 Lawrence County, Alabama, United States Census

1840 Lawrence County, Alabama, United States Census

1850 Lawrence County, Alabama, Agricultural Census

1850 Lawrence, Alabama, United States Census

1860 Lawrence County, Alabama, United States Census

1860 Lawrence County, Alabama, Slave Schedule

1870 Lawrence County, Alabama, United States Census

1880 Lawrence County, Alabama, United States Census

Albright, Edward, Early History of Middle Tennessee, Brandon Printing Company, Nashville, Tennessee, 1909.

Ancestry.Com

Borden, Myra, Footprints in Time, Borden's Genealogical Books, Mt. Hope, Alabama, 1993.

Bowling, Peggy A., A Recreated Journal from the life of Burchet (Curtis) King, 1785-1872, Colbert County, Alabama, Biographies, 2005.

Causey, Donna, First Families of Lawrence County, Alabama, Volume 1, Arthur Francis Hopkins (1794-1866), Donway Publishing Company, 2011.

Chancery Records of Madison County, Alabama, Circuit Court, April 25, 1831, Fall Term, 1836.

Cowart, Margaret Matthews, <u>Old Land Records of Colbert County, Alabama,</u>
7801 Tea Garden Road Southeast, Huntsville, Alabama, 1985.

Cowart, Margaret Matthews, <u>Old Land Records of Franklin County, Alabama,</u>
7801 Tea Garden Road Southeast, Huntsville, Alabama, 1986.

Cowart, Margaret Matthews, <u>Old Land Records of Lauderdale County, Alabama,</u>
7801 Tea Garden Road Southeast, Huntsville, Alabama, 1996.

Cowart, Margaret Matthews, <u>Old Land Records of Lawrence County, Alabama,</u>
7801 Tea Garden Road Southeast, Huntsville, Alabama, 1991.

Cowart, Margaret Matthews, <u>Old Land Records of Limestone County, Alabama,</u>
7801 Tea Garden Road Southeast, Huntsville, Alabama, 1984.

Cowart, Margaret Matthews, <u>Old Land Records of Madison County, Alabama,</u>
7801 Tea Garden Road Southeast, Huntsville, Alabama, 1979.

Cowart, Margaret Matthews, <u>Old Land Records of Morgan County, Alabama,</u>
7801 Tea Garden Road Southeast, Huntsville, Alabama, 1981.

Davidson, Donald Grady, <u>The Tennessee,</u> Rhinehart and Company, New York
City, New York, 1946.

Everett, Dianna, <u>The Texas Cherokees</u>, University of Oklahoma Press, Norman,
Oklahoma, 1990.

Find a Grave, www.findagrave.com

Foreman, Grant, <u>The Five Civilized Tribes</u>, University of Oklahoma Press,
Norman, Oklahoma, 1934.

Fowke, Gerard, <u>Forty-Fourth Annual Report of the Bureau of American
Ethanology</u>, United States Printing Office. Washington, D.C. 1928.

Gamble, Robert, <u>The Alabama Catalog, Historic American Building Survey: A Guide to the Early Architecture of the State</u>, University of Alabama Press, December 10, 1986.

Gentry, Dorthy, <u>Life and Legends of Lawrence County, Alabama</u>, Nottingham-SWS, Inc., Tuscaloosa, Alabama, 1962.

Hyatt, Ratford, <u>Last Indian and White Battle in Lawrence County. Melton's Bluff, Old Lawrence Reminscences</u>, Lawrence County Historical Commission, Moulton, Alabama, 1993.

James, Marquis, <u>Andrew Jackson, Portrait of a President</u>, The Bobbs-Merill Company, New York, 1937.

Lawrence County Archives, <u>Online Records</u>

Lawrence County Hertiage Book Committee, <u>The Heritage of Lawrence County, Alabama</u>, Heritage of Alabama Series, Volume 40, Heritage Publishing Consultants, Clanton, Alabama, 1998.

Leftwich, Nina, <u>Two Hundred Years at Muscle Shoals</u>, The American Southern Printing Company, Northport, Alabama, 1935.

M. A. H., <u>American Whig Review</u>, Volume 15, Issue 87, Cornersville, Tennessee-December 25, 1851, March 1852

Malone, Henry Thompson, <u>Cherokees of the Old South: A People in Transition</u>, University of Georgia Press, Athens, Georgia, 1956.

McDonald, William Lindsey, <u>Lore of the River</u>, Bluewater Publishing Company, Killen, Alabama, 2007.

Middle Tennessee University, <u>Wheeler Plantation, A Preservation Plan</u>, Murfreesboro, Tennessee, December, 1988.

Powell, John Wesley, Matthew Williams Stirling, Jesse Walter Fewkes, Frederick Webb Hodge, William Henry Holmes, <u>Annual Report</u>, Volume 5, Parts 1883-

1884, Library of American Civilization PCMI Collection, Smithsonian Institution, Bureau of American Ethnology, Government Printing Office, Pennsylvania State University, page 272, 1887.

Prucha, Francis Paul, Documents of United States Indian Policy, University of Nebraska Press, Lincoln, Nebraska, 1975.

Saunders, James Edmonds, Early Settlers of Alabama, Willco Publishing Company, Tuscaloosa, Alabama, 1961.

Sheridan, Richard C., Letter from John Coffee to General Andrew Jackson, October 22, 1813, Sheffield, Alabama, (private collection.)

Stone, James H., Surveying the Gaines Trace, 1807-1808, Alabama Historical Quarterly, Summer 1971.

Street, Oliver Day, Indians of Marshall County, Transactions of the Alabama Historical Society, Volume IV (1899-1903), Montgomery, Alabama, 1904.

Sugden, John, Tecumseh: A Life, Holt, Henry and Company, New York, New York, 1998.

Ramsey, James G. M., The Annals of Tennessee, Lippincott, Grambo, and Company, Philadelphia, Pennsylvania, 1853.

Royall, Anne Newport, Letters from Alabama 1817-1822, University of Alabama Press, Tuscaloosa, Alabama, 1969.

Wikipedia.org

Index

Hubbard, James, 16, 186, 187
Hubbard, Thomas, 186, 187
Hunt's Spring, 66, 138
Huntsville Road, 42, 64
Hutchings, John, 52, 53, 54, 55, 57, 59, 61
Indian, 5
Indian Removal Act, 8, 59
Indian Tomb, 45, 84, 88
Ingleside, 133, 136, 138, 139, 140
Ingleside Plantation, 133, 138, 139, 140
Ingleside Plantation Cemetery, 140
Jackson, Andrew, 8, 23, 24, 25, 28, 38, 49, 51, 52, 53, 54, 55, 57, 58, 59, 61, 172, 187, 194, 250, 254, 276, 279, 304, 305
Jackson, James, 103, 166, 169, 170
Jackson, Susan McKiernan, 169
Jackson, William, 166, 169, 226
James, Marquis, 54
Jarman Plantation, 106
Jarman, Amos, 191, 192, 193
Jasper Road, 42
Jefferson, Thomas, 17, 24, 89, 93, 139, 140, 141, 142, 143, 197, 221, 291
Johnson, John, 22, 134, 135, 193, 194, 195, 196, 197, 198
Johnson, John H., 193, 196, 197
Johnson, Lucinda, 66, 194
Johnson, Meredian, 135
Johnson, Meredian Cornelia, 134, 135
Johnson, Nicholas, 199, 200, 201
Jolly, John, 25
Jones, Benjamin B., 118, 202, 203, 204
Jones, Catherine Baker, 296
Jones, Daniel, 136, 204
Jones, Daniella Ellen, 59, 60
Jones, Frances, 206

Jones, Frances 'Fannie', 136
Jones, Frances Anna Mariah, 118
Jones, Francis Harwood, 205
Jones, Frederick, 96
Jones, John Nelson Spotswood, 178, 203
Jones, Littleberry, 281
Jones, Littleberry Hardyman, 132, 137, 204
Jones, Littlebury H., 93
Jones, Llewellen, 118
Jones, Martha Marie Davis, 204
Jones, Minerva Tazewell, 165, 166
Jones, Nancy Howard, 205
Jones, Richard, 59, 60, 61, 174, 206, 207, 208, 274
Jones, Richard Harrison, 206, 266
Jones, Sarah, 96
Jones, Sarah Maria Louisa, 118
Jones, Thomas, 96, 208
Jones, Thomas Morgan, 208
Jones, Tignal, 205, 210
Jonesboro, 122
Joseph Burleson's Trace, 126
Kaiser, Andrew, 290
Katagiskee, 7, 19, 20
Kattygisky, 13, 19, 20, 21, 22, 193, 194, 197
King Cemetery, 209, 211, 212, 214, 215
King, Cynthia Wright, 215
King, Hartwell Richard, 209, 210, 211, 212, 214
King, Margaret Peck, 212, 213, 214
King, Philemon, 210, 222
King, Robert, 210, 212, 213, 214
King, William Oswald, 210, 214, 215
Kinlock, 186, 188, 189, 190
Kittiakaska, 19, 196

Sherrod, W. C., 158, 257

Sherrod, William Crawford, 159, 256, 257, 261, 264

Sherrods Spring, 265

Shoal Town, 3, 4, 7, 19, 20, 24, 25, 43, 46, 193, 197

Sipsie Trail, 42, 57, 64, 65

Smith, David Hutchings, 57, 58

Smith, Susan, 166

Soldier's Wife, 5

South River Road, 29, 42, 43, 46, 50, 51, 54, 56, 61, 65, 264

Southdale Plantation, 93, 205

Spencer, Catherine, 14, 27

Spring Creek, 22, 25, 29, 294, 295

Standing Turkey, 13, 14

Stanley, Edward R., 231

Starr, Caleb, 27

Strain, Thomas, 244

Street, Oliver D., 38, 305

Sunnybrook, 116, 117

Swoope Cemetery, 110, 156, 273, 276

Swoope, C. C., 109

Swoope, Charles C., 138, 172, 275

Swoope, Charles Carroll, 274

Swoope, Cynthia Early, 206

Swoope, Edgar M., 272, 273, 275, 276, 294

Swoope, Elmira Watkins, 294

Swoope, Emma, 278, 279

Swoope, J. J., 116

Swoope, Jacob, 110, 260, 271

Swoope, Jacob K., 273, 274

Swoope, John, 225

Swoope, John M., 206, 273, 274, 275, 278

Swoope-Ussery Cemetery, 208, 275, 279

Sycamore Shoals, 4, 6, 12, 16, 51

Sykes Cemetery, 93, 94

Sykes, Andrew Jackson, 278

Sykes, Francis 'Frank' Winfield, 276

Sykes, Frank W., 276, 277, 278

Sykes, James Turner, 276, 278

Tabb, Thomas Bolling, 101, 225

Tahlonteeskee, 13, 24, 25

Tate, Caroline, 91, 92

Tate, Enos, 93

Tate, Waddy, 265

Tauquatehee, 16

Taylor, Margaret J., 101

Taylor, Robert, 101

Tecumseh, 11, 305

Tellico Blockhouse, 17

Ten Islands, 42

Terrell, Elizabeth, 115, 116

Texas, 18, 19, 110, 112, 113, 148, 149, 150, 166, 170, 171, 172, 177, 191, 213, 220, 221, 229, 231, 233, 235, 236, 238, 244, 255, 256, 261, 288, 300, 303

Thomas Smith Tavern, 114

Thomas, Martha W., 110

Thompson, Eleanor, 259, 275, 293, 294, 295

Tinker, Harris, 112, 279, 280

Tombigbee, 10, 42, 43, 44, 46, 66, 243

Toney, Charles Augustine, 222

Treaty of Philadelphia, 13, 17, 27, 36

Tripoli, 5

Turkey Town Treaty, 1, 13, 17, 23, 24, 37, 40, 49, 53, 56, 63, 137, 194

Tuscumbia Landing, 16, 24, 42, 46, 243, 269

Tuscumbia Road, 42, 46, 65, 169, 262, 264

I am extremely honored and humbled by the many people who read my books. I greatly appreciate the readers that enjoy truthful historical stories of the Warrior Mountains and the great Tennessee River Valley. I send all the followers of my books a heartfelt thank you; without people who love local history about North Alabama, all my research and work would be in vain.

I graciously request that each of you who acquire one of my books from Amazon to please post an honest review. A short two to three line evaluation of my books would be greatly appreciated. Again, thank you to all who take the time to read a book by Rickey Butch Walker.

Printed in the USA
CPSIA information can be obtained
at www.ICGtesting.com
CBHW060939241023
1422CB00009B/5